T0338503

Social Media Performance Evaluation and Success Measurements

Michael A. Brown Sr.
Florida International University, USA

A volume in the Advances in
Social Networking and Online
Communities (ASNOC) Book
Series

www.igi-global.com

Published in the United States of America by
IGI Global
Information Science Reference (an imprint of IGI Global)
701 E. Chocolate Avenue
Hershey PA 17033
Tel: 717-533-8845
Fax: 717-533-8661
E-mail: cust@igi-global.com
Web site: http://www.igi-global.com

                Library of Congress Cataloging-in-Publication Data

Names: Brown, Michael A., Sr., 1956- editor.
Title: Social media performance evaluation and success measurements / Michael
    A. Brown, Sr., editor.
Description: Hershey, PA : Information Science Reference, [2017]
Identifiers: LCCN 2016050382| ISBN 9781522519638 (hardcover) | ISBN
    9781522519645 (ebook)
Subjects: LCSH: Online social networks--Research. | Social media--Research. |
    Internet--Social aspects--Research.
Classification: LCC HM742 .S62835 2017 | DDC 302.23/1072--dc23 LC record available at https://
lccn.loc.gov/2016050382

This book is published in the IGI Global book series Advances in Social Networking and Online
Communities (ASNOC) (ISSN: 2328-1405; eISSN: 2328-1413)

British Cataloguing in Publication Data
A Cataloguing in Publication record for this book is available from the British Library.

Advances in Social Networking and Online Communities (ASNOC) Book Series

ISSN:2328-1405
EISSN:2328-1413

MISSION

The advancements of internet technologies and the creation of various social networks provide a new channel of knowledge development processes that's dependent on social networking and online communities. This emerging concept of social innovation is comprised of ideas and strategies designed to improve society.

The **Advances in Social Networking and Online Communities** book series serves as a forum for scholars and practitioners to present comprehensive research on the social, cultural, organizational, and human issues related to the use of virtual communities and social networking. This series will provide an analytical approach to the holistic and newly emerging concepts of online knowledge communities and social networks.

COVERAGE

- Leveraging Knowledge Communication Networks – Approaches to Interpretations and Interventions
- Knowledge Acquisition Systems and Networks
- Challenges of Knowledge Management
- Knowledge as a Competitive Force
- Local E-Government Interoperability and Security
- Citizens' E-participation in Local Decision-Making Processes
- Agent-Mediated Knowledge Management
- Knowledge as an Empirical Problem Solving Tool
- Knowledge as Capacity for Action
- Strategic Management and Business Process Analysis

IGI Global is currently accepting manuscripts for publication within this series. To submit a proposal for a volume in this series, please contact our Acquisition Editors at Acquisitions@igi-global.com or visit: http://www.igi-global.com/publish/.

Titles in this Series

For a list of additional titles in this series, please visit: www.igi-global.com

Power, Surveillance, and Culture in YouTube™'s Digital Sphere
Matthew Crick (William Paterson University, USA)
Information Science Reference ● copyright 2016 ● 317pp ● H/C (ISBN: 9781466698550)
● US $185.00 (our price)
Social Media and the Transformation of Interaction in Society
John P. Sahlin (The George Washington University, USA)
Information Science Reference ● copyright 2015 ● 300pp ● H/C (ISBN: 9781466685567)
● US $200.00 (our price)
Cases on Strategic Social Media Utilization in the Nonprofit Sector
Hugo Asencio (California State University – Dominguez Hills, USA) and Rui Sun (California
State University – Dominguez Hills, USA)
Information Science Reference ● copyright 2015 ● 375pp ● H/C (ISBN: 9781466681880)
● US $195.00 (our price)
Handbook of Research on Interactive Information Quality in Expanding Social Network Communications
Francisco V. Cipolla-Ficarra (Latin Association of Human-Computer Interaction, Spain &
International Association of Interactive Communication, Italy)
Information Science Reference ● copyright 2015 ● 449pp ● H/C (ISBN: 9781466673779)
● US $255.00 (our price)
Implications of Social Media Use in Personal and Professional Settings
Vladlena Benson (Kingston Business School, Kingston University, UK) and Stephanie
Morgan (Kingston Business School, Kingston University, UK)
Information Science Reference ● copyright 2015 ● 362pp ● H/C (ISBN: 9781466674011)
● US $195.00 (our price)
Identity and Leadership in Virtual Communities Establishing Credibility and Influence
Dona J. Hickey (University of Richmond, USA) and Joe Essid (University of Richmond, USA)
Information Science Reference ● copyright 2014 ● 321pp ● H/C (ISBN: 9781466651500)
● US $205.00 (our price)
Harnessing the Power of Social Media and Web Analytics
Anteneh Ayanso (Brock University, Canada) and Kaveepan Lertwachara (California Poly-
technic State University, USA)
Information Science Reference ● copyright 2014 ● 305pp ● H/C (ISBN: 9781466651944)
● US $215.00 (our price)

www.igi-global.com

701 E. Chocolate Ave., Hershey, PA 17033
Order online at www.igi-global.com or call 717-533-8845 x100
To place a standing order for titles released in this series,
contact: cust@igi-global.com
Mon-Fri 8:00 am - 5:00 pm (est) or fax 24 hours a day 717-533-8661

Table of Contents

Detailed Table of Contents

Section 1
Overview

Chapter 1
   Michael A. Brown Sr., Florida International University, USA

Organizations, researchers and academicians now have a new source for social networking methodology through Social Networking and Individual Performance (SNIP). This book will provide a scored survey instrument that, combined with research findings, relevant discovery and discussion will bring social networking into focus. The body of work focuses on the end state of social networking activities rather than the social media platform. This is an important distinction. This book addresses how to set an end state and devise a strategic approach to emphasize expectation, value, and return (EVR) in social networking. This approach is important because there are not enough references that have a similar approach to help those engaged in social networking and social media activities. In fact, there are none that focus on the current approach. SNIP addresses that limitation.

This chapter focuses on the development of a new assessment tool: Social Networking and Individual Performance (SNIP). This tool can provide valuable data for organizations and even individuals. The data provided through use of the tool can determine whether employees are exhibiting behaviors that are supportive of the organization's goals, thus allowing everyone to benefit based on a return on the investment in time or attention that could lead to improved skills. Employees might then reap benefits like availability of new challenges or increased standing in the organization. The data can also provide insight on improving personal social media activities.

Section 2
New Look Social Media

We use a gauge to make the point that public administrators have been busy working to take advantage of opportunities to participate in the digital conversation through increased social media activities. This is a daunting undertaking because of the speed at which digital conversations happen and transform to new interactions. This collection of chapters seeks to provide a new vision on social media interaction from the perspectives of several authors. This analysis goes from a history of social communication to organizational concerns to microblogging to social media marketing. We also include a look at crisis communication because social media has pushed itself to the forefront of activity and discovery in that area.

George Santayana said, "Those who cannot remember the past are condemned to repeat it." That statement is the reason social communication is covered here with a historical view. This review of computer mediated communications (CMC) is important in understanding some of the key developments that created the social media environment we know today. A discussion of the portable nature of these communications is relevant as the foundation for a deep understanding of social communication. This is an important analysis in helping people understand the way we can use information technology to interact without the limitations of geographical distance and time.

Chapter 4

Liston W. Bailey, University of Phoenix, USA

This chapter discusses the impact of social networking on participation in organizations across market sectors to include government, business and non-profit entities. The author relates the experiences of young adults working in various occupations on how smartphone use can influence social networking and interactions and whether that influence improves or hampers their learning and professional development. A review of literature and recent social media development trends are used to gather information in support of a conceptual model of media usage and social networked learning within organizations. Leaders and organizational members may want to refer to this 4 stage model when thinking about ways to improve their use of social media and informal learning opportunities found on the Internet and on smart devices.

Chapter 5

Yuanxin Wang, Temple University, USA

Micro-blogging is a popular, continuously developing form of communication that allows users to update their current life status in short posts around the clock with targeted websites and platforms. A significant blogosphere has developed in China where the prevailing micro-blogging websites comprise Internet coverage of issues not covered by mainstream media. This research will examine heavily shared and discussed blog posts on a popular micro-blogging website in China during an anti-animal cruelty campaign. The comments section of the blog posts will also be analyzed to identify discrepancies between the frames set by the bloggers and the perceptions by their audiences.

Chapter 6

Nozha Erragcha, Faculty of Law, Economics, and Management, Tunisia

Within the new economic and social environment, development of new technologies combined with Internet progress has had a profound impact on consumer lifestyles and, by extension, marketing concepts and practices. Understanding changes in marketing brought by a fast-acting development of digital social networks and Web 2.0 technology has become essential. The purpose of this chapter is to examine the impact of Web 2.0 on marketing and how marketers can use evolving technologies. Our contribution aligns changes in marketing techniques with Internet development and the changes introduced by the transition from Web 1.0 to Web 2.0. The chapter ends with a proposal of about potential implications for managers.

Chapter 7

This chapter covers crisis communication, focusing on the crucial activities before, during, and after a crisis occurs. An environmental scan identifies risks an organization may encounter. Prioritizing these risks informs the creation of crisis communications plans for each risk. These plans include a strategy to guide all organizational communications efforts. Timeline, budget, products, digital resources, and formative measurement all must be considered. Practice is essential. These actions can prepare an organization and its people to manage high-pressure, high-speed activities in real time. Once the crisis is controlled, it is time to evaluate the plan and institute adjustments as required.

Section 3
Examining Social Media Effectiveness

As the magnifying glass in Figure 1 illustrates, this section addresses a closer look at the challenge of analyzing online activities to get a sense of the effectiveness of online interactions. We take a broad view of measurement in an attempt to open the door to conversations, discovery, and research in this area. We cover two nonprofit situations to evaluate return on investment. Models of participation in social networks and social media use in election campaigns are also examined. This broad sampling of activity is an important step in starting a conversation about social media implications in these areas.

Chapter 8

Social media is increasing becoming a prominent tool in today's nonprofit sector. By 2010, the largest 200 nonprofit organizations in the United States used social media as a tool to meet their goals. According to those surveyed the top reason for using social media is for increasing awareness of the organization's mission (90%). In studying the American Red Cross' use of social media, Briones et al. found that the use of social media built relationships with the public. This chapter explores the success of a mid-sized nonprofit organization, CHOICES: Memphis Center for Reproductive Health, as it develops a strategic social media plan to increase awareness and support for the organization. Through this case study, we will address how this organization has used social media to advance its mission and the process used to develop performance metrics along the way.

Chapter 9

The use of social media technologies such as Facebook, Twitter, Instagram, and LinkedIn has enhanced and increased the communication and engagement strategies available to nonprofit organizations. This chapter focuses on and addresses the question of nonprofit use of social media by examining the main objectives for using social media, and whether social media has been effective in meeting these objectives. Existing research on nonprofit social media use tends to focus on finding out which social media tools nonprofit organizations are using and which one of these yields the most impact. To answer these questions, descriptive analysis is conducted on social media technologies and their usage to identify associations between effectiveness of social media in meeting objectives. These questions go beyond asking why nonprofit organizations use social media and analyzes how they meet their objectives using various social media tools.

Chapter 10

The most important technological trend of the last years has been the rise of social networking systems to social phenomena involving hundreds of millions of people, attracting users from several social groups. Social networking systems blur the distinction between the private and working spheres, and users use such systems both at home and in the workplace, both professionally and with recreational goals. Social networking systems can be equally used to organize a work meeting, a dinner with colleagues or a birthday party with friends. For example, the chat systems that are embedded in social networking platforms are often the most practical way to contact a colleague to ask an urgent question, especially in technologically oriented companies. Moreover, several traditional information systems have been modified in order to include social aspects. Currently, social networking platforms are mostly used without corporate blessing, maintaining their status as feral systems.

Chapter 11

Invest, Engage, and Win: Online Campaigns and Their Outcomes in an Israeli Election

Moran Yarchi, The Interdisciplinary Center (IDC), Israel
Gadi Wolfsfeld, The Interdisciplinary Center (IDC), Israel
Tal Samuel-Azran, The Interdisciplinary Center (IDC), Israel
Elad Segev, Tel-Aviv University, Israel

Though the use of social media for political campaigning has been widely studied, its correlation with electoral success has not received much attention. The current study uses the 2013 Israeli elections to examine the impact of social media on campaigns as a process. Findings indicate that parties and candidates that invest in social media are more likely to achieve social media success, which in turn increases their chances of achieving electoral success. Some may dispute the level of influence of social media; however, study findings suggest that being active in the digital arena has become a significant element in achieving ballot box success.

Foreword

IMPROVING CAPABILITIES IN THE SOCIAL MEDIA REVOLUTION

Twenty years ago, when I was doing doctoral research on citizen participation, the term social media did not mean what it does today. We were looking at the potential of the internet as a medium to communicate with the public. Researchers were fascinated by the prospect that one day a city budget would be announced on a website and that folks would be able to renew their license online. Today, most private, non-profit and public organizations are engaged in social media in multiple ways.

Private corporations similarly are using social media to engage with their customers. Non-profit organizations are connecting through social media with their donors and clients. Cities, counties, and state and federal agencies have followers on multiple social media outlets and use these media in a number of ways. They use these media to announce new initiatives, warn residents about pending disasters, announce public meetings, report crime, and solicit feedback on proposed policies or spending. As an academic in the area of public administration, I would like to highlight in this foreword the importance of social networking and its potential specifically in a government setting.

In my own neighborhood, the local police department and some city officials are on neighborhood social networks and they regularly post notices about burglaries, tree trimming, construction and other notices to the public. They also participate in resident conversations. In every sense, social media is allowing public officials to interact with residents in ways unimagined in the past. Many governments, especially those who provide services directly to citizens and residents, are finding a new outreach tool in social media.

The widespread impact of social media doesn't stop there. We live in an era where social organizing using the digital environment is becoming increasingly a reality to grapple with – online petitions in the United States, a people's revolution in Egypt, and shutting down a revolution in Turkey.

Engaging the public and communicating persuasive, informative or educational messages is vital to the success of individuals and organizations. But that communication is particularly important for two main reasons: enhancing popular sovereignty and providing consumerist type information to officials. Elias and Alkadry (2011) argue "that citizen participation should be grounded not only in democratic principles but also in the practice of joint knowledge creation through deliberation between public administrators and citizens. Deliberations about shared concerns hold the potential to "get things done" effectively via collaborative practices, thus bringing efficiency closer to democracy." Social media provides a deliberative medium which allows for that joint knowledge creation.

Social media for government empowers citizens and at the same time provides elected and non-elected government officials with critical knowledge to effectively deliver services. Most organizations today view social media skills as assets in the skill sets of employees. This is a big leap from the recent days when organizations created policies to prevent employees from participating on social media websites, especially from the workplace. The two bottom line questions are those iterated by Elias and Alkadry (2011):

1. Does engagement in social media enhance citizen participation and subsequently our participative democracy?
2. Does engagement in social media allow us to inform organizational decision making and ultimately yield more effective organizations?

To address the first question, I would like to engage one of the first scholars to write about citizen participation. Sherry Arnstein (1969) described a ladder of participation well before computers became personal computers. The ladder of participation is based on citizen empowerment or power in the process starting from what Arnstein labeled as non-participation all the way up to citizen power. The lowest non-participation rungs are labeled as therapy and manipulation. With these rungs, the goal of citizen engagement is to make citizens feel involved but without any substantive engagement or even transparency.

Arnstein labels the rungs informing, consultation and placation as tokenism in the sense that these forms of participation are one-way communications geared toward informing citizens about new initiatives and policies. Finally, the three top rungs are labeled as citizen power and include partnership, delegated power and citizen control. These three rungs go beyond communication and informing to allow citizens power to participate in decision making. While social media can be used to manipulate citizens, it introduces something that most other non-electronic media could not deliver – it introduces the potential for an online community where residents interact among themselves, with administrators, and with elected officials. Social media on its own will not yield citizen power, but it creates the potential for community mobilization against or in favor of public policies and/or administrative actions. Social media is also convenient and does not exclude lower income residents or people with families, people without cars, and people who are place-bound due to age or disability. Social media use can empower communities and can help communities organize.

Does social media involvement result in a more effective administration? If social media engages residents about their realities and their policy preferences, then administrators and elected officials can better design the right policy and deliver the right services. If accurate diagnosis is the pre-requisite for prescribing the right cure, then social media will help administrators and elected officials diagnose public issues, and will certainly enhance their ability to effectively find the right solution.

This book is a welcome addition to our libraries and training materials. It helps us be more strategic about introducing social networking into organizational cultures and traditions. The social media invasion into our culture has been neither expected nor gradual. Most organizations, and individuals, are catching up to this new reality. This book will be important for organizations, public, private, and nonprofit, which found themselves all of sudden having to integrate this new reality into their employee handbooks and training materials.

This book can help organizations create social media policies that address return on investment of time or resources and analyze performance implications. The time has come to identify measurement tools that allow organizations to impact online interactions as they happen. The conversation that begins with this book is about suggesting methods that can be used to affect behaviors in support of the organization's goals and objectives. Issues of participation, technology acceptance, trust, and social networking development are addressed by this edited collection of original research in this area. These are important first, or next, steps in digital interactions.

Social media is a revolution that is no less significant for people and organizations than the personal computer revolution. It is here to stay. Organizations in all sectors stand to gain from this new innovation. The authors of the various chapters of this book provide tools and illustrations of the use of social media in different sectors. It is our hope that we have created a rich sampling of information that will spark conversations and progress for years to come.

Mohamad Alkadry
Florida International University, USA

REFERENCES

Arnstein, S. R. (1969). A Ladder of Citizen Participation. *Journal of the American Institute of Planners, 35*(4), 216–224. doi:10.1080/01944366908977225

Elías, M. V., & Alkadry, M. G. (2011). Constructive conflict, participation, and shared governance. *Administration & Society*.

Preface

OUR OBJECTIVES

There are two major objectives for this book, the first of which is to help organizations identify social networking participation expectations, value, and return on investment of time. The second objective is to highlight the true value of social networking, examining individual performance in digital communication activities with a focus on differences in participation, behavior, technology acceptance, and trust. This is a new approach to social networking where the digital environment suggested a need for an edited collection of original thought and research in this area. The scored survey instrument, research findings, and relevant discussions from industry experts will be helpful in teaching and training applications. The resulting body of work herein is focused on the end state of social networking activities rather than the social media platform, an important distinction because there is no single reference that provides this digital examination.

OUR VALUE PROPOSITION

Our journey is about identifying valuable information to reinforce organizational training and improve internal and external communications through social media. There is an educational value for the reader because this work is primarily focused on public administration environments; however, the social networking experiences are relevant for any number of industries. A scored instrument called Social Networking and Individual Performance, or SNIP, provided herein, provides a social media aptitude measure and offers a vehicle by which organizations can analyze and improve social networking participation. Understanding the relationship between social networking and individual performance and employing a social networking plan are key steps to finding success in communication activities.

Success also relies on energizing social capital, taking advantage of the networks and relationships that are nurtured through exchanged value. A comparison of social networking and social media creates a baseline for effectively managing online activities. The planning and measurement journey in this book offers an opportunity for organizations to take advantage of unfettered, two-way communication with important audiences. The beauty of social networking lies not only in its immediacy but in its ability to let users get and give feedback in real time.

The social media revolution is upon us and it is not slowing down. Organizations, whether they want to or not, are going social on the inside, so it is important to listen to the digital conversation at every opportunity. Listening to the conversation strategically helps to engage stakeholders and friends using the channels they prefer.

Social networking and social media are great tools that enable organizations to unleash communication and improve listening ability by allowing the interaction of these concepts (Figure 1). Social capital is built this way and engagements start to take on organizational importance. This book is about accepting those opportunities. We will examine key concepts of social networking versus social media, performance keys, social capital, and social networking opportunities that will lead us to the next steps in our communication journey.

Figure 1.

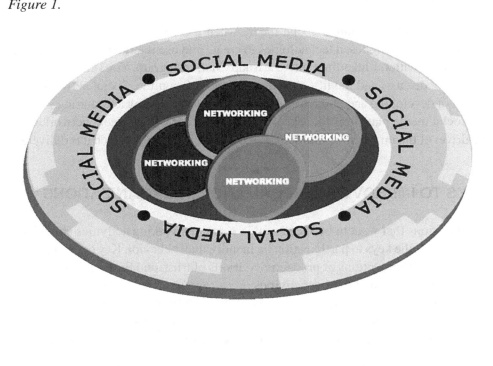

SOCIAL NETWORKING VS. SOCIAL MEDIA

Social networking is about trust and engagement. People form networks to build trusting relationships geared to reduce risk in business or personal decision by taking advantage of the skills and abilities of others. In terms of engagement, people who form networks want to give advice, share experiences and seek advice that they hope will make them better decision makers. Social networking is about the "why" of social relationships.

Social media provides the tools and venues that are used to communicate socially. These platforms transcend the boundaries of time and location. Using these platforms, organizations and people can send and receive information effortlessly, connecting with anyone participating in social media anywhere in the world.

But social networking can be so much more for organizations considering individual performance implications. Important discoveries can be made by changing the lens through which we view social networking. We take a different approach than what is discussed in current literature. We suggest an approach significantly different from the norm in social networking and social media circles today. It allows the destination, not the path or platform, be the focus of social media participation. Organizations should look beyond near-term financial benefits and leverage short-term costs (either time or expenses) that promote positive social and environmental change.

We most often encounter social media when there is an "app for that." Social media employs web-based technologies to create and use interactive platforms like Facebook, Twitter, LinkedIn, Pinterest, Snap Chat, Instagram, YouTube, etc. to create, share, discuss, and modify content at a rapid pace online. Social networking is the act of developing acquaintances and contacts by connecting and sharing, and we use social media platforms to make it happen. In other words, social networking is the driver of the information and social media is the method by which it is delivered.

KEYS TO IMPROVED PERFORMANCE IN ORGANIZATIONS

Organizations that want to be successful in social networking activities should understand that the keys to participation lie in individual behavior. Key considerations are individual perceptions of productivity, levels of trust, and the ability to conduct bonding, bridging, and linking activities.

Social networking is a voluntary process in which people are faced with choices. Organizations cannot achieve full success in social networking, however, unless they address acceptance and rejection of participation. Why? Because being social requires the exchange of valuable information and the resulting two-way interaction among participants. The relevant questions that organizations must ask have to do with finding out how people determine their connections and how they decide on how much time and effort they are willing to commit to the activity.

One basis for stressing this social networking and individual performance relationship is in the work of Svendsen and Sorenson (2006), which examined whether the levels of individual perception of productivity and levels of trust would be influenced by measuring social capital as the density of voluntary networking activities. The focus of social networking activities should be placed on the capacity of individuals to perform the necessary tasks. This book's performance and measurement resources offer a framework that organizations can use to affect creativity, idea exchange, and communication effectiveness.

It is important to note that a few key theories relate directly to this relationship between networking and performance and getting "social." Social networking characteristics can be examined through the Hawthorne Effect, social learning theory, and social network analysis (SNA). A primary focus is on behavioral intention which is defined as the extent to which a person believes that the technology is capable of being used advantageously and that the technology provides positive expected outcomes. Prior research related to these theories provides a participation foundation, one built on the understanding that social networking and individual performance share the activities of bonding (establishing strong ties), bridging (establishing informal ties), and linking (establishing voluntary ties).

In networking, strong ties are clusters of people in strong relationships who know what one another know (Granovetter, 1973; Granovetter, 1982). These typically long-term ties rely on collaboration and confidence and trust between people and networks. Weak ties are characterized by having no strong or established social group. The knowledge creation process in the network is supported by strong ties because they deliver strategic capabilities based on their personal connections, and they assist with finding new and valuable information opportunities. The benefit of weak ties is that they produce new information in the network.

Organizations can analyze employee behavioral intention to focus on strong ties that encourage the desired behaviors for maximum effectiveness. Organizational keys to improving social networking activities rely on three things:

1. **Small Wins:** Concrete incentives to participate in the kind of social media the organization values.
2. **Clear Instructions:** Improved definition of the work required through task analyzability.
3. **Deliberate Praise:** Continuous feedback through structured reinforcement.

ENERGIZING SOCIAL CAPITAL

As social networking activities are improved, energizing social capital means finding and taking advantage of meaningful engagements. Organizations that want a good corporate social media focus should be engaged in controlling and expanding their brand by relaying messages quickly while the subject, and the public's attention, is prevalent in the community conversation. It is important to generate conversation and gather feedback to build relationships and foster information sharing among employees.

The benefits begin with increased traffic and interaction on the organization's website or social media platform. Effective two-way communications can help organizations develop an understanding of their target audiences. That understanding is important to finding new and improved ways to find, collect, and share information. Social networking can develop an ability to reach audiences that are unavailable by other means, increasing the organization's reach in the community of interest. Finally, social networking develops transparency with important internal and external publics.

Bridging and bonding are types of social capital according to Robert Putnam (1993). Putnam says that bonding occurs when people socialize with others who have something in common with them: same age, race, religion, etc. Bonding is important, but Putnam contends that bridging is needed to create interacting societies in a diverse multi-ethnic country. Bridging is making friends with people who do not have something in common with us; they are not like us, they do not like our favorites, they do not eat what we eat, and they do not drive what we drive. However, both types of social capital are continuously at play, strengthening each other as online networks are created.

Social capital grows from relationships between and among organizations, individuals, communities, or societies. Social capital building can create close interpersonal relationships because of the valuable resources that are involved. Social networking relies on social capital and has some of the same characteristics; however, there may be no face-to-face communication and the relationships are more informal than those typically created in social capital building.

The resources offered in this book address the challenges of understanding social networking and social media platforms enough to assess the relevance of various approaches. A broader vision of social media participation and performance implications is suggested, using a goal-setting focus and social media plan advocated in the SNIP methodology. SNIP attempts to move the traditional frame of reference from solely which platform to use – Facebook, LinkedIn, Twitter, etc. – to a view of goal achievement and audience targeting.

SOCIAL NETWORKING OPPORTUNITIES

The SNIP scored survey instrument provides a social networking participation model that can help organizations predict and understand the value proposition that affects participation. Innovation adoption, governing by network, and social capital are important theories in developing an understanding of social networking behavior. Performance may be influenced when people are presented with evidence of a return on the investment of their time and effort.

SNIP provides information, techniques, and examples that address real or perceived benefits in order to assist in the social networking journey. This book is a new view of social networking that establishes and articulates the "why" of participation to help organizations find success. The digital conversation is uncontrolled and largely unorganized, an organic, complex series of communications in open space. Social networking uses that dynamic entity to highlight ways to connect and share content with anyone, anywhere.

These communications are simply based on opportunity. When people are presented with evidence of a return on the investment of their time and effort, participation becomes attractive. People may be inclined to participate even if there is only the hint or the perception of benefit. This value-based approach is what makes social networking relevant and what allows organizations to seek and encourage certain social media behaviors. This approach is about getting in touch with the thought processes behind social networking and social media.

SNIP offers an action plan for success. The historical perspective and theoretical evolution offered herein shows the growth and maturity of social media. That is followed by information about tools and techniques that build social capital and engage audiences in a meaningful way. How does it work? A checklist is provided in Table 1, and a SNIP Matrix is introduced.

IMPORTANT NEXT STEPS

We are now armed with general understanding of social networking, performance considerations, how social capital relates to online interactions, and the differences and similarities between social networking and social media. This book is divided into three parts that work together to help you take advantage of social networking opportunities and learn in new and different ways.

We begin with a digital communication overview. Chapter 1 provides an analysis of social networking in contrast with social media. This type of examination is missing from research about digital communication. Chapter 2 gives an overview of a powerful survey tool that people and organizations can use to start activities

Table 1. Social Networking and Individual Performance (SNIP) checklist

1. Set a social networking plan without deciding on the social media platform
2. Focus on the "act" of interacting by using the best platform for the plan
3. One construct, Perceived Improvement Potential (PIP), allows communicating parties to determine whether the activity will yield EVR (expectation, value, and return on investment of time) in terms of personal benefits
4. Employ key concepts:
a. Task analyzability of the activity
b. Modeling principles to promote or inhibit behavior
c. Structured reinforcement for continuous feedback
d. Trust to build strong ties between the parties involved

NOTE: PIP is based on a person's self-perception of effectiveness. PIP is about predicting a person's intention to behave in a certain way and determining whether they will actually exhibit that behavior.

in the best way, or to improve activities that are already underway. Either way, the knowledge can be used to get the maximum benefit from online interactions.

Section 1 is titled New Look Social Media. In *Understanding Social Communication*, Dr. Michael A. Brown Sr. discusses computer-mediated communication (CMC) history and development in recognition of their importance in setting a foundation for a deep understanding of social communication. This is an important analysis in understanding the way people use information technology to interact without the limitations of geographical distance and time. In *Social Media: A Discussion of Considerations for Modern Organizations and Professionals*, Dr. Liston W. Bailey examines the impact of social networking and participation both in schools and in the workplace. Leaders are offered knowledge gained through a review of literature as well as a survey instrument to assist in understanding media usage and social networked learning within organizations. In *Framing and Mis-framing in Micro-blogging Sites in China: Online Propagation of an Animal Cruelty Campaign*, Yuanxin Wang demonstrates that micro-blogging is an expanding form of communication featuring short posts around the clock. This convenient technology has caused the creation of a large and expanding blogosphere in China where the prevailing micro-blogging websites impact Internet coverage.

In *Using Social Media Tools in Marketing: Opportunities and Challenges*, Nozha Erragcha discusses the changing situation in the field of marketing and the ever-changing role of education in this area. The continuing growth of social media creates new dimensions for consumers and business and affects the practice of marketing in general and market dynamics in particular. In *Social Networking Engagement and Crisis Communication Considerations*, Dr. Mitchell Marovitz focuses on crucial crisis communication before, during, and after the unfortunate incident involved. It is necessary to conduct an environmental scan leading to plans for each potential risk an organization may encounter and to a strategy to guide all organizational efforts.

Section 2 is titled Evaluating Social Media Effectiveness. In *CHOICES: Measuring Return on Investment in a Nonprofit Organization*, Dr. Leigh Hersey argues that surveys show the top reason for nonprofits using social media is now for increasing awareness of the organization's mission (90%). The chapter explores the success of a mid-sized nonprofit organization, CHOICES: Memphis Center for Reproductive Health, as it develops a strategic social media plan to increase awareness and support. In *Nonprofit Organizations and Social Media Use: An Analysis of Nonprofit Organizations' Effective Use of Social Media Tools*, Dr. Aminata Sillah, PhD, focuses on the question of nonprofit use of social media by examining the main objectives for its use and whether it has been effective in meeting those objectives. Descriptive analysis was conducted on social media technologies and their usage to analyze effectiveness and to go beyond asking why nonprofit organizations use it.

In *Models of Participation in Social Networks*, Giulio Angiani, Paolo Fornacciari, Monica Mordonini and Michele Tomaiuolo point out that social networking systems blur the distinction between the private and working spheres, and users are known to use such systems at home and at work for personal and professional goals. Several traditional information systems have been modified to include social aspects, allow the use of external platforms, and to adjust to specific purposes in efforts to address objectives. In *Invest, Engage, and Win: Online Campaigns and their Outcomes in an Israeli Election*, Moran Yarchi, Gadi Wolfsfeld, Tal Samuel-Azran, and Elad Segev studied the 2013 Israeli elections to examine the impact of social media on campaigns as a process. The resulting findings indicate that parties and candidates that invest in social media are more likely to achieve social media success, which in turn increases their chances of achieving electoral success.

These works represent a call to action. There is an exciting digital conversation going on, and there are various ways to engage with social networking for success. Please join us in this exciting endeavor and let us communicate anytime, anywhere. Time to begin!

Michael A. Brown
Florida International University, USA

REFERENCES

Granovetter, M. S. (1973). The Strength of Weak Ties. *American Journal of Sociology*, *78*(6), 1360–1380. doi:10.1086/225469

Granovetter, M. S. (1982). *The strength of weak ties: A network theory revisited. In Social structure and network analysis* (pp. 105–130). New York: John Wiley and Sons.

Putnam, R. D. (1993). *Bowling Alone*. New York: Simon & Schuster Paperbacks.

Svendsen, G., & Sørensen, J. F. L. (2006). The socioeconomic power of social capital. *The International Journal of Sociology and Social Policy*, 26(9/10), 411–429. doi:10.1108/01443330610690550

Acknowledgment

I thank my family for being the driving force behind my efforts, and for being patient until the final word was penned. Without that support, this monumental task would have failed.

Thanks to my great friend Dr. Mohamad Alkadry for graciously agreeing to write the foreword to this book. This brilliant leader and scholar has been a tremendous help to me.

I want to thank every author in this book who contributed their priceless thoughts to this work. I want to thank my editorial board and all of my reviewers who volunteered their valuable time to make this project great.

Special thanks to Tracy Schario, Leigh Hersey, and James Goodwin for providing "last look" edits to finalize this project.

Finally, I am grateful to Nick Webb for continuing to collaborate with me and for providing outstanding graphics and color schemes.

Michael A. Brown
Florida International University, USA

Section 1
Overview

Chapter 1
Social Networking and Social Media Comparisons

Michael A. Brown Sr.
Florida International University, USA

ABSTRACT

Organizations, researchers and academicians now have a new source for social networking methodology through Social Networking and Individual Performance (SNIP). This book will provide a scored survey instrument that, combined with research findings, relevant discovery and discussion will bring social networking into focus. The body of work focuses on the end state of social networking activities rather than the social media platform. This is an important distinction. This book addresses how to set an end state and devise a strategic approach to emphasize expectation, value, and return (EVR) in social networking. This approach is important because there are not enough references that have a similar approach to help those engaged in social networking and social media activities. In fact, there are none that focus on the current approach. SNIP addresses that limitation.

DOI: 10.4018/978-1-5225-1963-8.ch001

SOCIAL NETWORKING ANALYSIS

We start our discussion of social media measurement and performance with an analysis of Social Capital Theory, which suggests that the efficiency of society can be improved by facilitating coordinated actions (Putnam 1993). Social networking provides a vital source of information and numerous opportunities for all participants to build social capital. Social media tools are increasingly provided by organizations to improve business processes, create new business, and enhance the lives of employees. The new and innovative ways to stay in touch with the environment and peers through social networking make for dynamic communication with internal and external audiences. Organizations that commit to social networking also commit to allowing employees to spend an unspecified number of hours making connections and joining communities. Many companies have embraced the fact that there are available benefits in terms of improved communication and morale, and in terms of connecting people on related projects or responsibilities (Madden and Jones 2008). The Pew Internet & American Life Project (2008) found that "Wired and Ready Workers" have improved their work lives through information and communications technology (ICT). According to the Pew Research Center, Wired and Ready Workers are the 96% of employed adults who are in some way making use of new communications technologies—either by going online, using email or owning a cell phone (Madden and Jones 2008). More information appears below:

- 80% say these technologies have improved their ability to do their job.
- 73% say these technologies have improved their ability to share ideas with co-workers.
- 58% say these tools have allowed them more flexibility in the hours they work.

The Wired and Ready Workers also note negative impacts of ICTs in the study:

- 46% say ICTs increase demands that they work more hours.
- 49% say ICTs increase the level of stress in their job.
- 49% say ICTs make it harder for them to disconnect from their work when they are at home and on the weekends.

Organizations need to find ways to encourage participation on a higher level, address any issues with acceptance of social networking policies, and address any negative perceptions that stand in the way of people "getting social" to their fullest capabilities. How can organizational leadership address social networking participation? The foundation provided through relevant theories in this book can help to define ways to create a decision matrix, which could lead to an active, lasting participation in an organization's chosen social networking activity. The decision matrix would provide a framework identifying determinants and opportunities that affect participation. As social capital builds in an effective social networking environment, the density of social networking activity should increase.

IMPORTANT SOCIAL COMPARISONS

The distinction between social networking and social media must be made clear before introducing a new focus. Social media refers to communication interactions which create, share, and exchange information and ideas in virtual communities and networks. If regular media is a one-way street, then social media is a two-way street that delivers unlimited ability to comment and discuss and offers a fast way to read the newspaper or digest a TV report.

Social networking is about getting people to collaborate and share experiences and get advice that may improve their lives or help them make better decisions. If we explore employee participation from a social information processing perspective, social interactions can be demonstrated in terms of the influences of actors, as in social exchange theory (Shetzer 1993). It is also important to consider how information relating to social interaction is cognitively organized and processed. This approach is informative for three reasons. First, it enables individuals to efficiently determine their relative influence in a workplace situation. Second, it allows individuals to respond efficiently to the situation on an emotional level. Third, it allows individuals to call upon scripted sequences of appropriate behavior.

Also, we reach out to people so that we can reduce risk in personal and/or business decisions by taking advantage of their expertise. Social media is about using different tools, or platforms to communicate socially. The tools allow us to communicate and store information without limitations of location or time. Anyone can connect with anyone anywhere if both parties are participating in social networking or social media.

This new view of social networking suggests identifying, achieving, and nurturing social capital. Organizations now have a partner in improving the pursuit of social networking by using social capital to leverage value propositions in two-way, online communications. There is benefit in the pursuit of shared expectations that focus on finding common value and a worthy return on investment of each party's contribution of time and effort.

The social network focus can be made clearer with the existence of connected-ness and dependency. Connectedness is about being in touch with people who are similar in thought or action. In this way, connectedness is a value that powers a challenging adventure into digital conversations. Dependency is valuable, but it is sometimes viewed in a negative light. That is because some believe that people are dependent on posting or tweeting the most insignificant, the most negative, the craziest bits of information one can imagine. That can be true, but it can also be true that dependency is as positive as connectedness.

Why? Social media is a way to get in touch anytime, anywhere with organizations and people who have similarities and ask questions, share information, and take the risk of getting to know each other. That is exciting and invigorating at times, and that is a reason that some cannot resist sharing anything, or everything. Think about Maslow's Hierarchy of Needs, in which love, belonging, and esteem are primary concerns. People need friendship, family, confidence, and respect to feel good about themselves. Social media can be an outlet for those feelings.

Whatever participation choice is made should be based on an understanding of both benefits and risks. Start by weighing the pros and cons of social media to understand negative AND positive implications. Organizations should keep in mind that the digital conversation is never-ending and it may be harder to catch up later if they decide to delay participation. That advice is good for individuals as well.

Social networking is already being used by many organizations because they believe that the benefits of increased or improved communications outweigh the potential problems associated with social networking. Organizations want employees to exhibit behaviors that support social networking efforts. That means there can be performance implications. To address the issues, organizations should base social networking activities on task analyzability, modeling principles, and structured reinforcement.

The SNIP methodology provides additional tools that can support business and employee development for organizations involved in social networking. If employees perceive that there is some return on the investment of their time and attention in terms of improved skills, the availability of new challenges, or increased standing in the firm, they may be more inclined to participate in the organization's social media choice. Many organizations want to understand the social networking return on investment. An improved understanding of employee perceptions and motiva-tions for participation provides a better chance of arriving at social networking that permeates the culture. Igbaria and Tan (1997) demonstrated the impact of social networking acceptance on employer and employee perceptions of performance and productivity. Some of that impact will be investigated here.

There is a relationship between social networking and perception of individual performance (Brown 2011). Organizations seeking improvements in social networking activities must first understand the nature of the network. This understanding is vital, because improvement requires identifying levels of participation, setting a standard or level for desired participation, and convincing employees that their participation has the potential to improve their job performance. Organizations should also ensure that their social networking activities are efficient. Efficiency is best achieved by providing the highest quality task analyzability, using modeling principles to affect behavior, and employing structured reinforcement to provide continuous feedback.

In the search for improvement and efficiency, SNIP methodology focuses on five types of relationships.

1. Relationship between trust in organizational leadership and participation in social networking.
2. The impact of perceived improvement potential (PIP) on participation in social networking.
3. The relationship between modeling opportunities and social networking participation.
4. The importance of task analyzability.
5. Structured reinforcement as it relates to individual improvement.

Social networking activities should focus on whether or not individuals see a value proposition in terms of their performance. In other words, do individuals believe that they will improve their skills, increase their promotion chances, or get some other benefits as a result of their participation? Will that value proposition convince them to increase their participation? These questions reflect the notion of individual impact (Igbaria and Tan 1997), which refers to the influence of online interactions on the perceived performance of the individual on the quality of his or her decision making.

As organizations assess their social networking programs and their outcomes, it is important to understand the role of trust in leadership and of perceptions of individual improvement. Any investigation should attempt to address whether social media engagement and networking foster a supportive and cooperative structure and result in increases in generalized trust. The company should seek a trusting structure that will lead to an accumulation of social capital in the form of inclusive, cooperative networks that are economically productive. Part of the research of Svendsen and Sorenson (2006) was to determine whether the levels of individual perception of productivity and levels of trust would be influenced by measuring social capital as the density of voluntary networking activities. The research determined that that any inquiry of this type should also focus on capacity of individuals to perform the necessary tasks in social networking activities.

There are many reasons for getting involved in social networking. Possibly the most important reason is that social media is viral, offering potentially unlimited ability to participate in a connected, secure, and information-rich environment that can be tailored to individual needs. Just as important, social media tools are no cost or low cost, allowing a full range of participation in many different situations and organizations.

Any analysis of characteristics of participation must begin with a thorough understanding of the social networking construct. Activities that integrate technology, telecommunications, and social interaction, including the construction of words, pictures, videos, and audio, fit under the social networking umbrella. Social networking is an umbrella term that refers to sharing and discussing information, then using social media, which are primarily Internet- and mobile-based tools. Social media sites are web-based services that allow individuals to use a protected system to construct a public or semi-public profile, maintain a list of people with whom they share a connection, and build and share their list of connections through interactive activities (Brown 2011). The explosion of new network connections in the workplace suggests an exploration of the various ways managers can affect and improve performance, or ways that workers can get better help from their leadership, is in order.

Every day, organizations and individuals sign up to take advantage of social networking benefits. But once they are participants, there is an almost inevitable desire to seek information about return on investment of time and effort. The most basic question raised is whether the participant, or the company, is better off because of social networking. Many are quick to accept social networking and the tools it offers. The large and growing numbers of people and organizations involved in social networking suggests that they are, by and large, quick to accept social networking and the tools it offers. Organizations tend to "get in the game" after short periods of deliberation over its use. Once organizations are engaged and leaders decide that an acceptable number of employees are participating, there is inevitably a question posed concerning return on investment. That question might be "Are my employees better off because we expended money or effort in social networking?" Employees who have limited participation or those who do not participate might ask "Will my participation make me a more skilled or more productive worker?"

As we continue to look at online participation, we examine several factors: trusting relationships, individual potential to improve activities, modeling opportunities, task analyzability, and structured reinforcement. But we start with trust. Social networking activities require a trusting atmosphere that allows dependence, satisfaction, and commitment between participants. Trust comes from the ongoing decision to give most people the benefit of the doubt during communication interactions. In the sense of weak ties, trust can even be extended to people one does not know from direct experience. When trust is present, one participant may make a unilateral transfer of control over certain information or resources to another participant, based on the hope or expectation that the other person's actions will satisfy his or her interests. This is an important feature of trust, because one can only be certain about the outcome after the transfer of value has been made.

The independent and interactive effects of trust and dependence on satisfaction and commitment significantly improve organizational effectiveness (Andaleeb 1996, Schöbel 2009). Sharing expectations and making inspirational appeals are examples of how leaders can promote trust from the workers. The implied benefit is that workers reciprocate and increase their commitment to the task at hand and, in a larger sense, to the organization by actively participating in activities.

In addition to trust, PIP involves a conscious determination of whether the activity or commitment involved will bring personal benefits (Brown 2011). The success of social networking as it relates to performance is based on normative practices as well as on relationships that will build trust, foster interaction, and address participant needs. PIP is based on a self-perception of effectiveness. PIP has a twofold purpose: to predict the intention to behave in a certain way and to determine whether participants will actually exhibit that behavior.

PIP seeks synergy through integration of network activities. There are three important central tasks.

1. Identify the nature and extent of the social relationships characterizing a particular community, its formal institutions, and the interaction between them.
2. Develop institutional strategies based on an understanding of these social relations, particularly the extent of bonding and bridging social capital in a society or a community.
3. Identify ways and means by which positive manifestations of social capital – widespread cooperation, trust institutional efficiency – can offset and/or be created from its negative manifestations – sectarianism, isolationism, corruption.

Organizations should find value and cooperation in social networking activities based on satisfaction of the requirements of the central tasks. At this point, aspirations are translated into realities through problem resolution, facilitation of community network building, and increased awareness of how people interact through shared information.

First, social capital allows citizens to resolve collective problems more easily... Second, social capital greases the wheels that allow communities to advance smoothly. Where people are trusting and trustworthy, and where they are subject to repeated interactions with fellow citizens, everyday business and social transactions are less costly... A third way in which social capital improves our lot is by widening our awareness of the many ways in which our fates are linked. People who have active and trusting connections to others – whether family members, friends, or fellow bowlers – develop or maintain character traits that are good for the rest of society. (Putnam 1993)

Next, we consider modeling opportunities. Organizations can enhance the social networking experience through understanding and employment of effective modeling techniques. Employees can learn social networking behaviors by observing someone else, by examining the outcomes of another employee's participation, or by behavior facilitation. Behavior facilitation occurs when a participant is reminded of a previous learned behavior, or organizational norm, through modeling another participant (Manz & Sims 1981)."

Outcome expectations are also viable for organizational use. This is modeled where participants see others successfully navigating the social networking endeavor. They may even see others being openly recognized for their efforts, and this may create positive expectations. Participants may also gain information from the evidence of a model's behavior that will help form outcome expectancies. Therefore, observing a model is a type of what Manz & Sims (1981) called vicarious learning. Vicarious learning can lead to behavioral change without the learner actually performing the behavior or without directly experiencing the consequences.

Social networking activities can also benefit from social learning theory, which suggests four component processes of observational learning. This theory stresses continuous reciprocal interaction between cognitive, behavioral, and environmental influences (Bandura 1977):

1. Attention, using modeled events and observer characteristics.
2. Retention, including symbolic coding, cognitive organization, symbolic rehearsal and motor rehearsal.
3. Motor Reproduction, including physical capabilities, self-observation of reproduction and accuracy of feedback.
4. Motivation, including external, vicarious and self-reinforcement.

There is a very basic approach to modeling that organizations can use that we will refer to as MTT: Model, Train, and Test. MTT requires that organizations model the skill, use training to achieve mastery, and test the new skills in key projects. MTT is based on guided mastery modeling (Bandura 1986) and is beneficial in addressing task breakdowns and structured reinforcement that coincides with social network interactions. This is how organizations develop intellectual, social, and behavioral competencies.

Begin with modeling the relevant skills for basic competencies. General rules and strategies for dealing with different situations are taught to help people learn how to apply the general rules to specific situations. Once rules and norms are established, provide guidance and create opportunities for skill perfection. This is done in simulated situations where employees can learn without worrying that they might be inadequately skilled or that they will make mistakes. This modeling and guided performance under simulated conditions has been shown to be an excellent way to create competencies (Wood and Bandura 1989). The skills probably will not be used for a prolonged period unless individuals have a sense that they will be useful skills when put into practice in work situations.

Finally, MTT requires provision of opportunities to find self-directed success. Experiencing a level of success with new-found skills can create high beliefs in both individual abilities and in the new emphasis on social networking activities. Allow newly-trained employees to employ their skills in high-level job situations that are likely to produce good results.

Porras (1982) suggested that mastery modeling, MTT for our purposes, can improve not only employee performance and affect morale and productivity in organizations, it can also affect supervisors' skills in a positive way. Supervisors who had the benefit of the modeling program maintained and even improved their supervisory problem-solving skills in ratings provided by their employees. The plant in which the modeling program was applied had a lower absentee rate, a lower turnover of employees, and a higher level of productivity in follow-up assessments.

The next important consideration has to do with task analyzability and behavioral indicators. Behavioral indicators can prove invaluable to activities that promote new uses of social networking, that seek to increase the current level of participation, or that seek to provide a value proposition that affects participation in a positive way. Elton Mayo's Hawthorne studies from 1924 to 1932 addressed aligning human resources with organizational factors and showing, in part, that workers respond to group norms, social pressures, and observation (Ivancevich 2008). A group norm is a major factor that the studies have in common with social networking. Task analyzability is a way to allow organizations to take advantage of group norms and other similarities.

When determining how to measure performance, it is useful to start with media richness theory, which is derived from contingency theory (Rice 1992). The theory proposes that when information processing capabilities match information processing demands, performance will improve. The Rice study examines communication media that differ in media richness or social presence, focusing on conditions of differing task analyzability. The findings show that the effect is on self-reported performance components such as quality of work, effectiveness, productivity, ability to obtain information, decision-making ability, access to others, etc. Rice measured media usage as the reported percentage of information used in one's work that was obtained from online databases.

That brings this examination to task analyzability, which is computed as the mean of four items assessed and standardized by Withey, Daft, and Cooper (1983):

1.   Is there a clearly known way to do the major types of work you normally encounter?
2.   Is there a clearly defined body of knowledge matter which guides you in doing your work?
3.   Is there an understandable sequence of steps that can be followed in doing your work?
4.   To do your work, do you actually rely on established procedures and practices?

Task analyzability requires identification of procedures that define the steps to follow in performing a task. That means building social networking activities into a plan that features well-defined steps that are analyzable and that lend themselves to fit well into the organization's planning activities.

Finally, our social networking and improved performance focus turns to structured reinforcement. Continuous reinforcement is important because learning experts believe that it is the most important principle of learning (Ivancevich 2008). A structured reinforcement plan that provides feedback during critical performance times allows real-time information concerning whether the relevant actions are correct or incorrect. Structured reinforcement is characterized by on-demand training, real-time results, ongoing recognition and reinforcement tied to specific actions, and assistance to continue value-plus actions or eliminate value-minus actions.

Structured reinforcement can be accomplished by finding the most appropriate uses of social ties, both weak and strong, and then employing their relevant strengths and weaknesses (Hossain and de Silva 2009). Weak ties are characterized by absent or infrequent contact and lack of emotional closeness and reciprocal services. They are considered best suited for innovation (Granovetter 1973). Strong ties are those that demonstrate strong investment of time and reciprocity. Barry Wellman (1997) argued that sets of actors who maintain strong ties are more likely to trust each other in knowledge sharing, behavior modeling, and the decision-making process (Wellman and Wortley 1990). The research suggests that organizations should create as many weak ties as possible to foster open communications and innovation. However, to influence behavior and affect performance, the organization should look to create strong ties.

The bottom line of structured reinforcement is to go beyond simply identifying others who are engaged in the same specialty area and who are taking on the same tasks. Go beyond simply modeling behaviors. The goal is to identify what steps are taken and determine whether the employee's right-now actions are value-plus or value-minus. That type of goal-seeking venture requires more information in the social networking experience. Table 1 offers valuable social networking concepts.

Table 1. Social networking concepts

Social Networking Matrix		
The matrix provided below provides concepts that organization leaders and planners can apply to social networking programs as a checklist for program feedback and follow up. The concepts represent important social media program building blocks.		
Characteristic	**Definition**	**Success Requirements**
Trust	Trust is about believing that another party is reliable and that they will act in a manner that is favorable to the relationship between parties. *	• Increase openness in digital activities • Focus on employee perceptions and motivations • Clearly identify acceptable participation • Set a participation standard • Offer opportunity for personal benefits
Performance Improvement Potential (PIP)	A conscious determination of whether the activity or commitment involved will bring personal benefits which is based on a self-perception of effectiveness.	• Obtain acceptable SNIP Score • Plan to focus on strengths and address weaknesses
Modeling	Learn social networking behaviors by observing someone else, by examining the outcomes of another employee's participation, or by behavior facilitation (remind employees of prior learned behavior).	• Emulate effective programs • Research emerging technologies • Benchmark successes
Task Analyzability	Identification of procedures that define the steps to follow in performing a task.	• Establish a clear way to do the work • Define the relevant body of knowledge • Understandable sequence of steps • Establish procedures and practices
Structured Reinforcement	On-demand training, real-time results, ongoing recognition and reinforcement tied to specific actions, and assistance to continue value-plus actions or eliminate value-minus actions.	• Relevant training on social networking platforms • Publish results of the activity • Reinforce of desired behaviors

NOTE: * When trust is present, one participant may make a unilateral transfer of control over certain information or resources to another participant, based on the hope or expectation that the other person's actions will satisfy his or her interests.

NEW SOCIAL NETWORKING

This book is a new source for social networking methodology. It presents ways to focus on expectation, value, and return on investment of the era in social networking. A foundation is now established to help in defining ways to create a decision matrix, which could lead to improved performance and more effective social networking participation. The matrix uses trust in organizational leadership, PIP, modeling, task analyzability, and structured reinforcement as the basis of a plan of action.

The distinction between social networking and social media should now be clear. Social networking is about using online interactions and building communities to share experiences, get advice, and make decisions. Social media is about the platforms that allow us to work in those communities.

Trusting relationships are essential to social networking, allowing open and ongoing communications to prosper. PIP seeks synergy through integration of network activities, creating valuable social interactions. MTT, or Model, Train, and Test, ensures that organizations address task breakdowns and structured reinforcement that coincides with social network interactions. Organizations must focus on well-defined steps that enhance training in social networking activities. Structured reinforcement is important because it provides on-demand training, real-time results, ongoing recognition, and reinforcement tied to specific actions.

REFERENCES

Andaleeb, S. S. (1996). An experimental investigation of satisfaction and commitment in marketing channels: The role of trust and dependence. *Journal of Retailing*, *72*(1), 77–93. doi:10.1016/S0022-4359(96)90006-8

Bandura, A. (1977). *Social learning theory*. Englewood Cliffs, NJ: Prentice Hall.

Bandura, A. (1986). *Social foundations of thought and action: a social cognitive theory*. Englewood Cliffs, NJ: Prentice-Hall.

Brown, M. Sr. (2011). *Social networking and individual performance: Examining predictors of participation Ph.D*. Old Dominion University.

Granovetter, M. S. (1973). The Strength of Weak Ties. *American Journal of Sociology*, *78*(6), 1360–1380. doi:10.1086/225469

Hossain, L., & de Silva, A. (2009). Exploring user acceptance of technology using social networks. *The Journal of High Technology Management Research*, *20*(1), 1–18. doi:10.1016/j.hitech.2009.02.005

Igbaria, M., & Tan, M. (1997). The consequences of information technology acceptance on subsequent individual performance. *Information & Management*, *32*(3), 113–121. doi:10.1016/S0378-7206(97)00006-2

Ivancevich, J. M., Konopaske, R., & Matteson, M. T. (2008). Organizational Behavior and Management. New York.

Madden, M., & Jones, S. (2008). *Networked Workers*. Washington, DC: Pew Research Center.

Manz, C. C., & Sims, H. P. Jr. (1981). Vicarious Learning: The Influence of Modeling on Organizational Behavior. *Academy of Management Review*, *6*(1), 105–113.

Porras, J. J., Hargis, K., Patterson, K. J., Maxfield, D. G., Roberts, N., & Bies, R. J. (1982). Modeling-Based Organizational Development: A Longitudinal Assessment. *The Journal of Applied Behavioral Science*, *18*(4), 433–446. doi:10.1177/002188638201800405

Putnam, R. D. (1993). *Bowling Alone*. New York: Simon & Schuster Paperbacks.

Rice, R. E. (1992). Task Analyzability, Use of New Media, and Effectiveness: A Multi-Site Exploration of Media Richness. *Organization Science*, *3*(4), 475–500. doi:10.1287/orsc.3.4.475

Schöbel, M. (2009). Trust in high-reliability organizations. *Social Sciences Information. Information Sur les Sciences Sociales*, *48*(2), 315–333. doi:10.1177/0539018409102416

Shetzer, L. (1993). A social information processing model of employee participation. *Organization Science*, *4*(2), 252–268. doi:10.1287/orsc.4.2.252

Svendsen, G., & Sørensen, J. F. L. (2006). The socioeconomic power of social capital. *The International Journal of Sociology and Social Policy*, *26*(9/10), 411–429. doi:10.1108/01443330610690550

Wellman, B. (1997). *An electronic group is virtually a social network. In Culture of the Internet* (pp. 179–205). Hillsdale, NJ: Lawrence Erlbaum.

Wellman, B., & Wortley, S. (1990). Different Strokes from Different Folks: Community Ties and Social Support. *American Journal of Sociology*, *96*(3), 558–588. doi:10.1086/229572

Withey, M., Daft, R. L., & Cooper, W. H. (1983). Measures of Perrows Work Unit Technology: An Empirical Assessment and a New Scale. *Academy of Management Journal*, *26*(1), 45–63. doi:10.2307/256134

Wood, R., & Bandura, A. (1989). Social Cognitive Theory of Organizational Management. *Academy of Management Review*, *14*(3), 361–384.

Chapter 2
SNIP:
A Survey Instrument

Michael A. Brown Sr.
Florida International University, USA

ABSTRACT

This chapter focuses on the development of a new assessment tool: Social Networking and Individual Performance (SNIP). This tool can provide valuable data for organizations and even individuals. The data provided through use of the tool can determine whether employees are exhibiting behaviors that are supportive of the organization's goals, thus allowing everyone to benefit based on a return on the investment in time or attention that could lead to improved skills. Employees might then reap benefits like availability of new challenges or increased standing in the organization. The data can also provide insight on improving personal social media activities.

DOI: 10.4018/978-1-5225-1963-8.ch002

SNIP: SOCIAL NETWORKING AND INDIVIDUAL PERFORMANCE

SNIP allows organizations to include performance considerations in the beginning stages of the social media journey and the subsequent policy decisions that must be created and adjusted. The survey offers leaders and planners three very important assets. First, the data analysis provides tools that address online interactions as they happen. Second, the data analysis suggests strengths, weaknesses, and perceptions, information that can be used to affect behaviors supportive of the organization's goals and objectives. Finally, a focus on positive performance and supportive participation is built into the process, not bolted on after the program is already running. The process of developing and validating an effective instrument on a new population is extensive and requires data from many subjects collected from different samples on variables beyond what is contained in the instrument. SNIP can help with that process as explained in Table 1.

SNIP SURVEY INSTRUMENT

Dr. Michael Brown and Jeremy Albright of Methods, Ann Arbor, Michigan collaborated on the SNIP assessment tool you see in these pages. The project got its focus from an interest in using Performance Improvement Potential (PIP) to create an assessment tool that would allow organizations to take full advantage of the relationship between social networking and individual performance. PIP is important because organizations may be more successful in getting employees to support a particular social media tool or follow a social media plan if they perceive there is a benefit in exhibiting those behaviors. If employees make a choice that organizations value, everyone could benefit based on a return on the investment in time or attention that could lead to improved skills, for example. This cooperation could

Table 1. SNIP value

> The true value lies in evaluating social networking and individual performance differences in participation, behavior, technology acceptance, and trust. A formal evaluation of a person's "SNIP score" could be instrumental in measuring acceptance and rejection. This is important because it is almost effortless for organizations to get involved in social networking activities. The questions about performance are inevitable based on the amount of time people spend online.
>
> The SNIP approach urges organizations to ask questions about relationships between social networking and individual performance much earlier in the process. If that does not happen as part of the goal-setting that should precede social networking startup, it should happen as early in the process as possible.

bring additional benefits to employees in the form of availability of new challenges or increased standing in the organization.

A SNIP survey can help organizations profit from a value proposition that can lead to enhanced social networking participation. The wealth of knowledge and information exchange that could result from increased and/or improved performance could also provide a clear view of the dynamics of changes processes. The digital conversation is so dynamic and fast-paced that organizations should welcome any opportunity to have an influence on behaviors that enhance participation. SNIP presents that opportunity through a scoring system that provides empirical evidence of important relationships and adds measurement and feedback to these important activities.

The survey instrument is valuable because it allows organizations to collect data that can be analyzed quickly. If the response rate is sufficient based on the population demographics, the results can be generalized to other populations. This is an important benefit for organizations interested in aligning good social networking practices with other organizations and stakeholders. The findings to date suggest a reliable direction for planning programs and may set the stage for longitudinal studies that could help identify a range of best practices for organizations.

Why SNIP? Many organizations do not consider performance when they create social media policies aimed at improving online interactions and providing security protections. In the course of my research, I've noticed that companies normally do not worry about return on investment or performance implications until they've been running social networking activities for months or years. SNIP allows leaders and planners to include performance considerations, or PIP, and other factors in the beginning stages of the social media journey and in the subsequent policy decisions that must be created and adjusted. The survey offers leaders and planners three very important assets. First, the data analysis provides tools that address online interactions as they happen. Second, the data analysis suggests strengths, weaknesses, and perceptions, information that can be used to affect behaviors supportive of the organization's goals and objectives. Finally, a focus on positive performance and supportive participation is built into the process, not bolted on after the program is already running.

Using this survey, leaders can develop the social networking process with the mission in mind. In other words, determine the end state *BEFORE* starting or changing social networking activities. This is a critical change to the norm of deciding on a process and then trying to fit it to a mission. This truly allows the destination, not the path, to be the focus around which the components and interactions of the network are built (Goldsmith & Eggers, 2004).

Social Networking Background

Before examining use of the survey, we should closely examine social networking and performance. Success requires three things:

1. Support for the organizational approach.
2. Good task analyzability.
3. A structured process.

The SNIP survey is useful because organizations that commit to social networking also commit to allowing employees to spend an unspecified number of hours making connections and joining communities. Focusing on the three items mentioned ensures that leaders can derive benefits that go beyond connecting people and address improving individual performance. The basis of the survey is the Hawthorne effect and social learning theory, while social network analysis (SNA) is used to clarify important characteristics. An examination of prior research serves as a foundation to show that social networking and individual participation share the activities of bonding (establishing strong ties), bridging (establishing informal ties), and linking (establishing voluntary ties). So, the survey addresses the idea that the key to improving performance in an organization relies on three things:

1. Concrete incentives to participate in the kind of social media tools that the organization values,
2. Improved definition of the work required through task analyzability, and
3. Continuous feedback through structured reinforcement.

Let us begin with information about Hawthorne, social learning, and SNA before moving on to understand performance characteristics. We must understand characteristics that promote performance through social networking in support of organizational goals. To begin, behavioral intention is about measuring the extent to which a person believed that the technology was capable of being used advantageously and provided positive expected outcomes (Davis 1989). Mark S. Granovetter discussed the use of social ties that are strong or weak as major factors in assessing performance (Granovetter 1973). Weak ties are absent or infrequent contact, lack of emotional closeness and reciprocal services. Strong ties, on the other hand, demonstrate a strong investment of time and reciprocity. Trust is increased when pairs of actors who maintain strong ties collaborate in knowledge sharing (Wellman 1997) and in the decision-making process (Wellman and Wortley 1990). An organizational focus that results from attention to these characteristics promotes the following capabilities:

- **Advanced Consulting Skills:**
  - **Data Gathering:** Improves ability and greater access to information.
- **Analysis:** Leverages strong and weak ties.
- **Improved Assignment Performance:**
  - **Task Execution:** Uses technology to improve capability,
  - **Individual Contribution:** Archives and shares information via the network.
- **Improved Functional Skills:**
  - **Functional Knowledge:** Increases capacity by leveraging access to greater number of people, programs, and information,
  - **Professional Growth:** Embraces technological capability and leverages it to multiply skills and abilities,
  - **Firm/Industry:** Uses technological capability to understand firm concerns and increase scope of firm involvement.
- **Enhanced Client & Market Development:**
  - **Market Focus and Strategy:** Leverages technological capability to enhance current service delivery in market and identifies additional service delivery possibilities.

Figure 1 is a kind of flowchart for the relationship between individual performance and social networking. The focus of individual performance is on strong ties that support structure. The focus of social networking is on weak ties that support innovation and trust in people who one might otherwise have no reason to trust. Some experts believe that weak ties promote trust because of the absent or infrequent contact and lack of emotional closeness. It is believed that people feel comfortable with virtual strangers who will not judge them like friends and family might.

To understand the existence of social ties and the strength at which they are present, we refer to the Hawthorne effect. Mayo's work with the Hawthorne studies (1949) is helpful in illustrating the need for an understanding of the task at hand and for reinforcement of the employee's effort. The importance of tasks, how they are analyzed in terms of the type of work that is necessary, and the amount of knowledge matter that is available was examined by Withey et al (1983). These researchers also discussed a clear progression of how the work should be done and easy access to information on relevant procedures and practices. This discovery is important in assisting organizations with employee perceptions that are crucial to acceptance or rejection of social networking programs and initiatives. Leaders and

Figure 1. Examining the communicative process

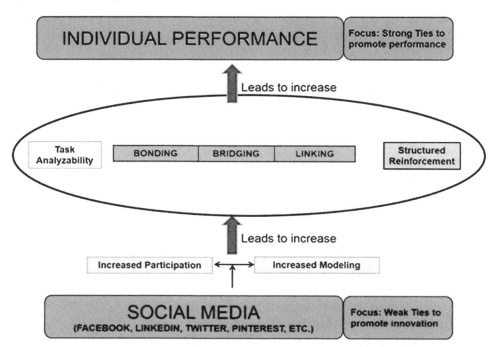

planners can enhance success by ensuring employee opportunity in the areas of knowledge sharing, behavior modeling, and the decision-making process.

Mayo's Hawthorne Effect, Emotional Intelligence (EI), and radical change are behavioral indicators that can prove invaluable to activities that promote new uses of social networking or that seek to increase the level of current use. The Hawthorne Effect suggests that providing complementary structure to the networking environment could deliver positive results. Major findings from Elton Mayo's Hawthorne studies from 1924 to 1932 addressed aligning human resources with organizational factors. Mayo's studies showed that workers respond to group norms, social pressures, and observation (Ivancevich 2008). A group norm is a major factor that the studies have in common with social networking. The way to take advantage of group norms and other similarities is through effective task analyzability practices and structured reinforcement.

There is another construct that is interesting in this context of Mayo's work – EI. Similar to Mayo's discovered focus in the Hawthorne studies, EI is relevant in understanding established behaviors, which is a necessary first step in redirecting or changing a person's actions.

EI (Cooper 1997) is a theory that organizations can use to determine desired behaviors for success. EI provides a basis to understand employees because it is the ability to sense, understand, and effectively apply the power and acumen of emotions as a source of human energy, information, trust, creativity, and influence. Those who possess emotional intelligence can effectively acknowledge and value feelings in themselves and in others and can respond to those feelings in an effective way.

Paying attention to emotions can save the leader time by directing energies more effectively, and expanding opportunities. Emotional Intelligence has three driving forces: build trusting relationships, increase energy and effectiveness, and create the future. Research shows that Emotional Intelligence far outweighs IQ and raw brainpower as the primary success factor in decision making, creating dynamic organizations, and achieving lifestyle satisfaction and success (Cooper 1997).

To some employees, social networking is a radical change. The effect of emotion on radical change dynamics can be best understood by looking at the change process in separate components. There are three critical steps required to achieve radical change: receptivity, mobilization, and learning (Huy 1999). Receptivity is a person's willingness to consider change and it is characterized as both a state and a process. At any fixed point in time, a person can accept the need for the proposed change if there is an interpretive, attitudinal state on the cognitive and emotional level.

The concrete action a person takes in the direction of change is mobilization. This is the process of rallying and propelling different segments of the organization to undertake joint action and to realize common change goals (Huy 1999).

Receptivity and mobilization are linked to, or lead to, learning. Individuals learn by thinking and then acting, using the outcome of action to revise his or her belief system (Kim 1993). Receptivity is an observed change where individuals exhibit various stages of willingness to accept the proposed change, from resigned, passive acceptance to enthusiastic endorsement.

Huy's (1999) characterization of the radical change process maintains that when receptivity leads to motivation, individuals and organizations also can learn from the outcomes of the changes they enact, and learning provides a feedback loop from the outcomes of behavioral change back to receptivity. In other words, the learning process is a beginning, but that beginning leads back to using the process to sustain receptivity at the desired level. In turn, sustained receptivity at the correct level leads to continued mobilization and so forth. All of the characteristics of radical change are important as one evaluates how to enhance performance through social networking.

According to social learning theory, increased participation and modeling can improve social networking activities. Any activity that the organization conducts, leads, or values should address satisfying needs that promote employee productivity and mission accomplishment. Similarly, SNA uses bonding, bridging, and linking to bring participants together and foster performance improvements. This approach requires a mutual effort using bonding, bridging, and linking to build standards that are identified, operationalized, and achieved.

Social learning theory uses four component processes – attention, retention, motor reproduction, and motivation – to explain observational learning, which stresses continuous reciprocal interaction between cognitive, behavioral, and environmental influences (Bandura 1977). Attention is about using modeled events and observer characteristics, which retention involves including symbolic coding, cognitive organization, symbolic rehearsal, and motor rehearsal. Physical capabilities, self-observation of reproduction, and accuracy of feedback are motor reproduction characteristics. Motivation processes are external, vicarious, and self-reinforcement. For instance, an example of vicarious reinforcements would be seeing people who train hard win gold medals at the Olympics, reinforcing physical exercise in observers.

Additionally, Bandura's guided mastery modeling is beneficial in addressing task breakdowns and structured reinforcement that coincides with social network interactions. The construct is used widely to develop intellectual, social, and behavioral competencies, with the best results coming from the use of three elements: skill modeling, guided skill mastery, and a transfer program (Bandura 1986). The process begins with modeling of the appropriate skills to convey the basic competencies. General rules and strategies for dealing with different situations are taught to help people learn how to apply the general rules to specific situations.

Once individuals are equipped with an understanding of the rules, the next step is to give them guidance and opportunities to perfect their skills. Simulated situations are important in putting communicators in relationships in which they do not have to fear the possibility that they might be inadequately skilled or that they will make mistakes. This modeling and guided performance under simulated conditions has been shown to be an excellent way to create competencies (Wood and Bandura 1989). The skills probably will not be used for a prolonged period unless individuals have a sense that they will be useful skills when put into practice in work situations.

Therefore, the next requirement for effective mastery modeling is a transfer program aimed at providing self-directed success. People need the experience of a level of success with their new set of skills that is high enough to allow them to believe equally in themselves and in the value of the new ways of doing business. An effective transfer program achieves this by allowing the new skills to be employed on the job in situations that are likely to produce good results.

Porras (1982) suggested that mastery modeling can improve not only employee performance and affect morale and productivity in organizations, it can also affect supervisors' skills in a positive way. Supervisors who had the benefit of the modeling program maintained and even improved their supervisory problem-solving skills in ratings provided by their employees. The plant in which the modeling program was applied had a lower absentee rate, lower turnover of employees, and a higher level of productivity in follow-up assessments.

Behavior self-management to affect performance is another area suggested by social learning theory (Davis and Luthans 1980). Awareness of the contingencies that regulate behavior is acquired mainly through self-observation and self-monitoring.

This approach requires awareness of the contingencies regulating behavior, which is acquired mainly through self-observation and self-monitoring. Self-monitoring demonstrates frequency of the behavior and defines contingencies like antecedent cues, cognitions, and response-consequences that are taking place (Davis and Luthans 1980). Self-monitoring also promotes objectivity in evaluating behavior and designing an intervention strategy. Done effectively, this effort usually establishes a new behavior, increases or maintains an existing behavior, or reduces or eliminates a behavior (Mahoney and Thoresen 1974, Watson and Tharp 1977).

Beyond social learning theory, SNA literature discusses connecting people to others with similar interests and attitudes. The shared relationship does not, however, indicate ways to use social network benefits to influence, or even to drive, individual performance in a positive direction. Social capital, contingency theory, and social exchange theory provide additional insights for social networking and individual performance relationships. Woolcock and Narayan (2000) discussed the evolution of social capital research that identified four distinct approaches: communitarian view, networks view, institutional view, and synergy view. The synergy view is relevant for this research effort because it lends itself to the most comprehensive and coherent policy prescriptions. This view emphasizes incorporating different levels and dimensions, and recognizes the positive and negative outcomes that social capital can generate. Social capital can be defined as the value and cooperation that is created by social networks and other human relationships.

Contingency theory argues that organizations must respond to new and changing environmental conditions by redesigning their internal processing capabilities through structures and technology (Rice 1992). The theory is that no particular organizational design assures performance. Performance is contingent on an appropriate match between contextual variables such as task demands and organizational arrangements such as communication structures and media.

Social exchange theory proposes that social behavior is the result of an exchange process. This exchange is intended to maximize benefits and minimize costs, requiring people to weigh the potential benefits and risks of social relationships. When the risks outweigh the rewards, people will terminate or abandon that relationship.

A synergy view comes from Woolcock and Narayan (2000) as an attempt to "integrate the compelling work emerging from the networks and institutional camps." They list three central tasks for theorists, researchers, and policymakers. The first is to identify the nature and extent of the social relationships characterizing a particular community, its formal institutions, and the interaction between them. Next, it is important to develop institutional strategies based on an understanding of these social relations, particularly the extent of bonding and bridging social capital in a society or a community. Finally, identify ways and means by which positive manifestations of social capital – widespread cooperation, trust, and institutional efficiency – can offset and/or be created from its negative manifestations – sectarianism, isolationism, corruption.

Millen and Fontaine (2003) noted that study participants agreed that community activities influence various personal benefits, specifically productivity. That study's finding indicates further development of the work of Dennis and Valacich (1994), part of which addressed synergy. Synergy develops when a participant builds on information provided by another participant to create new ideas, typically because that participant has additional information, different skills, or a different view of the problem. Through social networking, organizations have ways to archive shared experiences and then give community members opportunities to recreate that success or to apply the same experience to a new effort.

When determining how to measure performance, it is useful to start with media richness theory. This theory is derived from contingency theory (Rice 1992). The theory proposes that when information processing capabilities match information processing demands, performance will improve. The Rice study tests whether using communication media that differ in media richness or social presence in conditions of differing task analyzability affects self-reported performance components such as quality of work, effectiveness, productivity, ability to obtain information, decision-making ability, access to others, etc. Rice measured media usage as the reported percentage of information used in one's work that was obtained from online databases. Task analyzability was computed as the mean of four items assessed and standardized by Withey, Daft, and Cooper (1983):

1. Is there a clearly known way to do the major types of work you normally encounter?
2. Is there a clearly defined body of knowledge matter which guides you in doing your work?
3. Is there an understandable sequence of steps that can be followed in doing your work?
4. To do your work, do you actually rely on established procedures and practices?

ANALYZING PERFORMANCE

The notion of task analyzability leads us to a discussion of the performance characteristics that were listed earlier in this chapter. Those characteristics are support for the organizational approach, good task analyzability, and a structured process.

Support for the organization is an important consideration, but studies on social influence have not shown a lot of focus on the process through which social influence unfolds to impact individual IT use. There is not a lot of research that demonstrates how individual users actively use social information in their decisions regarding IT adoption and use (Jasperson, Sambamurthy, & Zmud, 2000). Also, although social ties have been examined under a wide range of social science disciplines (Lee et al., 2003), relatively little attempt has been made to integrate both factors into user's adoption of information technologies in the virtual environment. Furthermore, no attempt has been made to distinguish between the influence brought about by strong and weak ties separately in accepting a technology. The examination in this book incorporates these social ties as major factors of user acceptance of information technology in the context of a virtual community.

The strength of a tie affects the level of resource exchanged, which is shown with the path analysis in Figure 2. Where a stronger tie relation takes place, resources can be more freely exchanged and shared than where a weaker tie relation takes place (Garton, Haythornthwaite, &Wellman, 1997). Although weak ties have the ability to provide people with information and resources that are usually unavailable to them within their social circle, stronger ties can provide better assistance overall and this service is freely available (Granovetter, 1982). Strongly tied individuals are

Figure 2. Path analysis
Based on Hossain and de Silva (2009).

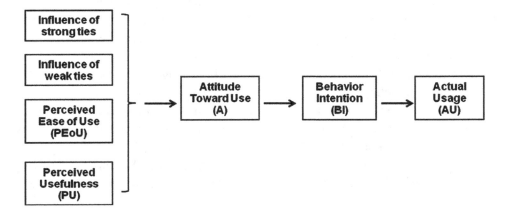

motivated to share what information or resources they have and thus provide ready access to information circulating their network, and provide help whenever needed to any of their stronger ties. However, due to the close association within strong tie networks, they are often left with access only to the same resources as others with whom they are closely tied (Haythornthwaite, 2002).

Individuals adopt innovations with mainly private, personal, individual consequences. Such innovations depend on interactions through strong ties, such as the community ties and face-to-face interactions (Wejnert, 2002). Furthermore, whether or not an individual considers an innovation for adoption is strongly determined by compatibility between the characteristics of an innovation and the needs of the individual (Valente & Rogers,1995). Strong ties impose greater demand for conformity on the individuals and they are expected to heed the advice of their stronger ties. The affective content of these relationships strengthens the role of their influence (Ruef, 2002). As such, if one individual in such a network adopts something new, it is likely that the others will conform. However, it would be unlikely that an individual in such a network would adopt anything new since they have pressure to conform.

Individuals who directly interact with each other and have a strong social tie may tend to mimic each other's behavior because of direct communication and influence. These individuals are said to be structurally equivalent. Structurally equivalent individuals are subject to similar normative pressures and standards and are therefore more likely to adopt the same innovations. These individuals model their behavior after those with whom they have direct relations and those to whom they have similar roles or, to put it simply, their strong social ties (Burt, 1987). According to Wellman (1997) pairs who maintain strong ties are more likely to share their knowledge and when such knowledge is from a strong social tie it is likely that this knowledge is accepted as true. Strong ties also provide broader support in one's decision making (Wellman & Wortley, 1990). These provide evidence that the influence of stronger ties have a positive effect on one's technology acceptance process. However, the influence of weak ties cannot be undermined since many researchers believe that weak ties provide a similar influence to that of strong ties.

The networks to which people belong affect knowledge and resource exchange. In network interactions, weakly tied persons are less likely to share resources, however they have the ability to provide access to more diverse types of resources because each of these people operates in distinct social networks and therefore has access to different knowledge and resources (Garton et al., 1997). It is expected that one's weak ties do not have relations with one another, but one's strong ties are more likely to be a densely knit group. However, each of these weak ties has a densely knit cluster of their own, which means that the tie forms an important bridge between the two densely knit clusters. Therefore, these two clusters would not be connected to each other if it were not for the existence of the weak tie (Granovetter, 1982). This connection provided by weak ties helps in diffusion of knowledge and resources between the connecting social networks.

According to the "strength of weak ties" theory of Granovetter (1973), an innovation is diffused to a larger number of individuals and traverses a greater social distance when passed through weak ties rather than strong ones. As such individuals with more weak ties have greater mobility and can live up to the expectations of different people in different places and at different times, which makes it possible to withhold inner attitudes while conforming to various expectations. However, people with strong ties share norms so strongly that little effort is needed to determine the intentions of others, since they are all alike. As such, weak ties allow for the adoption of innovation, which is made difficult by the conformity present within strong ties (Borgatti, 2000). Weak ties allow for more experimentation in selectively combining ideas from one source with another and impose fewer concerns regarding social conformity (Ruef, 2002). As such, individuals relying on weak ties as sources of ideas are more likely to be innovative.

Much of the research conducted so far on the influence of ties has focused on offline relationships. However, it is also necessary to consider online ties since there is an increase in communities built online, and as such the influence of ties formed online becomes as important as the influence of ties formed offline. According to Wellman et al. (1996) computer supported social networks (CSSNs) should not support much reciprocity, because many online ties are between people who have never met face-to-face and are therefore weakly tied. They are socially and physically distant and not bound into densely knit work or community structure. As such, Wellman et al. (1996) assume that it is unlikely that there are strong ties found online and that the majority of the ties online are weak ties.

However, many other researchers such as Haythornthwaite (2002) assume that the characteristics held in offline environments are the same as those in the online environment. Thus, online ties, like offline ties, are expected to be stronger to the extent that they demonstrate greater varieties of interaction, exchange, and emotional support. This work is about exploring online ties, showing that online exchanges are as real in terms of their impact on the tie as are offline exchanges, where social support given online or offline is an exchange that adds to maintaining a tie. Therefore, it is said that the number and types of exchanges determine the strength of a tie, rather than whether it is maintained online, offline, or both (Haythornthwaite, 2002).

Perrow's task analyzability (1967) defines the way in which individuals are able to respond to problems encountered in the process of task completion. Analyzable tasks are useful because they have predetermined responses to potential problems or well-known procedures, allowing outcomes that can be easily understood. Task analyzability seeks information in four areas (Withey, Daft et al. 1983):

1. Clear definitions for accomplishing the major types of work,
2. Clearly defined and available body of knowledge,
3. Clear sequence of steps for tasks, and
4. Reliance on policy and procedures.

If there is good task analyzability, the next consideration for improving performance is structured reinforcement. Continuous reinforcement is important because learning experts believe that it is the most important principle of learning (Ivancevich 2008). A structured reinforcement plan that provides feedback during critical performance times allows real-time information concerning whether the relevant actions are correct or incorrect. Structured reinforcement is characterized by on-demand training, real-time results, ongoing recognition and reinforcement tied to specific actions, and assistance to continue value-plus actions or eliminate value-minus actions.

Structured reinforcement can be accomplished by finding the most appropriate uses of social ties, both weak and strong, and then employing their relevant strengths and weaknesses (Hossain & de Silva 2009). Weak ties are characterized by absent or infrequent contact and lack of emotional closeness and reciprocal services, and they are considered best suited for innovation (Granovetter 1973). Strong ties are those that demonstrate strong investment of time and reciprocity. Barry Wellman (1997) argued that sets of actors who maintain strong ties are more likely to trust each other in knowledge sharing, behavior modeling, and in the decision-making process (Wellman and Wortley 1990). The research suggests that organizations should create as many weak ties as possible to foster open communications and innovation. However, to influence behavior and affect performance, the organization should look to create strong ties.

Additional research illustrates various uses of Performance Support Tools (PSTs), which provide workers with on-the-job help, advice, information, examples, or assurance. Like Electronic Performance Support Systems (EPSSs), PSTs describe the technological tools that help people make decisions, plan for activities, and perform tasks (Paino and Rossett 2008). This study requires identifying the relevant PSTs for assisting employees with their most critical tasks.

Simply using PSTs correctly, however, is not the answer. The idea is to go beyond simply identifying others who are engaged in the same specialty area and who are taking on the same tasks. The goal is to identify what steps are taken and determine whether the employee's right-now actions are value-plus or value-minus. That type of goal-seeking venture requires more information in the area of social influence.

In addition, contingency theory argues that organizations must respond to new and changing environmental conditions by redesigning their internal processing capabilities through structures and technologies (Rice 1992). A basic underlying principle is the "law of requisite variety." It states that the variety of the conversion process must match the variety of the input demands. Thus, contingency theory makes at least one very explicit proposition: performance is not assured by any particular organizational design, but is contingent on an appropriate match between contextual variables (such as task demands) and organizational arrangements (such as communication structures and media).

Any examination of task analyzability requires a look at productivity. In research effort, productivity was measured in two ways (Cerulo 1990). One measure was objective, and one was a subjective, self-reported count. The objective measure of productivity was created by scanning seven computerized abstracting/indexing services for the three-year period immediately prior to interviewing the subjects in this sample. The subjective measure of productivity was created from interview data. Each subject in the sample was asked to indicate the number of professional articles he or she had published (actually in print) over the past three years.

Productivity, according to the Bureau of Labor Statistics, "is a concept that expresses the relationship between the quantity of goods and services produced – output – and the quantity of labor, capital, land, energy, and other resources that produced it – input" (Bearman, Guynup et al. 1985). Simply expressed, the relationship is: Productivity = output/input. Increasing the organization's productivity could mean huge savings. An examination of the activities of knowledge workers indicates that a substantial portion of time is spent on unproductive tasks. One of the most comprehensive studies of knowledge worker activities was conducted by Booz Allen in 1980 (Booz and Hamilton 1982). In a year-long study, 300 "typical" managers recorded their daily activities. Research was conducted at 15 major manufacturing, banking, insurance, and government institutions. The results show that 15-40% of knowledge worker time is spent on activities that the subjects themselves usually recognized as less than productive. Some of the less productive ways managers and professionals spend their time include searching for information, searching for people, copying, scheduling, and travelling.

The challenge for the information community is to identify techniques for improving productivity of information workers and to encourage the use of these techniques (Bearman, Guynup et al. 1985). Among these techniques is improvement of the communications process. A second important mechanism for improving productivity is the honing of information finding and using skills. A basic objective of education should motivate each student to learn how to identify needed information, locate and organize it, and present it in a clear and persuasive manner. A third mechanism for increasing the productivity of information workers involves the integration of information technology into the workplace. The technology must link the knowledge worker to the appropriate sources of information whether internal to the organization (such as other employees) or external (such as databases) and facilitate information flow.

Productivity should be viewed as the amount of output per unit of input. Leaders and planners should focus on creating worker productivity through personal responsibility for online activities and by making informed choices in the social networking systems that are available. Understanding the range of social networking applications and what features exist in those applications as related to worker productivity is crucial to making digital selections that support the organization's mission and goals.

Now we move to a synergistic view of social media that can lead to a structured process. Evolution of social capital research identifies four distinct approaches: communitarian view, networks view, institutional view, and synergy view (Woolcock and Narayan 2000). Social capital is defined as the norms and networks that enable people to act collectively. The authors suggest that the synergy view has the greatest empirical support and that it lends itself to the most comprehensive and coherent policy prescriptions. The synergy view emphasizes incorporating different levels and dimensions in the interaction, and recognizes the positive and negative outcomes that social capital can generate. The communitarian view equates social capital with local level organizations, namely associations, clubs, and civic groups. This view, measured most simply by the number and density of these groups in a given community, implies that social capital is inherently "good," that "more is better," and that its presence always has a positive effect on a community's welfare. The networks view attempts to account for both its "upside" and "downside." This view stresses the importance of vertical as well as horizontal associations between people and relations within and among other organizational entities such as community groups and firms. An institutional view argues that the vitality of community networks and civil society is largely the product of the political, legal, and institutional environment. Where the communitarian and networks perspectives largely treat social capital as an independent variable giving rise to various "goods" and/or "bads," the institutional view instead puts the emphasis on social capital as a dependent variable. In this view, the capacity of social groups to act in their collective interest depends crucially on the quality of the formal institutions under which they reside. Emergency qualities, such as high levels of "generalized trust," correspond to superior rates of economic growth.

Synergy also comes from mutual stimulation or "piggybacking," because it develops when a participant builds on information provided by another participant to create new ideas, typically because that participant has additional information, different skills, or a different view of the problem. For any given project team, synergy should be enhanced if all members work as one intact group rather than as several smaller sub-groups or nominal groups because the intact group has more opportunities for information to be shared among members.

In *Social Media Programs: Cultivate, Don't Control*, Ed Schipul discusses cultivating the environment to allow social media activities to blossom and succeed organically (January 2009). The author also discusses focusing on the four pillars of social media success: planning, recruiting, training, and promoting.

- Planning to assess if social media makes sense for your organization and integrating efforts with the rest of the PR program.
- Recruiting social media participants from within the organization.
- Training the organization's social media participants to ensure high standards and mitigate risks (working offline can help).
- Promoting your initiative to build awareness.

Now that we have some common knowledge concerning social networking and performance, we can focus the SNIP survey.

Building SNIP

The basis for SNIP comes from my May 2011 published dissertation leading to my PhD in Public Administration and Urban Policy (Brown 2011). The scored instrument was needed to satisfy two of my four "implications for future research." The intent was to study one organization that is fully engaged in social networking and/or replicate the survey with a larger sample. To do that, methods researcher Albright was asked to first analyze the original survey data. The results of that analysis follow.

The intent of this analysis was to determine if it is possible to take items from existing, previously validated scales and create a single scale tapping the concept of social media participation. Towards this end, factor analysis and principal components analysis were performed in order to determine if the items were measuring a single dimension of participation or instead representing different subscales that get at different aspects of participation.

The results show that both are true. Factor analysis revealed multiple dimensions of participation rather than one single, overarching concept reflecting participation.

This outcome is not surprising, given that the items are taken from pre-existing and previously validated scales, and the dimensions from the factor analysis presented here line up with the previous scales. Nonetheless, a subsequent principal components analysis and an examination of Cronbach's alpha revealed that, even if the items can be broken down into subscales, they can also be combined reliably into a single scale. This approach was further validated by comparing the scores that result from the single participation scale to the number of hours spent using social media. Higher participation scores correlate with greater use of social media.

Thus, the researcher can determine how deeply he or she wants to drill down into the concept of participation. The broad scale can be used consisting of all items or the separate subscales can be used if these are of more specific interest.

The first step taken in this analysis was to perform an exploratory factor analysis (EFA). An EFA takes a correlation matrix and determines if the items making up the matrix can be collapsed into a smaller number of dimensions, allowing a clearer examination of the relationships in the data. The number of dimensions is determined by examining the eigenvalues associated with the matrix, measuring the amount of change in the data. A common cutoff for identifying the number of dimensions in the data is the number of eigenvalues greater than one.

Figure 3 presents a scree plot of eigenvalues, allowing visual assessment of which components or factors explain most of the variability in the data. The scree plot shows that there are four values clearly larger than one, plus two more that are right at the cut-off. Had there been only a single eigenvalue greater than one, the interpretation would be that the items make up a single participation scale. Figure 3 suggests instead that the items make up four distinct dimensions.

The next step in an EFA is to determine how to interpret the dimensions. Towards this end, the EFA was re-run to retain four factors, and the factor structure matrix (the correlation between each item and the respective factors) was examined to identify the items whose relationship was strongest with each factor. Direct oblimin rotation was applied to the factor loadings, which is a method that makes the values easier to interpret.

Table 2 presents the rotated loadings. Values less than .25 are suppressed to make the patterns stand out more clearly. What is evident is that items near each other in the survey – and hence part of the same previously validated scale – tend the cluster together. This is not always the case (assistance with high priority tasks and identification of available resources do not fit as well with the other three importance items), but the patterns do support the interpretation that the original, previously validated scales demonstrate the expected construct validity.

Figure 3. Scree plot showing eigenvalues by factor number. Plot suggests four to six sub dimensions of participation. Subsequent analysis retains four factors for parsimony.

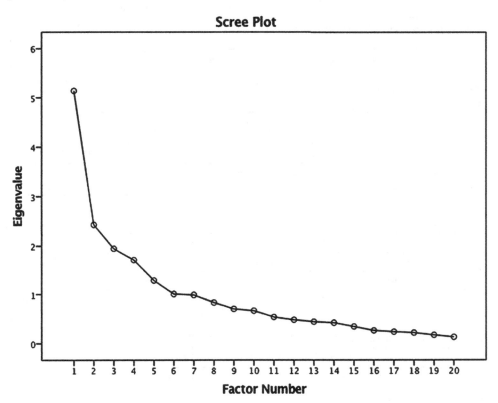

Although these results favor interpreting the items as separate scales, it is possible that they may be thought of as subscales of a broader concept of participation. If so, then the researcher can either keep the scales as separate measures of more distinct facets of participation or combine them to create a single participation measure.

A reliability analysis supports combining all of the items into a single scale. Next, Table 3 presents Cronbach's alpha, including the value of alpha if the item were deleted. Together, the items generate a highly reliable scale (alpha = .837), which can scarcely be improved (if at all) by dropping items. This suggests a high level of internal cohesion to the larger participation scale.

Another way of testing the possibility of creating a single scale is to perform a principal components analysis (PCA) on the items. A PCA identifies the linear

Table 2. Principal axis factor analysis with Oblim rotation

	Factor			
	1	**2**	**3**	**4**
1. Enables me to acquire more information and/or meet more people.			0.289	
2. Improves my efficiency in sharing information and connecting with others.				0.317
3. Useful for communication with colleagues with similar issues and challenges.				0.836
4.Useful for interaction with colleagues from with similar issues and challenges.				0.836
5. Learning to use Social Media services is easy for me.			0.682	
6. The process of participating in Social Media is clear and understandable to me.			0.782	
7. Social Media easy to use.			0.658	
8. Importance: Personal quality of output.	0.671			
9. Importance: Work group quality of output.	0.619			
10. Importance: Performance in comparison to others.	0.551			
11. Importance: Assistance with high priority tasks.	0.318			0.328
12. Importance: Identification of available resources.				0.305
13. Stay in touch: Personally with family and friends.	0.585			
14. Stay in touch: Professionally within my organization.	0.787			
15. Stay in touch: Professionally outside of my organization.	0.685			
16. How effective?: Collecting best practices.		0.796		
17. How effective?: Archiving best practices.		0.782		
18. How effective?: Sharing best practices.		0.843		
19. How effective?: Improving citizen via technology.		0.582		
20. How effective?: Improving communication via technology.		0.305		0.280

combination of items that can explain the maximal amount of variance among all survey items. It is similar to factor analysis in that it can identify different dimensions in the data. The distinction is that the first principal component (as opposed to the first factor) will always contain loadings that explain the most total variance. Thus, if loadings on the first principal component are similar in size, the interpretation is that the items are capturing overall participation similarly. The loadings on the subsequent principal components can be interpreted as clusters of items that together explain the largest amount of remaining variance after accounting for participation, broadly speaking.

Table 3. Reliability analysis supports combining all of the items into a single scale

	Corrected Item-Total Correlation	Cronbach's Alpha if Item Deleted
1. Enables me to acquire more information and/or meet more people.	0.342	0.832
2. Improves my efficiency in sharing information and connecting with others.	0.495	0.827
3. Useful for communication with colleagues with similar issues and challenges.	0.403	0.830
4.Useful for interaction with colleagues from with similar issues and challenges.	0.412	0.829
5. Learning to use Social Media services is easy for me.	0.291	0.835
6. The process of participating in Social Media is clear and understandable to me.	0.307	0.834
7. Social Media easy to use.	0.340	0.833
8. Importance: Personal quality of output.	0.535	0.823
9. Importance: Work group quality of output.	0.615	0.819
10. Importance: Performance in comparison to others.	0.417	0.829
11. Importance: Assistance with high priority tasks.	0.410	0.830
12. Importance: Identification of available resources.	0.276	0.838
13. Stay in touch: Personally with family and friends.	0.452	0.828
14. Stay in touch: Professionally within my organization.	0.514	0.824
15. Stay in touch: Professionally outside of my organization.	0.583	0.820
16. How effective?: Collecting best practices.	0.384	0.831
17. How effective?: Archiving best practices.	0.328	0.833
18. How effective?: Sharing best practices.	0.397	0.831
19. How effective?: Improving citizen via technology.	0.428	0.830
20. How effective?: Improving communication via technology.	0.409	0.830
Scale total		0.837

We now go to Table 4, which presents the loadings for the first four principal components. Consistent with the interpretation of a single "participation" dimension, the loadings are all between .3 and .7 for the first principal component. The remaining principal components show clusterings of items that can be interpreted as subsequent dimensions that remain after the general participation dimension has been accounted for. These again show some tendency for items from the same previously validated scale to clump together.

Table 4. Loadings for the first four principal components

	Component			
	1	**2**	**3**	**4**
1. Enables me to acquire more information and/or meet more people.	0.387		0.332	
2. Improves my efficiency in sharing information and connecting with others.	0.582			
3. Useful for communication with colleagues with similar issues and challenges.	0.500			0.621
4.Useful for interaction with colleagues from with similar issues and challenges.	0.495			0.584
5. Learning to use Social Media services is easy for me.	0.348		0.598	
6. The process of participating in Social Media is clear and understandable to me.	0.355		0.711	
7. Social Media easy to use.	0.380		0.618	
8. Importance: Personal quality of output.	0.615	-0.429		
9. Importance: Work group quality of output.	0.707			
10. Importance: Performance in comparison to others.	0.506		-0.358	
11. Importance: Assistance with high priority tasks.	0.458	-0.392		
12. Importance: Identification of available resources.	0.306			
13. Stay in touch: Personally with family and friends.	0.523			-0.39
14. Stay in touch: Professionally within my organization.	0.605			-0.444
15. Stay in touch: Professionally outside of my organization.	0.651			-0.338
16. How effective?: Collecting best practices.	0.492	0.668		
17. How effective?: Archiving best practices.	0.430	0.683		
18. How effective?: Sharing best practices.	0.516	0.662		
19. How effective?: Improving citizen via technology	0.549	0.404		
20. How effective?: Improving communication via technology.	0.518			

A final means of validating the participation scale is to compare its value to another measure of participation, namely levels of usage. Analyzing the means across items after they had been standardized as z-scores allows creation of the general participation scale. Figure 4 presents a bar chart of average participation scores at different participation levels. As expected, the participation scale has a higher mean in the higher participation group. This provides external validation that the participation scale is measuring participation, but in a manner that captures many facets of participation beyond simply hours in front of the computer.

Figure 4. Bar chart showing mean participation scale scores by hours spent on social media. Consistent with expectations, higher mean participation scores occur among those who use social media more often.

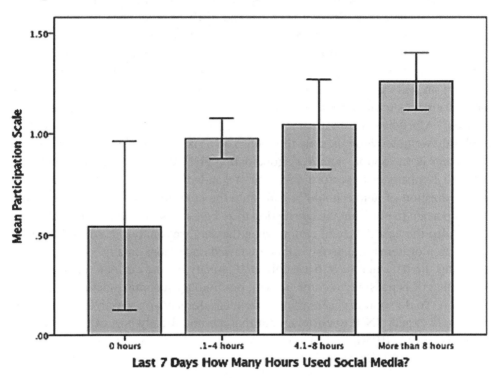

NEXT STEPS

There are limitations in the work that has been done to date. The primary concern is that the survey has not been built for and validated for one company, one population. That needs to be done.

The process of developing and validating an effective instrument on a new population is extensive and requires data from many subjects collected from different samples on variables beyond what is contained in the instrument. As SNIP is a new survey tool with limited data available, the guidelines presented below should be taken as preliminary and subject to revision over time. In addition, the validation is performed on only a small set of indicators, meaning that further testing should be carried out comparing SNIP scores to observable implications not captured with current survey questions. For example, SNIP scores may be validated against a sample completing a social media-related project to verify that the different categories defined here predict with high accuracy performance on that project.

Methods researcher Albright explains and justifies guidelines for interpreting SNIP scores administered within the context of organizations. In addition to the population limitation mentioned earlier in this chapter, another caveat to keep in mind moving forward is that the SNIP instrument combines multiple surveys that measure answers on both six-point and seven-point scales. "Future revisions of the instrument should harmonize these items so that all have the same number of choices," Albright said. "When they [do]not, items on a seven-point scale will be implicitly weighted more heavily than those on a six-point scale. Converting these to z-scores is one option, not a very good option given that managers will likely not have the competence to perform this type of standardization on their own. Instead, standardization of items should be built into the next iteration of the instrument." It is important to note that the conversion to z-scores was the method used because it provided the best course of action when the data was analyzed. Albright's standardization of items suggestion can be reviewed once more data is collected.

Using the data that have been collected already on the current version of the instrument, it is possible to come up with preliminary recommendations for interpretation. To do so, it is necessary to have measurements on variables with which one would expect SNIP to correlate but that are not already part of the survey. A new version of SNIP was recently developed. The methodology used was to remove three items from the instrument to use as the benchmarks. These three items were:

1. I use social networking sites to stay in touch personally with friends and family.
2. I use social networking sites to stay in touch professionally within my organization.
3. I use social networking sites to stay in touch professionally outside my organization.

SNIP scores were calculated by summing up all of the items in the instrument after dropping these three. Of the 190 subjects in the sample, complete data – including for the hold-out questions – were available for 107 subjects. The range of SNIP scores was from a minimum of 26 to a maximum of 102. The mean response was 69.71, and the standard deviation was 18.38. Cronbach's alpha was .826.

After calculating SNIP scores, the three hold-out questions were used as benchmarks (Responses on the hold-out questions equal to 1 or 2 were coded "low"; 3 or 4 were coded "medium"; 5 or 6 were coded "high."). This allowed the researchers to determine at which point along the SNIP continuum responses shift from low to medium or medium to high. This was done by fitting an ordered logistic regression separately for the three social networking questions using SNIP as the predictor. SNIP was always a significant ($p < .01$) predictor of the outcomes, meaning that the concurrent validity is high, as expected.

We present several graphics to illustrate SNIP. We show Figures 5 through 7 to demonstrate the probability of giving an answer of low, medium, and high for each level of SNIP.

The first figure focuses on usage of social networking sites being used to stay in touch with friends and family. The blue area corresponds to the 95% confidence interval around the probability of answering in the low category, red corresponds to the 95% confidence interval around the probability of answering in the medium category, and green corresponds to the 95% confidence interval around the probability of answering in the high category. It is clear that as SNIP increases, the likelihood of answering "low" decreases while the likelihood of answering "high" increases. The confidence intervals for these two anchoring responses are clearly distinct below SNIP scores of 45 and above SNIP scores of 68. In between, there is some ambiguity, meaning that SNIP scores in this range represent respondents with a mix of propensities for use of social media.

Figure 5. SNIP probability 1

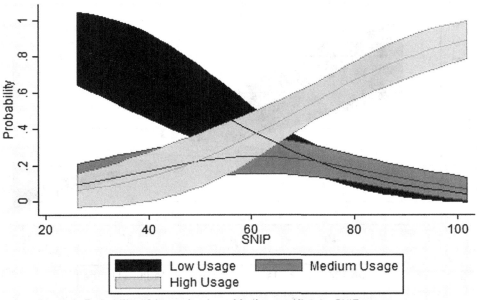

Y-axis is Probability of Answering Low, Medium, or High by SNIP score

Figure 6 focuses on social networking use within the same organization as the survey taker. In this case, the blue area – the 95% confidence interval around the probability of answering "low" – shows that SNIP scores up to a little over 60 predict minimal usage. One has to get above 88 before SNIP scores indicate a high propensity for social networking use within the organization.

Figure 7 considers social networking for professional reasons outside the organization. In this case, the probability of providing a "low" answer is clearly the largest for SNIP scores up to 36. The probability of giving a "high" answer is greatest when SNIP scores exceed 70. In between there is again ambiguity.

Now we can look at an overview of these results. Table 5 summarizes these results and shows that interpretation of SNIP scores varies according to the outcome in which one is interested. SNIP scores have to be quite high before it is likely a respondent is using social media within the organization. This may in part be due to the fact that not all organizations utilize social networking extensively among employees, and hence the suggested SNIP guidelines are least reliable here.

The other two outcomes do show similarities, especially for determining who is most likely to be a user. Those above 70 are very active social media users for networking outside the organization, both personally and professionally. On the low

Figure 6. SNIP probability 2

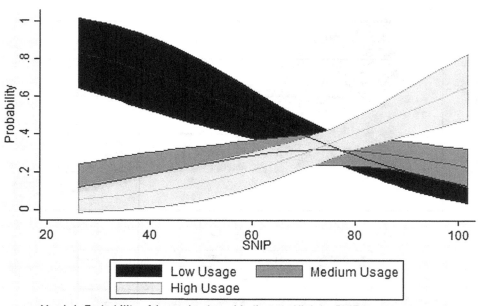

Y-axis is Probability of Answering Low, Medium, or High by SNIP score

Figure 7. SNIP probability 3

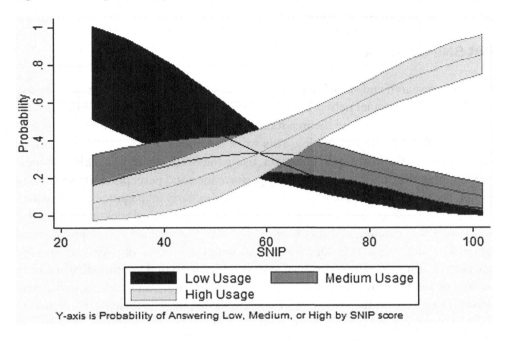

Y-axis is Probability of Answering Low, Medium, or High by SNIP score

Table 5. SNIP score summary

Most Likely Answer	Family and Friends	Professionally Within Organization	Professionally Outside Organization
Low	44 and lower	60 and lower	36 and lower
Mixed	45 up to 67	61 up to 87	37 up to 69
High	68 and higher	88 and higher	70 and higher

Note: Summary of SNIP scores ranges and predicted outcomes.

end, those falling below the 36-44 range are least likely to be users. Taking the mean, the following guidelines can be used:

- SNIP scores 40 and below indicate low frequency users,
- SNIP scores between 41 and 69 indicate medium frequency users,
- SNIP scores 70 and above indicate high frequency users.

These criteria are based on the SNIP instrument without the three hold-out items, and hence SNIP scores should be determined by summing across all items except these three. In addition, more work is necessary to further validate this categorization with more data, other populations, and using other observable outcomes for which SNIP is to serve as a proxy.

Put SNIP to Work

All of the research and subsequent survey findings are important because it is easy to get involved in social networking activities. Organizations jump right in and are up and running long before the inevitable questions are asked about how long employees spend on online activities. This work recommends asking those questions much earlier in the process or, better yet, using the SNIP survey. This kind of questioning, planning, and measurement of performance and perception of the activity should not be neglected. They should be involved as early in the process as possible.

With this book, people and organizations have the theoretical background of SNIP and how it was created, and it is now ready for use to manage and improve social networking activities. This survey can help with the success of social networking activities and individual performance, both of which are based on normative practices as well as relationships that build trust, foster interaction, and address participant needs. The results of the survey show whether or not there is focused interaction in social networking, both in person-to-person and task-specific activities. The survey provides important data for analyzing a social network perspective characterized by a variety of factors. Some of those factors are "centrality (betweenness, closeness, degree), position (structural), strength of ties (strong/weak, weighted/discrete), cohesion (groups, cliques), and division (structural holes, partition)." Armed with this information, leaders and planners may be able to understand the following social networking characteristics:

- Social interaction for centrality (Ivancevich 2008),
- Involvement and need fulfillment for position (Mayo 1949),
- Formal and informal ties for strength of ties (Ivancevich 2008),
- Two-way personal selection for cohesion (Mayo 1949),
- Self-importance for division (Mayo 1949).

Any of these characteristics may create instances where the individual's inward focus contributes to disconnected activities in terms of the organization and its mission. The survey provides a detailed organizational analysis of relationships that began with a thorough understanding of the social networking construct.

The overriding importance of the survey lies in its potential to give companies additional tools that can support business and employee development. It offers people and organizations a deeper understanding of digital conversations, relationships, and activities.

REFERENCES

Bandura, A. (1977). *Social learning theory*. Englewood Cliffs, NJ: Prentice Hall.

Bandura, A. (1986). *Social foundations of thought and action: a social cognitive theory*. Englewood Cliffs, NJ: Prentice-Hall.

Bearman, Guynup, & Milevski. (1985). Information and Productivity. *Journal of the American Society for Information Science, 36*(6), 369.

Booz, Allen, & Hamilton. (1982). *New products management for the 1980s*. New York: Booz, Allen & Hamilton.

Brown, M. Sr. (2011). *Social networking and individual performance: Examining predictors of participation Ph.D*. Old Dominion University.

Cerulo, K. A. (1990). To Err Is Social: Network Prominence and Its Effects on Self-Estimation. *Sociological Forum, 5*(4), 619–634. doi:10.1007/BF01115394

Cooper, R. K. (1997). Applying Emotional Intelligence in the Workplace. *Training & Development, 51*(12), 31–38.

Davis, F. D. (1989). Perceived Usefulness, Perceived Ease of Use, and User Acceptance of Information Technology. *Management Information Systems Quarterly, 13*(3), 319–340. doi:10.2307/249008

Davis, T. R. V., & Luthans, F. (1980). A Social Learning Approach to Organizational Behavior. *Academy of Management Review, 5*(2), 281–290.

Dennis, A. R., & Valacich, J. S. (1994). Group, Sub-Group, and Nominal Group Idea Generation: New Rules for a New Media? *Journal of Management, 20*(4), 723–736. doi:10.1177/014920639402000402

Granovetter, M. S. (1973). The Strength of Weak Ties. *American Journal of Sociology, 78*(6), 1360–1380. doi:10.1086/225469

Hossain, L., & de Silva, A. (2009). Exploring user acceptance of technology using social networks. *The Journal of High Technology Management Research, 20*(1), 1–18. doi:10.1016/j.hitech.2009.02.005

Huy, Q. N. (1999). Emotional Capability, Emotional Intelligence, and Radical Change. *Academy of Management Review, 24*(2), 325–345.

Ivancevich, J. M. Konopaske, R., & Matteson, M. T. (2008). *Organizational Behavior and Management*. New York: McGraw-Hill/Irwin.

Kim, D. H. (1993). The link between individual learning and organizational learning. *Sloan Management Review*, *35*(Fall), 379–500.

Mahoney, M. J., & Thoresen, C. E. (1974). *Self-control: power to the person*. Monterey, CA: Brooks/Cole Pub. Co.

Mayo, E. (1949). *Hawthorne and the Western Electric Company: The Social Problems of an Industrial Civilisation*. New York: Routledge.

Millen & Fontaine. (2003). Improving individual and organizational performance through communities of practice. *Proceedings of the 2003 international ACM SIGGROUP conference on Supporting group work*. Sanibel Island, FL: ACM. doi:10.1145/958160.958192

Paino, M., & Rossett, A. (2008). Performance Support That Adds Value to Everyday Lives. *Performance Improvement*, *47*(1), 37–44. doi:10.1002/pfi.177

Perrow, C. (1967). A Framework for the Comparative Analysis of Organizations. *American Sociological Review*, *32*(2), 194–208. doi:10.2307/2091811

Porras, J. J., Hargis, K., Patterson, K. J., Maxfield, D. G., Roberts, N., & Bies, R. J. (1982). Modeling-Based Organizational Development: A Longitudinal Assessment. *The Journal of Applied Behavioral Science*, *18*(4), 433–446. doi:10.1177/002188638201800405

Rice, R. E. (1992). Task Analyzability, Use of New Media, and Effectiveness: A Multi-Site Exploration of Media Richness. *Organization Science*, *3*(4), 475–500. doi:10.1287/orsc.3.4.475

Schipul, E. (2009). Social Media Programs: Cultivate, Don't Control. *Public Relations Tactics, 16*(1).

Watson, D. L., & Tharp, R. G. (1977). *Self-directed behavior: self-modification for personal adjustment*. Monterey, CA: Brooks/Cole Pub. Co.

Wellman, B. (1997). *An electronic group is virtually a social network. In Culture of the Internet* (pp. 179–205). Hillsdale, NJ: Lawrence Erlbaum.

Wellman, B., & Wortley, S. (1990). Different Strokes from Different Folks: Community Ties and Social Support. *American Journal of Sociology*, *96*(3), 558–588. doi:10.1086/229572

Withey, M., Daft, R. L., & Cooper, W. H. (1983). Measures of Perrows Work Unit Technology: An Empirical Assessment and a New Scale. *Academy of Management Journal*, *26*(1), 45–63. doi:10.2307/256134

Wood, R., & Bandura, A. (1989). Social Cognitive Theory of Organizational Management. *Academy of Management Review*, *14*(3), 361–384.

Woolcock, M., & Narayan, D. (2000). Social Capital: Implications for Development Theory, Research, and Policy. *The World Bank Research Observer*, *15*(2), 225–249. doi:10.1093/wbro/15.2.225

Section 2
New Look Social Media

We use a gauge to make the point that public administrators have been busy working to take advantage of opportunities to participate in the digital conversation through increased social media activities. This is a daunting undertaking because of the speed at which digital conversations happen and transform to new interactions. This collection of chapters seeks to provide a new vision on social media interaction from the perspectives of several authors. This analysis goes from a history of social communication to organizational concerns to microblogging to social media marketing. We also include a look at crisis communication because social media has pushed itself to the forefront of activity and discovery in that area.

Figure 1. Assessing activities

Chapter 3
Understanding Social Communication

Michael A. Brown Sr.
Florida International University, USA

ABSTRACT

George Santayana said, "Those who cannot remember the past are condemned to repeat it." That statement is the reason social communication is covered here with a historical view. This review of computer mediated communications (CMC) is important in understanding some of the key developments that created the social media environment we know today. A discussion of the portable nature of these communications is relevant as the foundation for a deep understanding of social communication. This is an important analysis in helping people understand the way we can use information technology to interact without the limitations of geographical distance and time.

DOI: 10.4018/978-1-5225-1963-8.ch003

INTRODUCTION

This chapter covers computer-mediated communication (CMC) history and development, but first we must look at full-range communication. History and development are important to understand in order to set the foundation for finding a deep understanding of social communication. For instance, James Arthur Baldwin, American novelist, essayist, playwright, poet, and social critic, said, "Know from whence you came. If you know whence you came, there are absolutely no limitations to where you can go." Success in social networking relies on creating relationships and building strong ties.

This analysis of CMC is important because it is a popular way people use information technology to interact. CMC is portable and it removes the boundaries or limitations of geographical distance and time. Computer-mediated relating (CMR) is another term relevant for our learning journey because it addresses interpersonal dimensions of interactions, encompassing a broader spectrum of exchanges than CMC might, such as online friendships and romantic communications (Cooper and Sportolari 1997, Whitty and Gavin 2001).

This examination is important because it demonstrates all of the tools available to communicators and it suggests limitations that exist in strictly online communications. For instance, the feedback cycle is crucial in communication importance because we know that messages are rarely fully "one-way" activities. The sender needs clarification that the receiver or receivers decode the message in the way it was intended or that they received the value that the sender intended to provide in the communication. A mutual agreement between the communicating parties is vital to ensure effective interactions that are true to the original message and its meaning. This agreement sets the stage for the continuing, cyclic conversation that should follow the original engagement. A truly effective communication features all parties accepting responsibility to exhibit authenticity and accuracy. Human contact or interaction can be important to improving the engagement, but they are not normally available in digital communications.

CMC is so powerful today in making connections with people. Studies on Gen Y and Millennials demonstrate their constantly growing numbers in terms of participation. These groups are known to prefer the use of instant messaging or other social media over stopping by an office for a talk (Tardanico 2012). That preference makes it a real challenge to build and nurture a team and corporate culture unless you can create real relationships and strong ties. Social media allows us to communicate on very serious topics like contracts, purchases, and love. The feedback cycle is very important because the sender needs to know that the other party or parties interpreted the message correctly, or that they received the intended value from the message. In management issues, feedback is necessary because the leader needs to know how subordinates respond to directives and plans. There is a need to understand how work is progressing and to get a sense of how employees are invested, or not invested, in the work environment.

The need for a common understanding is the cornerstone of communicating. It is critical to measure effectiveness through a mutual agreement between the parties about the message and its meaning. Effectiveness is achieved when there is an indication that the receiver understands the message in the manner intended by the sender. This should be the goal of any communication, but digital senders sometimes assume or take for granted that this agreement is reached. The agreement can be forged and continuously improved while achieving deeper meaning in the exchange when there is a developing level of trust between the parties that is supportive and complementary to the interaction. Feedback should be accomplished through a continuous loop between the parties involved. It should start when the message is received and subsequently decoded. After that, it should reengage the communicative process, generating a newly-encoded message as the receiver becomes sender. This cycle is vital to providing information that can enhance, clarify, or restate the previous message. In this way, feedback fosters common understanding and mutual agreement. To do this, digital senders must continue sending until there is a verification of receipt and understanding.

Senders and receivers should conduct diachronic communications, which are activities in which the parties share the "spotlight." The communication emphasis alternates between voices with each taking the lead at the appropriate time based on the requirements of message delivery. In this way, the conversation is conducted via an ongoing and dynamic process. Communication is a flexible and exponential process in which participants, contexts, and the future communication probabilities change and adapt (Dance 1970). Communication participants are players in a contest of meaning construction that allows the discourse to shape the conversation in ways that give it meaning and allow for continued interaction (van Ruler 2015).

These issues are at play in CMC, which is also referred to as computer-mediated relating (CMR). CMR contrasts with CMC in that it emphasizes a larger area of interest that includes varied interpersonal dimensions of interactions (Cooper and Sportolari 1997, Whitty and Gavin 2001). CMR encompasses a broader spectrum of interactions, such as online relationships that are friendships and romantic communications. There is an intimacy without emotional investment in online interaction that can lead to strong relationships. "This situation is demonstrated in the 'boom or bust' phenomenon, in which a rapid process of intimate self-disclosure leads budding relationships to become quite intense, quite quickly." (Whitty and Gavin 2001, p. 623) Boom or bust explains a communication evolution that is an accelerated process of revelation, increasing the chance of exhilaration at the outset, followed by a quick erotic episode. Unfortunately, experts in this area contend that this relationship cannot be sustained because it lacks the underlying trust and true knowledge between the participants that is required to support long-term interaction. Still, there are benefits to be derived from this communication approach.

Theory is important in deciding the best approach to communicating. A very important theory for our examination of digital communication is social presence. The theory evaluates "the degree to which a person is perceived as a 'real person' in mediated communication." (Gunawardena 1995, p. 147) The theory focuses on intimacy in communication and psychological distance. In terms of CMR, lower levels of social presence make for more impersonal conversations. The lack of contextual cues can hinder online communications.

The absence of social content cues can lead to more uninhibited behavior, such as verbal aggression, blunt disclosure, and nonconforming behavior. This type of behavior, known as 'flaming,' has been observed across a range of online settings, including business, governmental, educational, and public networks. Such findings lend further support to the argument that online relationships are less intimate and more aggressive than face-to-face relationships. (Whitty and Gavin 2001)

Trust and relative anonymity, then, are often listed as benefits of online communication. For instance, social distance has been increasing since the telegraph and telephone were invented. Social distances increase every day, as technology allows us to be anywhere and communicate online. Many rich and valuable communications that take place despite social distance considerations and these internet conversations can create dynamic first impressions. In face-to-face communication, for instance, the first impression is derived when physical attractiveness, gender, or age are immediately revealed or implied. However, those who prefer online communication would argue that there are opportunities for more radical first impressions because of a lack of inhibition, possibly resulting in effective relationship development.

Trust is important in building relationships that are good for communication, allowing the participants to develop dependence, satisfaction, and commitment. Trusting relationships in organizations involve an ongoing decision to give most people the benefit of the doubt, and it can be extended even to people one does not know from direct experience (Brown 2011). There is a rich body of literature to help with the examination of trust. A group of guest editors addressed the widespread influence of trust in a special issue on trust in an organizational context (McEvily, Perrone et al. 2003). The discussion addresses the importance of trust, examining its current importance and finding that the current emphasis on trust was caused by changes in technology, and the changes they examined reconfigured exchange and the coordination of work across distance and time.

The changes are still evident today in personal and organizational forums and in knowledge-intensive organizations. The relevant research indicates that new ways of communicating "alter the patterns of interdependencies and the nature and extent of uncertainty." (McEvily, Perrone et al. 2003) These new ways make people rely more on the decisions and actions of others, creating both dependency and vulnerability. These factors are crucial to building and maintaining trust, and senders must pay attention them. The authors continue to demonstrate that organizational science has made some important advances that promote understanding of the meaning of trust and how it relates to certain factors that characterize organizations and that are important for the current communication discovery. An increasing number of journal articles and special issues (Rousseau, Sitkin et al. 1998, Bachmann, Knights et al. 2001) and books (Gambetta 1988, Kramer 1996, Lane and Bachmann 1998) are devoted to the topic of trust in and between organizations. The special issue published seven papers that represent a wide range of methodological approaches, a diverse set of theoretical disciplines, a variety of levels of analysis, and a blend of empirical models (McEvily, Perrone et al. 2003). These views are valuable in understanding trust as a factor in CMC.

There are two important issues that are central to any examination of trust. The first involves trust as a means for dealing with uncertainty. The second focuses on trust and acceptance of vulnerability (Newell and Swan 2000). Trust occurs in situations of risk and uncertainty, because any system must have trust as an input condition to stimulate supportive activities in situations with these two factors (Luhmann 1988). This understanding suggests that trust is an attitudinal mechanism that allows individuals to subjectively assess whether or not to expose themselves to situations where there may not be an acceptable trade-off in terms of possible damage versus received advantage. The attitude develops when individuals have accepted vulnerability to others.

Trust is multidimensional and it helps values, attitudes, emotions, and moods interact (Newell and Swan 2000). There are three reasons someone may be able to develop trust (Sako 1992):

1. Because of a contractual agreement that binds the parties in the relationship,
2. Because of a belief in the competencies of those involved,
3. Because of a belief in the goodwill of those involved.

It is common knowledge that electronic communication has surpassed face-to-face methods. The new age of business communications and the lack of comfort with traditional interpersonal communication contribute to the rise of digital communication. Some experts attribute this move to the influence of Gen Y and Millennials who tend to favor the instant kind of messaging afforded by social media and digital applications over sitting down in front of another person and interacting.

One barrier that communicators must face is the need to create cultural compatibility, or find common ground. Senders can foster long-standing, mutually beneficial relationships by achieving shared values in the communication. This enhances shared understanding. Another barrier is resistance to participate based on fear, disbelief, underestimation of the benefits of communication, lack of a sense of return on investment of time and effort, misunderstanding, and misperception. Other barriers are not new. Senders must deal effectively with the pace of communication to ensure that information exchange is timely and holds the receiver's interest. Online communication requires that the physical surroundings of the sender are conducive to getting the message across. All communicators deal with attitudes and language in their own way. Lack of common experience and information overload are other barriers that are at play in any kind of communication. There are other barriers to communication, but the ones mentioned here are most relevant for our discussion.

The key consideration in terms of barriers to communication is that the sender must recognize them and address them when and if they interfere with the interaction. Barriers are often the key to driving receivers away from the communication, either not fully getting the message or not staying long enough to provide the valuable feedback that keeps communication alive as a cyclical process. Effective communications feature shared understanding between the participants and cannot be taken for granted. Senders must pay attention to any signs and signals to determine whether the message reaches its target. The communication goal is simple: encode, send, decode, and provide feedback. Senders must accept responsibility for this whole process, and for continued communications. Online communicators must search for ways to request, evaluate, and respond to feedback. This is important because online communications happen so fast that the sender often has no time to even consider making adjustments.

SOCIAL NETWORKS AND INTERPERSONAL COMMUNICATION

In addition to barriers to the interaction, sometimes called noise in the channel, social networks may adversely affect communication by imposing superficial communications experiences, and grammatical and spelling erosion of the language. Therefore, current studies seek to capture data about the spread of social networks and their use and impact on interpersonal communication. More specifically, they look for the answer to the question: what is the nature of interpersonal communication that is found on social networking sites: personal, emotional, private or shared, informal, and public? (Gheorghiță and Pădurețu 2014) These are important considerations that may not get enough emphasis in organizational and personal settings.

So the next time you communicate online, ask yourself if you are getting feedback and true value from the interaction. You just might be missing a critical part of a message you need! The most obvious benefits in digital conversations are the pure speed at which they can occur and the lack of limitations on the times and places at which communication can occur. Senders and receivers have complete freedom in the timing of their responses. Some experts say that online communicators benefit from being able to think about what they say before sending the message. We can edit and revise the communication before sending to make sure we get the right message out. Digital communication allows participants to enter and leave the conversation at any time, often without the other party even knowing that we are gone. Online participants, good or bad, can interact privately and can hide or mask their identity. This allows these senders and receivers to avoid phone calls or other human interactions that may or may not be convenient, necessary, or desired. Participants can relay or forward messages verbatim. Despite online limitations for developing verbal, in-person communications, digital communicators can engage in that area at a later date. Online proponents believe that their communications make it easy to communicate accurately (say what we mean), to be genuine (mean what we say), and to filter out unnecessary details or negative messages (determine whether to say everything we think based on the situation). And, of course, digital interactions allow us to navigate great geographic distances easily without the limitations of time.

These are all great benefits, but we must also view the challenges in the online environment. First, there is the impersonal nature of some communications, which can be caused in part by the fact that we do not know who is listening or if anyone is listening. While it is true that online communicators can check what they say before sending, the reverse can be true. The sheer speed and convenience can betray the sender and the message can be sent before the thought process is complete. The digital environment does not allow the sender to determine the receiver's tone or demeanor. Online conversations are not recommended for bad news, emotional messages, apologies, or sharing affections because the sender cannot engage to make sure the receiver understands the seriousness or gravity of the message and is relatively safe and comfortable with the information. Many people use online communication for these situations to achieve anonymity, reduce stress, alleviate accountability, etc. The sender should take those actions at their own risk.

Experts used to say that 90% of communication is nonverbal, but digital communication makes that statistic unrealistic. When online, senders cannot determine facial expressions, eye contact, tone, pitch, speed, body language, etc. Emoticons are supposed to help, but their applicability is limited. What if you have a feeling that does not match any of the emoticons? Other ways to help include video messaging or skyping, but they still do not have the full capabilities available in face-to-face interactions. It can be difficult to impossible to convey compassion in the online communication. Messages may come across as words without real emotion. Basically, the digital conversation seeks to balance its "human" limitations with the ability to promote faster connections between individuals and within groups.

Table 1 provides a handy reference for the benefits of digital message encoding.

The beginning of this chapter discusses the pros and cons of CMC. The opening quote of this section suggests the importance of understanding how we get "here." Let us explore the evolution of online communication.

The Departure from Human Interaction

Social media and digital communication have taken over the world. But what happened to face-to-face communication? What happened to human interaction?

Technology has grown almost out of control over the past few decades. Gone is the time when we would gather in a room and talk together as the primary mode of communication. Today, the phone and the tablet dominate the way we communicate. Look around you while you are driving through town, on the highway, or at a stop light. How many of the people you observe are looking at an electronic device? How many people are texting, reading e-mail, or searching for the best location for

Table 1. Digital message encoding comparison

Action	Benefit
Sending messages	Fast
Message accuracy	Can be reviewed before sending
Receiver response	Fast
Sender identity	Public persona promotes openness
Sender-receiver relationship	Impersonal nature promotes creativity
Message environment	No time/distance requirement

NOTE: Practice message empathy: do not deliver messages containing bad news, emotional messages, apologies, or sharing affections.

lunch? If they are driving, they are not fully watching the road and any feedback they may get will be further distracting. Now you are at a restaurant and you see a table of five or six people together. None of them are looking at each other. Their eyes are on their phones, and the waitress is trying to get their attention about their order. Technology has their almost undivided attention.

Let me tell you about what might comprise someone's typical day when technology drives everything that happens. The alarm clock on Erica's phone rings at 5:30 a.m. She has a big meeting today so she has to get up and get going. Erica connects her phone to a Bluetooth speaker so she can listen to her favorite tunes while getting ready. As she gets dressed, she gets a weather alert from her phone: that storm is moving out to sea so her weekend plans may work after all. Erica gets her coffee and opens a news site on her tablet. While she is watching the news, the tablet sends a traffic alert for her route to work.

Erica is all ready for work now and heads for the car. The meeting is at a location she is not familiar with, so she pulls up "Maps" her smartphone to get directions. The phone connects music to the vehicle for her drive to the meeting. The phone rings, suspending the music, because Erica has a call. One of her colleagues is going to the same meeting and wants a ride. There is time to pick up the friend, so Erica reprograms "Maps" for that location on the way. Erica picks up Susan and asks if she is still planning the vacation trip. But Susan is not listening because she is playing a game on her phone with a Bluetooth earpiece on.

They arrive at the meeting and Erica turns the music off and puts her phone on vibrate to it will not interrupt the meeting. She meets Larry, who is running the meeting. Larry lets Erica know that this is a Skype call and there will only be four total people in the room. The call is connected and the meeting starts. Erica and the other three people in the room monitor their phones during the meeting. A person on the Skype call asks a question for Susan, but she misses the question while working on her phone. The meeting goes well and everyone is ready to head out to lunch. Larry asks where they can go, and they all check Google for "food near me." At lunch, there is some conversation but very little eye contact.

After lunch, Erica gives Susan a ride. Now Erica has to return to her house and get the phone charger because her phone charge has gotten very low. We can keep going, but the idea should be clear by now. Today, technology in the form of phones and tablets is getting the attention that humans used to get. This story is typical of many situations we see today. Today, many people would rather text than talk, and they prefer mediated communication to face-to-face interaction.

CMC, also known as mediated communication, mediated discourse, or mediated interaction, uses information technology to interact with others. CMC does not employ the senses or facial expressions or symbolic cues. The emergence of

CMC has even caused changes in our romantic relationships. Experts say that those who maintain long-distance friendships rate face-to-face communication fourth in importance behind telephone, email, and instant messaging (Wright and Webb 2011). Apparently the real change from face-to-face to CMC was caused by access. Technology has been around for many years, but the size and price of cell phones and tablets have made it progressively more accessible to many more people. Let us look at some history.

The evolution of cell phones and tablets has occurred at breakneck speed. The demand and accessibility have grown dramatically over the years. There has been remarkable movement since 2000 with changes upon changes. We now have the smartphone (and tablet) which has evolved from a large semi-functional phone, to a smaller semi-functional phone, to a smaller fully functional phone, to a larger fully functional phone. As phones get larger to provide more screen size to watch videos, tablets tend to get larger as well. Now, the smartphone is a mega-functional, somewhat pocket-sized computer that includes a mobile app for virtually all of the capabilities that we used to find only on our desktop or laptop computer.

Experts look at two developments which are related: mobile-friendly design and mobile-app development. Countless mobile applications now exist and the smart-phone marketplace is out of control. There is virtually nothing you cannot get from the marketplace and if something is missing, you typically hear people say "We need an app!" Digital communicators can now use their smartphones to access the web quickly and effectively, thanks to the continuing development of high-speed, large-bandwidth mobile networks (3G, 4G, Wi-Fi). In fact, some would say smartphones can be just as good and capable as desktops.

"Today, the mobile phone market is outstripping ownership and use of landline phones in virtually every country on Earth. The steady conversion of more and more of these phones into smarter, more multimedia-friendly devices that work off Wi-Fi, 3G, or 4G networks suggests that the future of mobile development and design will only grow stronger." (Reagle 2012)

People used simple wireless analog-based (1G) portable phones through the 1990s when mobile phones changed in sophistication. The technology continued to improve and numerous features were developed, and those features were much more complex than anything that had been imagined before. The evolution started with our desires to have a phone that had some great communication accessibility and that gave us mobility to go anywhere without being restricted by coverage area. The next development was Europe's Global System for Mobile communication (GSM), a digital mobile telephony system that was also used in other parts of the world. Sometimes called 2G, GSM allowed a huge leap in available mobile services during the mid to late 1990s.

As pre-smartphone devices came on the scene, data transmission changed from analog to digital, allowing the devices to handle the earliest smartphone features. Those features led to today's explosion of app development. Consumers started to get downloadable content, text messaging, and very low-level web access. This basic access let consumers send emails, take a look at a limited selection of online multimedia, and download music files, ringtones, and other simple digital applications. Advances in 2G technology convinced many to give up the landline communication tools in favor of the new capabilities in the mobile phone. These were still relatively basic devices, but that did not stop widespread popularity worldwide that touched all income levels.

The 2000s brought into being the first 3G wireless digital networks with more sophisticated development and service offerings. These true smartphones were remarkable, and in 2002 and 2003 widespread 3G access was offered by network operators. More powerful transmission technology took over for the 2G networks circuit switching mechanism. This was unprecedented wireless transmission technology that depended on efficient packet switching data transmission. This started the modern era of wireless mobile smartphones as pocket-sized computers. Phone networks now offered web-based data options for smartphones, and these offerings exploded from small quantities into out of control development. The growing apps market drove the redesign of the devices to better display interactive systems and digital media.

The more powerful 4G network with packet-switching based data optimization was next. Some digital experts characterize the increases as "10-fold" based on improved data transmission's ability to further improve access to digital media. The demand for media-rich mobile applications also increased, again. Around this time in the overall development, the touchscreen phone with large visual screen interface was created. This technology has virtually replaced small display screens and buttons. The replacement of technology was so rapid that in some countries, it is not possible to purchase anything older than 3G. Almost all new phones today feature button less touch screen design.

Reading the GSMA Intelligence report "The Mobile Economy" yields fascinating information about the unbridled growth of technology and, in turn, online communication. "The mobile industry continues to scale rapidly, with a total of 3.6 billion unique mobile subscribers at the end of 2014. Half of the world's population now has a mobile subscription—up from just one in five 10 years ago. An additional one billion subscribers are predicted by 2020, taking the global penetration rate to approximately 60%. There were 7.1 billion global SIM connections at the end of 2014, and a further 243 million machine-to-machine (M2M) connections." (GSMA 2016)

The technology facilitates online communication and tablets are growing bigger, faster, and lighter, just like the smartphone. There are three forms of mediated communication: mediated interpersonal communication, interactive communication, and mass communication (Lundby 2009). This broad spectrum of facilitated communication demonstrates social media's effect on our interaction and collaboration. We know that people are building social capital and seeking social identity online, leading to more interactive communication. That has changed the basic style of communicating and has continued to limit and/or hinder face-to-face communication. Some experts say that people are more interactive than before, but it comes with a price. Digital conversations create weak ties characterized by less personal feeling than we have when we are face-to-face with our receiver. Still, communicators tend to send open and honest messages because we tend to trust the people on the other end, even if we have not met them. Because of weak ties, it is harder to advance the relationship in online communication. Also, diversity of communication may suffer because in the online environment, we typically interact with people who agree with our points of view. People ride the wave of new technology without considering the implications for closer relationships.

One research project took a broad look at technology and communication, analyzing previous studies, conducting field observations, and completing an online survey. This research was intended to determine the level of engagement that individuals have with their cell phones, with other technologies, and with each other in face-to-face situations. The study's findings showed a negative effect on the quality and quantity of face-to-face communication. The study shows that U.S. Census reports that 76% of households reported having a computer in 2011, compared with only 8% in 1984 (Drago 2015). The report went on to list that the number of households reporting that they accessed the internet rose from 18% in 1998 to 72% in 2011. Also, in 2013 90% of American adults had a cell phone of some kind and that number was closer to 97% for people under age of 44. Other studies tell us that people age 8 to 18 spent more than 7 hours online per day, easily more than any other activity. There appears to be no credible, similar research at this depth that addresses tablets, but we can be sure some of those numbers are included. We can definitely be sure that the conversations that are conducted via tablet are at least as involved as those of the smartphone. Also, the new compatibility between smartphones, tablets, and laptops allows us to sync all of those devices and conduct more online communication and activity.

What these reports and others tell us is that billions of people can easily connect with others short distances or millions of miles away. The prevalence of these devices influences the departure from face-to-face interactions. A 2011 study highlighted mobile communication and its influence on the extent to which people engage face-to-face with new people in public settings (Campbell & Kwak 2011). The study examined different types of cell phone uses and found that mobile phone use actually enhanced information exchange with strangers. In another study, researchers demonstrated that the presence of mobile communication devices in social settings caused problems in human relationships (Przybylski & Weinstein 2013). In conducting two experiments, the researchers uncovered evidence that the devices negatively influenced closeness, connection, and conversation quality. The research concluded that the negative influence increases when people discuss personally meaningful topics.

The relationship between mobile device availability and the quality of in-person social interactions was the subject of another study, one in which researchers discovered that conversations without the use of mobile communication technologies were rated as significantly superior to those in the presence of a mobile device (Misra, Cheng et al. 2016). People who had to communicate without the benefit of mobile devices said they had higher levels of empathetic concern, while those who used a mobile device reported lower levels (Misra, Cheng et al. 2016). These and other studies provide evidence that mobile phone use actually facilitated talking with strangers to get and exchange information. There were some findings that indicated that "cyber-youth" have grown up with cell phones and the internet in education, communication, and entertainment, resulting in a significant decrease in face-to-face interaction among this group. All of this information about online activity, identity, and communication points to the reality that there is some level of degradation of our social skills and our presentation of self-identity to others resulting from the use of new communications technologies. There are indications that there are consequences for personal relationships as well.

In Alone Together: Why We Expect More from Technology and Less From Each Other, Sherry Turkle (2012) examined the effects of technology on familial relationships. After interviewing more than 300 young people and 150 adults, Turkle found that children were often times the ones complaining about their parents' obsession with technology. Turkle discovered that many children believed their parents paid less attention to them than to their smartphones, often times neglecting to interact with them face to face until they had finished responding to emails. (Drago 2015)

The evidence above tells us that while there are great benefits to online communication, those benefits also cost us. CMC typically results in a negative effect on face-to-face interactions with strangers, acquaintances, and family. Online communication puts people in touch and helps with managing daily activities. The interesting part is that it does not create strong, long-lasting relationships. It creates weak ties, as we said earlier. We sacrifice connection and empathy for speed and ready access. This is anytime, anywhere connectivity that allows communication in a variety of ways. The very public use of this technology causes issues. It is interesting that we can connect with anyone, anywhere, but when using the technology in public we do not connect with the people sitting next to us or right across from us. This is true even if those people are family and friends. We are committed to the technology.

Public use challenges behavioral norms, and many people are still uneasy or irritated when someone else is using technology in public. This is most often a concern when people are taking and participating in calls. This bothers co-present others. Co-presence can be defined as the perception by a communicator that another person in a mediated or online environment is real, immediate, or present. The mobile communicator can be oblivious to the objection around him or her. This is interesting because it is the basis for many of the arguments against sole reliance on digital communication. Human interaction is necessary to keep a sense of society and build real relationships.

Remember our example of Erica from earlier in the chapter? Figure 1 illustrates how she might view the concept of co-presence.

Figure 1. Co-presence relationships

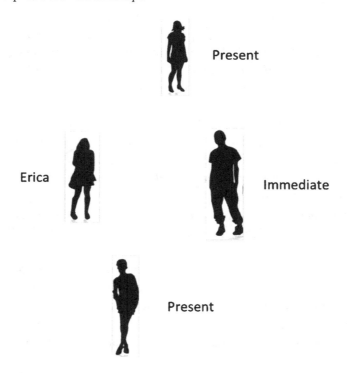

Regardless of which method you value the most between online communication and face-to-face interactions, there is no disputing the sheer value of digital communication. The amount of growth we have seen over the years should tell us that online communication is here to stay. By looking at the history of this type of communication, we can address the pros and cons, enabling us to find the best way to use it for our purposes. More importantly, our need to measure levels of performance requires that we have a full understanding of this method. In-depth knowledge will almost certainly facilitate in-depth analysis and measurement.

REFERENCES

Bachmann, R., Knights, D., & Sydow, J. (2001). Special Issue: Trust and control in organizational relations. *Organization Studies*, *22*(2). doi:10.1177/0170840601222007

Brown, M. A. (2011). *Social networking and individual performance: Examining predictors of participation*. Old Dominion University.

Campbell, S. W., & Kwak, N. (2011). Mobile Communication and Civil Society: Linking Patterns and Places of Use to Engagement with Others in Public. *Human Communication Research*, *37*(2), 207–222. doi:10.1111/j.1468-2958.2010.01399.x

Cooper, A., & Sportolari, L. (1997). Romance in cyberspace: Understanding online attraction. *Journal of Sex Education and Therapy*, *22*(1), 7–14.

Dance, F. E. (1970). The concept of communication. *Journal of Communication*, *20*(2), 201–210. doi:10.1111/j.1460-2466.1970.tb00877.x

Drago, E. (2015). The Effect of Technology on Face-to-Face Communication. *Elon Journal of Undergraduate Research in Communications, 6*(1).

Gambetta, D. (1988). *Trust: Making and breaking cooperative relations*. New York, NY: B. Blackwell.

Gheorghiță & Pădurețu. (2014). Social Networks And Interpersonal Communication. *System, 2*(3), 5.

GSMA. (2016). London, UK: GSMA Mobile Economy.

Gunawardena, C. N. (1995). Social presence theory and implications for interaction and collaborative learning in computer conferences. *International Journal of Educational Telecommunications*, *1*(2), 147–166.

Kramer, R. M. (1996). *Trust in organizations: Frontiers of theory and research*. Thousand Oaks, CA: Sage Publications.

Lane, C., & Bachmann, R. (1998). *Trust within and between organizations: Conceptual issues and empirical applications*. New York: Oxford University Press.

Luhmann, N. (1988). *Familiarity, confidence, trust: Problems and alternatives. In Trust: Making and breaking cooperative relations*. New York: Basil Blackwell.

Lundby, K. (2009). *Mediatization: Concept, changes, consequences*. Peter Lang.

McEvily, B., Perrone, V., & Zaheer, A. (2003). Introduction to the special issue on trust in an organizational context. *Organization Science*, *14*(1), 1–4. doi:10.1287/orsc.14.1.1.12812

Misra, S., Cheng, L., Genevie, J., & Yuan, M. (2016). The iPhone Effect: The Quality of In-Person Social Interactions in the Presence of Mobile Devices. *Environment and Behavior*, *48*(2), 275–298. doi:10.1177/0013916514539755

Newell, S., & Swan, J. (2000). Trust and inter-organizational networking. *Human Relations*, *53*(10), 1287–1328.

Przybylski, A. K., & Weinstein, N. (2013). Can you connect with me now? How the presence of mobile communication technology influences face-to-face conversation quality. *Journal of Social and Personal Relationships*, *30*(3), 237–246. doi:10.1177/0265407512453827

Reagle, D. (2012). *10 Years of Mobile Industry History in 10 Minutes*. Academic Press.

Rousseau, D. M., Sitkin, S. B., Burt, R. S., & Camerer, C. (1998). Not so different after all: A cross-discipline view of trust. Academy of Management. *Academy of Management Review*, *23*(3), 393–404. doi:10.5465/AMR.1998.926617

Sako, M. (1992). *Prices, quality, and trust: inter-firm relations in Britain and Japan*. Cambridge, UK: Cambridge University Press. doi:10.1017/CBO9780511520723

Tardanico, S. (2012, April 30). Is social media sabotaging real communication? *Forbes*. Retrieved from http://www. forbes. com/sites/susantardanico/2012/04/30/is-social-media-sabotaging-real-communication/Published

Turkle, S. (2012). *Alone together: Why we expect more from technology and less from each other*. Basic books.

van Ruler, B. (2015). Agile public relations planning: The Reflective Communication Scrum. *Public Relations Review*, *41*(2), 187–194. doi:10.1016/j.pubrev.2014.11.008

Whitty, M., & Gavin, J. (2001). Age/Sex/Location: Uncovering the Social Cues in the Development of Online Relationships. *Cyberpsychology & Behavior*, *4*(5), 623–630. doi:10.1089/109493101753235223 PMID:11725656

Wright, K. B., & Webb, L. M. (2011). *Computer-mediated communication in personal relationships*. New York: Peter Lang.

Chapter 4
Social Media:
A Discussion of Considerations for Modern Organizations and Professionals

Liston W. Bailey
University of Phoenix, USA

ABSTRACT

This chapter discusses the impact of social networking on participation in organizations across market sectors to include government, business and non-profit entities. The author relates the experiences of young adults working in various occupations on how smartphone use can influence social networking and interactions and whether that influence improves or hampers their learning and professional development. A review of literature and recent social media development trends are used to gather information in support of a conceptual model of media usage and social networked learning within organizations. Leaders and organizational members may want to refer to this 4 stage model when thinking about ways to improve their use of social media and informal learning opportunities found on the Internet and on smart devices.

DOI: 10.4018/978-1-5225-1963-8.ch004

INTRODUCTION

What a world we live in today! Our ability to engage in social media and to entertain ourselves at any time of day or night is remarkable. Social media, which is sometimes referred to as Web 2.0 or the read-write web, is growing as part of our professional lives each day. Social media includes blogs, business networks, collaborative projects, enterprise social networks, forums, microblogs, photo sharing platforms, product/service reviews, social bookmarking, social gaming, video sharing and virtual worlds. As the power of personal computers and smartphone devices increases, so does the public's appetite for maintaining an online presence. Our online presence allows us to stay current on world events and allows our minds to wander through volumes of information and images as we surf the web. Is this a good thing? Can we get smarter or more professional by viewing our journey across the playing field of the internet as a remedy rather than just a form of amusement?

The internet will evolve and change over time to provide richer forms of content (media, news, information, services) available at our fingertips. It will become the fountain of learning for all of mankind in the 21st century. Amazingly, the unique authoring, storage, and sharing capabilities of the web and the cloud will make it possible for us to learn just about anything both formally, informally, and at our own pace. We see this already starting to happen across major educational institutions and university systems that now offer courses through the internet. Social media is also driving informal learning wherein online tutorials and mini courses are more frequently appearing on the web in different venues as free learning options. In fact, social media is becoming a source of learning that we all regularly interface with in order to get smart about things quickly. Daily, people using personal devices such as smartphones gather information on how to live their lives better by consulting social media applications (Apps). The internet, now with its multiple venues for connecting socially, drives our collective memory and is a bubbling cauldron of activity. Moreover, to be effective actors in this world, we are now increasingly compelled to participate in social media much in the manner that the German Philosopher Martin Heidegger (McConnell-Henry, Chapman et al. 2009) described when he coined the term *Dasein* to contextualize the need to "be there" amongst other things.

But the downside to all this frenetic activity is that we tend to discount the importance of face-to-face (f2f) communication and interpersonal connections with people. Writers in the field of social psychology have painted internet communications as an impoverished and sterile form of social exchange compared to traditional face-to-face interactions. Members of the digital generation are prepared to spend longer hours using virtual reality and social media to connect superficially than to connect with others f2f. One could then argue that social media allows one to build relationships that are superficial and far flung, but that are not necessarily ideal for building social capital and lifelong relationships. If this premise it true, then this gives one cause to pause and think about ways to reduce instances of our limited time being dedicated to superficial connections. Perhaps instead we need to put in the additional effort to ensure that the business and social relationships we cultivate also have a physical and real world dimension to them. One could make the prediction that in a period in which social media and virtual reality are becoming a mode for developing workplace relationships, we, as humans, will begin to place a higher value on authentic relationships in the family, in the church, and within the diverse communities in which we live. Interestingly, a loss of connection to authentic relationships is still not a major problem in places once referred to as part of the third world, such as Africa and South America, where access to the internet is much lower than in the United States. But those nations are also developing a higher exposure to the web and so these questions of how we connect and engage in realistic forms of relationship and community will also need to be addressed in what are largely less affluent societies when compared with the United States.

DISCUSSION

There are a few noticeable trends happening now with regard to social learning and the networking of ideas. The *Internet of Things* (Williams, 2016), now serves not only as a venue for socialization, but also as a fountain for other key areas of knowledge acquisition, which we will discuss here. Figure 1 shows four areas I want to discuss which relate to the personal and professional benefits of social media in our lives are

1.   Learning,
2.   Access to technical information,
3.   Competitive posture, and
4.   Social connectedness.

The magical world of social media today supports these four areas of benefits for users of social media and professionals need to understand this theory.

A great deal of our formal learning still continues to be delivered through traditional schooling in universities, both in online and in face-to-face formats. But, as stated earlier, people are also learning quite a lot through informal channels that arise out of social media. The number of blogs accessible on the internet doubles

Figure 1. Social media advantages for users

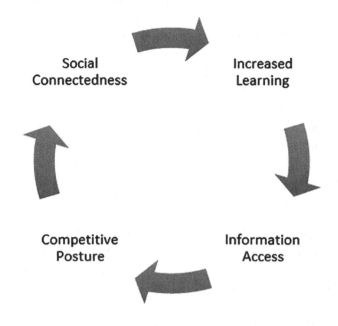

each year. When you add in user generated content in the form of WhatsApp, Linke-dIn, Twitter, Facebook, and personal web pages, it is easy to understand the unique role that social media plays in terms of providing opportunities to learn about what is going on globally, both politically and socially.

This pile of social media information that we find online in different venues provides an opportunity for the extension of socialized learning opportunities beyond what one typically finds in a college or university setting. More specifically, our smartphones and the growth of mobile learning applications today provides us with access to information in the form of text, voice, video, electronic books, location services, and personal assistance Apps, along with on-demand access to educational resources.

In the past, universities were the main source of learning for the young and upcoming professional who wanted to grow his/her competencies (understanding) and skills (ability to do things). College was intended to provide learners with exposure to foundational knowledge provided by experts. Most professionals prepared for the world of work in this manner. It is still assumed that university education gives the learner insights on the ways in which what they have learned may be applied in a postmodern world, where meaning is often continuously revised, and where the definition of truth is often constructed. But can we also achieve required learning as a result of exposure to virtual reality applications, learning content, or other informational sources found on the social media blogosphere? People are spending hours each day connecting with the internet. For example, a majority of U.S. adults – 62% – get news on social media, and 18% do so often, according to a recent survey by Pew Research Center (Gottfried, J. & Shearer E. 2016). These PEW results indicate that YouTube, Facebook and Instagram news users are more likely to get their news online mostly by chance, when they are online doing other things.

In 2015 it was estimated that somewhere around 92% of American adults own a smartphone. This information is based on telephone interviews conducted June 10 through July 12, 2015, among a national sample of 2,001 adults, ages 18 years and older, living in all 50 U.S. states and the District of Columbia. Not surprisingly, adult consumers of social media now tend to get the majority of their entertainment, news, and information from the web and aggregator websites that pool information. How can this online activity be used as a way to learn and develop professionally?

Social learning theory as espoused by Albert Bandura (1977) can provide insight on how to answer this question. Bandura, a social psychologist, proposed a theory of social intelligence wherein we all learn through observation or exemplars in the environment. He suggested that humankind has evolved to have an advanced capacity for observational learning that enables them to acquire knowledge, attitudes, values, emotional proclivities, and competences through modelling. Bandura (2002) discussed social cognitive theory and a cultural context under which people learn from others and the environment.

If we bring this theory forward to the social learning environment of today, we know that people model and imitate the behavior of others they observe through the media and the web. Perhaps life has always imitated art, but today it seems like social media may be having a dampening effect on our collective intellect. For sure, this massive information available in social media is influencing both younger and older generations of consumers who go to the web to get news and information. We are socially and informally learning from everything that is happening in arts, media, politics, and world affairs on a 24/7 basis. Even more striking is the arrival of a new generation of millennials who have never known life without access to media and the internet. One obvious facet of their learning habits surrounds a desire for learner autonomy and also the capacity to get access to information and news on demand.

There is also an ever expanding rationale for the connection between social media and human learning and performance across today's workforce. If you are working in any industry today, you need to connect to others to stay on top of all things that may affect your ability to compete or outperform rivals. Forums, web hangouts, and blogs are places to share news and information about the state of the marketplace and your professions. This growing trend is driving renewed interest in the ability of organizations to leverage social media platforms in order to drive cross-organizational learning and knowledge management. Some organizations are using social media as a cauldron in which ingredients are stirred and mixed together to create learning organizations.

Technical Information Everywhere

The amount of technical information related to science and technology found in online media is astounding. We have blogs that cover technical areas in disciplines as far ranging as chemistry, medicine, physics, and engineering across the internet. Information on how to build, design, or organize things is practically limitless. For example, a Google search of the term technical manuals online yields some 53 million results. Some of those search results may not be actual manuals, but one can assume that many are technical manuals filled with schematics and details on how machines, systems, and other interfaces work. The trick for the media consumer is to be able to validate sources of information and also find the most up to date technical information.

Having access to technical information does not mean that you will instantaneously become an expert. We know that true expertise or mastery in any field of importance comes from disciplined practice. The 10,000-hour rule applies. In other words, social media and the web provide one with a portal through which information and recent knowledge can be attained. Quick referencing information pertinent to an area of interest by using web searches and reading blogs allows one to gather information at a much faster rate than ever before. Therefore, you are likely to do better professionally when you are able to use the capabilities of the web to get smart quickly, especially if you need to cultivate technical knowledge that will make you a more valuable employee or leader.

Social Media Increases the Competition

Social media is driving competition in all areas of our professional lives. Yes, even if you do not see yourself as having a competitive spirit, you need to work aggressively to earn a decent living in today's world. Social media gives you access to networking tools needed to compete for employment, earn more, and do more professionally. Getting access to job opportunities is more than ever before dependent on social media and websites that employers use to advertise openings. Through social media, we learn about popular career trends, best employers to work for, and those "hot" fields to get into. Just go to a popular website like CNN Money and find all you need to know about careers and personal finance. Visit PEW Research and you can find recent blogs and other media on things like being a part of the middle class in America or marriage patterns for college educated adults. Access to powerful forms of information like this helps us to know where we need to put our efforts in terms of building a career or even a business.

Regardless of whatever field you choose to be a part of as a professional, you will need to master a few social media skills in order to remain competitive with rivals. If you want to run a business, you will need to be culturally competent enough to understand the diverse possibilities there are for potential customers. You will also need to have a social media presence through which to market your services and products. This is also referred to as social marketing. For example, if you want to find stable employment you can benefit from having a LinkedIn page or a personal website to market the best aspects of who you are. And then of course there is Twitter where you can follow someone of stature and potentially weigh in on the conversation on a particular topic.

For professional entrepreneurs, there are quite a few places on the internet where one can get access to information to help their business. Figure 2 provides

Figure 2. Tools for businesses

1. ForEntrepreneurs.com

2. OneVest.com

3. AudienceBloom.com

4. Dutiee.com

5. Quora.com

6. AngelList.com

7. EpicLaunch.com

8. BusinessOwnersToolkit.com

9. ChicCEO.com

10. AllBusiness.com

11. ForteFoundation.com

a sample listing of 20 such websites that typically allow would-be business found-ers to socialize ideas for new companies or find sources of capital for start-ups or business franchises.

Why Can't We Live Without that Smartphone?

Walk through a major airport, shopping center, or recreational event in your local town. What you will most assuredly see is people everywhere with their heads glued to their smartphones. They are reading, listening, conversing, taking pictures and doing a myriad of things that contribute immensely to their intelligence of what is happening socially. A room full of people can seem strangely quiet and cold. In many instances, people are learning informally, searching for information on things that grab their interests, or for which they crave more information. Our phones, filled with Apps and storage capacity, are also our external hard drive that we use to pull content from the internet. Having said all this, it is hard to imagine a world where we do not have an external device that connects us to the social version of ourselves. We also seek artificial connectedness with like-minded individuals through social media which has as a downside. We do not deeply debate or share true feelings with people we do not really know.

Many of us feel an immense amount of trepidation when we cannot communicate freely or load our favorite App for too long a period of time. Some have suggested that it is either a fear of missing out (FoMO) or Nomophobia (i.e. "no mobile phone" and phobia) that drives our anxiety at this point. One idea is The Extended iSelf, which is the Impact of iPhone Separation on Cognition, Emotion, and Physiology. Researchers examined the effects on self, cognition, anxiety, and physiology when iPhone users are unable to answer their iPhone while performing cognitive tasks (Clayton, Leshner et al. 2015).

So what does this mean? Apparently many of us are addicted to social media and the web and we do not even know it. There are also physiological conditions associated with our addiction. When we get online, our pupils dilate, our blood pressure rises, and our brain syncs with the media and content on our device. The circuitry in our brain becomes overloaded and we are unable to remain aware of anything outside of what we are doing on the web. Cellphone addition along with an inability to manage the amount of time one spend on the internet is really worth discussing with a peer (or even a therapist) because it can lead to wasted time and depleted energy levels. We all have to strike a healthier balance in terms of social media use versus time we allocate to non-electronic forms of communication and face-to-face interaction with family and friends.

The Social Media Frenzy

The next generation of employees coming into our business, government, and non-profit sectors thrive on the use of social media for what they view as fact gather. However, there is a problem with this phenomenon, which leaves us with a question about our future as a nation. We risk becoming a nation of lazy thinkers who would rather have simplistic answers to complex problems than do deep thinking about the components of problems and issues. Will a generation of people who rely on social media for news and information be willing to meet with people who do not share the same views? What we see is that many people who engage in social media are attracted to flocking to venues where they find like-minded people.

When we spend too much time with people who think like we do, there is less need to engage in dialectic thinking or to defend our views on an issue. Online digitalization of social communities is being leveraged by media companies to corral users into groups based on demographics and their income level. Unknowingly, people are being segregated into groups where there is a predominant political or social viewpoint on society. How does this affect our ability to think creatively or independently about the arc of our professional lives and how we make personal decisions? If I do not like what I am hearing on TV or in the press I can self-select where and from whom I choose to get information. The idea of group polarization, a theory from social psychology, comes to mind.

People in groups tend to have more extreme views than they would have as individuals. Group polarization is described as instances where individuals identify with a particular group and conform to a prototypical group position that is more extreme than the group mean. Online social media often drives people into camps of the like-minded and this is something we have to think more broadly. We see the effect of group polarization in our politics on a whole range of issues in regards to things like gun owner rights, LGBT issues, political campaigns, heavy handed police tactics, and wealth distribution in our country. This is not to say that social media is to blame for these issues because the majority of these issues were present before social media was born. But where social media does have an effect is in driving our conversation as an American people and what is reported on in the mainstream press. Young people are more likely to believe what they see in social media than what they see or read in the press. For them, social media is becoming the press of the future. At the same time, millennials are seen as cash cows with large amounts of disposable income ripe for the taking by corporations. The upside for businesses is that advertising and media executives are always working to get maximum exposure of the products and services they want to sell to potential consumers.

Companies and Their Use of Social Media

Businesses across the country are making use of social media to drive stakeholder interest in their products and services. This is an area in which companies that want to compete in the marketplace must have some skin in the game. When we look at the majority of mid-to-large sized companies, we see that almost all of them engage in some form of social media, either directly or indirectly linked to their company websites. Many companies have their own Facebook or LinkedIn pages. Remember that as of January 2014, Facebook was the largest global social network, with a total of 1.19 billion active users monthly and an annual growth rate of 18%. Researchers looked at degree of corporate social media use how much companies are exploiting the capabilities of single or multiple social media platforms (Aichner & Jacob 2015). LinkedIn describes itself as the world's largest professional network on the Internet, with more than 350 million members.

Many companies, for example, host online venues for product and services reviews. In such instances, customers can evaluate products or certain attributes (e.g. product quality) and write or read product reviews. Companies have also put millions of dollars in recent years into social media to support their brands and to market directly to the consumer. But this approach has not always paid off because social media may build icons, however, it has not always produced the same results for consumer product brands. This is because the chaotic world of social media includes many subcultures that are fickle and somewhat unresponsive to the idea of social media being used to sell products to them. Companies that want to use social media to drive their products must be nimble and smart enough to use a cultural branding approach that is responsive to societal trends and the concerns of consumers they want to attract. The big question a business or agency has to ask is: *Who do we want to engage with using social media and what do these people care about in their professional and private lives?*

Due to the power of social media, a shift in the landscape of advertising and marketing has taken place where industries that used to dominate media buying, television, and print advertising no longer dominate corporate messaging unchallenged. Today 67% of adults use Facebook and 44% get their news from the site. Shoppers today are more likely to buy products and services online using store websites that have a social media component to them. People in local government agencies and nonprofit organizations are also harnessing the web to stay connected and to organize activities in the community.

Companies that smartly use the power of social media to drive business have another arsenal in their quiver to beat their rivals. Harvard professor Michael Porter's five forces theory of the competitive marketplace suggest that companies must take into account buyer power, supplier power, threat of new entrants, threat of substitutes, and industry rivalry (Gamble et al., 2017). The power of social media to manage these forces is remarkable. Social media use allows businesses to market products and services relatively cheaply to potential buyers in the marketplace. Companies can also manage aspects of their value chain and demonstrate the quality of their supply network using social media. Hosting a social media page on the Web provides an entity the opportunity to build a powerful brand and to dissuade new entrants from competing head to head. As stated earlier, there is no doubt that a healthy amount of social media presence is necessary if a business owner wants to achieve comparative advantage versus industry rivals.

Managing for Social Networking Participation

Managers of employees must now take into account the use of social media as a part of work communication. If your workforce is not using social media to be more productive at work, then how are they using their time? The truth is that people spend quite a bit of their day online anyway. So, it makes sense for business and organizations to have a strategy to leverage Web 2.0 technologies to be more productive at work. This may include using social networking sites (SNS) like Tumblr, Facebook, LinkedIn, or a company blog to drive conversation and excitement about an organization and its mission. It is also important to think about how much we have evolved and moved past the idea of all pertinent knowledge being resident within an all knowing firm. A business must now also take into account what customers are saying about the value and utility of their products and services. This is important because fickle consumers are more eclectic in their tastes and buying decisions than ever before.

A social media strategy for a business should include considerations related to social capital, network theory, and knowledge management. Social media strategy applied within organizations should drive a sense of community and culture among organizational stakeholders and customers. This can be accomplished through streaming media and short films about a product or service. It can be a hosted on internal or external networks for customers to access whenever they want to know more about the business or products. The purpose of streamlining media and film must be to develop a brand that supports a crowd culture of users and subscribers. Networking strategies for businesses can be operationalized through the use of platforms like LinkedIn or by developing a company website that stakeholders may use to share thoughts or write directly to the company. Knowledge management efforts that are steeped in the use of polling and online surveys can be great techniques to get information on which consumers use your products and services. This is must have as a knowledge management requirement for development of market segmentation and differentiation strategies for your business or group.

Another consideration for the use of social media by individuals has to do with the extent to which social capital can build social capital. Social capital refers to one's relationships with others which in turn serve as a basis for gaining benefits from those relationships. Individuals today do this through SNS applications like LinkedIn. Organizations also have the ability to build social capital and sell their goods and services using the power of social media.

A great user case for social media within organizations is that of creating online venues where people can share opinions about the business, workplace projects, or outreach to the broader community on issues related to social responsibility. In most instances, where people perceive such opportunities as having usefulness to support their professional and personal growth, they will more frequently log into SNS to build their selected network of relationships. Companies can also reap the benefits of this kinetic online networking activity by sponsoring organizational pages on venues like LinkedIn, Facebook, or YouTube. When organizational stakeholders (employees, customers, investors) go to these online venues, they can interface with various forms of content sponsored by the business or individual contributors (i.e., user generated content).

CONCLUSION

Urban professionals and companies have the choice and power to use social media in a manner that positively supports their work and learning every day. For the individual, the challenge is to find the most productive ways to spend time on social media, maintaining a virtual persona, and networking to build a career. For businesses, the power of social media can mean getting new customers and creating a buzz around products and services. Businesses and entrepreneurs that want to use social media need to devise a strategy that attracts customers. A company today that does not have a website, an App, or a YouTube channel will probably be unable to compete very well against rivals. There is much to consider for businesses that want to drive success through establishing a social media presence.

Now more than ever it is important to manage your time, energy level, and effort put into social media and being on the web. Too much time spent surfing through social media on the web can be harmful in terms of your ability to focus energy. We can connect socially and be entertained by the stories and experiences of others we get access to through social media, but too little time spent finding useful ways to apply your media habits can leave you blind to learning opportunities, access to pertinent information, or those survival facts you need to live in your community. We have to strike a balance and use our time with social media for the purpose of making ourselves more aware of ways to improve in all aspects of our lives. At the same time, we need to remember that finding opportunities for true face-to-face communication is that little thing we can do to be more human each day. Meeting someone for the first time in person rather than via a cold and impersonal tweet is often preferable. This is especially true in our professional lives where we need to establish relationships with new clients or with our organizational peers. Based on the readings in this book and this chapter, you should be thinking about the personal and potential business value of your relationship to social media and ways to use your connections to get ahead socially and professionally in the modern world of work.

REFERENCES

Aichner, T., & Jacob, F. (2015). Measuring the degree of corporate social media use. *International Journal of Market Research*, *57*(2), 257–275.

Bandura, A. (2002). Social cognitive theory in cultural context. *Applied Psychology*, *51*(2), 269–290. doi:10.1111/1464-0597.00092

Bandura, A., & Walters, R. H. (1977). *Social learning theory*. Academic Press.

Clayton, R. B., Leshner, G., & Almond, A. (2015). The extended iSelf: The impact of iPhone separation on cognition, emotion, and physiology. *Journal of Computer-Mediated Communication*, *20*(2), 119–135. doi:10.1111/jcc4.12109

Gamble, J., Peteraf, M., & Thompson, A. (2017). Evaluating a company's external environment. In Essentials of Strategic Management: The quest for competitive advantage (5th ed.; pp. 40-50). New Yok: McGraw-Hill.

Gottfried, J., & Shearer, E. (2016). *News across social media platforms*. PEW Research Center.

McConnell-Henry, T., Chapman, Y., & Francis, K. (2009). Husserl and Heidegger: Exploring the disparity. *International Journal of Nursing Practice*, *15*(1), 7–15. doi:10.1111/j.1440-172X.2008.01724.x PMID:19187164

Williams, J. L. (2016). Privacy in the age of the internet of things. *Human Rights (Chicago, Ill.)*, *41*(4), 14–22.

ADDITIONAL READING

Anderson, M. (2015). *Technology device ownership*. PEW Research Center.

Holt, D. (2016). Branding in the age of social media. *Harvard Business Review*, *94*(3), 40–50.

Chapter 5

Framing and Mis–Framing in Micro–Blogging Sites in China:
Online Propagation of an Animal Cruelty Campaign

Yuanxin Wang
Temple University, USA

ABSTRACT

Micro-blogging is a popular, continuously developing form of communication that allows users to update their current life status in short posts around the clock with targeted websites and platforms. A significant blogosphere has developed in China where the prevailing micro-blogging websites comprise Internet coverage of issues not covered by mainstream media. This research will examine heavily shared and discussed blog posts on a popular micro-blogging website in China during an anti-animal cruelty campaign. The comments section of the blog posts will also be analyzed to identify discrepancies between the frames set by the bloggers and the perceptions by their audiences.

DOI: 10.4018/978-1-5225-1963-8.ch005

INTRODUCTION

The concept of micro-blogging became popular with the emergence of Tumblr and Twitter in 2006 (Li, Hoi, & Chang, 2010). The basic elements in such connected social network communities (aka blogospheres) include individual postings, comments, and articulated connections through hyperlinks, replies, or re-tweet (share or repost in Chinese blogging sites) between (micro) blogs from networks of interconnected texts (Schmidt, 2011). A typical micro-blogger has tens if not hundreds of friends in his or her network, which may translate to hundreds of micro-blog updates every day. Therefore, the medium holds the potential for powerful information flow.

Micro-blogging, a platform for Web-based and mobile applications that allows users to exchange small elements of their life status, has experienced rapid growth and gained popularity worldwide. Compared to traditional blogging, micro-blogging allows for more instant and flexible communication due to its real-time news-update function and multiple tools for exchanging ideas with immediacy. Schmidt (2011, p. 160) defined blogs as "frequently updated websites that display content in reverse chronological order." Single blog entries have unique URLs and can be linked to individual users, rather than to the site as a whole.

Micro-blogs differ from blogs in that micro-blogs are limited in the number of characters in a single post and in the aggregated size of audience (Ho, Li, & Lin, 2011). For example, the popular U.S. micro-blog site, Twitter, limits each post's length to 140 English characters. One of China's prominent micro-blog sites, Sina. com, requires its users to post no more than 140 Chinese characters in each post. Micro-blog users explicitly establish connections among themselves by "following" or "being followed by" other users and by explicitly referring to other users by replying to or "re-tweeting" (i.e., "forwarding") their posts (Schmidt, 2011, p. 160).

Micro-blog data provide a useful resource for studying the dynamic flow of change or exchange of information due to micro-blog's embedded timeline (Ho, Li, & Lin, 2011). Marolt (2008) suggested that blogs should be perceived as a conscious and intentional effort to alter perceptions in and of everyday life: Bloggers express their opinions and produce shared meanings, and they may inspire societal transformation resulting in (perceived and actual) changes in their everyday lived realities. In China, because mainstream media is under heavy censorship from the central government, and because the general public usually does not have access to information that may be perceived by the government as a threat to public security, blogging sites have become a major channel for ordinary people to voice their concerns about sensitive issues (e.g., political and environmental issues) and to make an effort to facilitate changes in their daily lives.

Research examining micro-blogging is relatively slim compared to studies addressing other Internet-based new media. Due to the early inception and development of blogging sites in the U.S., most studies on blogging have examined the topic in the U.S. Nonetheless, micro-blogging technology has prospered in China due to its huge netizen (Internet users) population and the prevalence of Wi-Fi availability in public areas. Yet only limited amount of published research examining micro-blogging in China exists. The lack of research may be partially due to the political pressure from the Chinese government, which has attempted to block and delete sensitive words, controversial posts, as well as diverse viewpoints on blogging sites (Yu, 2007). This study fills a gap in the literature by offering a close look at micro-blogging in China. This paper explores how micro-blogging messages originating in China are initiated, designed or tailored, and distributed to a large audience, and how its audience perceives the micro-blog messages.

Specifically, this study examines micro-blogging in the context of efforts to prevent animal cruelty. This research examines the elements within the 140-character micro-blogging posts that make messages about the anti-bile farm campaign appealing to a specific audience and influence mass media and policy-makers. Bile is a digestive fluid produced by the liver and stored in the gallbladder, which is used by some traditional Chinese medicine practitioners. The bile bear farm keeps the animals in captivity to harvest their bile and they are housed in small cages which often prevent them from standing or sitting upright, or from turning around.

BACKGROUND ON CHINA'S ANIMAL CRUELTY CAMPAIGN

On February 1, 2012, Guizhentang, a pharmaceutical company based in the southeastern province of Fujian, received approval from the China Securities Regulatory Committee (CSRC) for its plans to raise millions of dollars through a stock exchange listing to enable expansion of its bile bear farm, facilities where the animals are kept so that bile can be retrieved over a long period of time. Guizhentang quickly found itself at the heart of an angry Internet campaign accusing it of violating animal welfare. Graphic and disturbing videos of bear bile extraction circulated on the Chinese internet. Initiated by a handful of protesters through their micro-bloggings, this anti-cruelty to animal campaign was quickly joined by public figures, celebrities, NGOs, politicians, and tens of thousands of netizens. The CSRC faced a dilemma: follow the law or respond to human conscience. As the pressure culminated, Qiu Shuhua, the founder of Guizhentang, burst into tears in a television interview by the China Central Television. In April 2013, Guizhentang suspended its IPO application to Shenzhen stock market (Yang, 2013). In May 31, 2013, animal activist across the country were thrilled when CSRC terminated the Guizhentang's IPO's application (Li, 2013).

More important than the complex emotions that resulted from the public debate were the social and political changes this campaign initiated, including the instant information relay among blogging and news websites, the awareness of the influence of the opinion leaders, the participation of the accused in debates through online media, and the accelerated legislation process regarding anti-cruelty to animal. The inception and development of the huge online organization helped to create an online campaign that possessed all the elements contained in a face-to-face campaign, but was less noisy and more time and space-consuming.

This study examines the influence that micro-blogs can have in general and more specifically on this campaign to prevent animal cruelty.

The Power of Micro-Blogs

Micro-blogging features short posts published through a variety of channels (e.g., web, text messaging, instant messaging, and other third-party applications). Micro-blogging communities share a constantly changing information stream and repository where trustworthiness and credibility may be challenged, which can impact the mass media industry. Blogging has been used extensively as a new source of news produced by amateur journalists, who "criticize, supplement, comment, check, and challenge the accountability of mainstream journalism" (Reese & Dai, 2009, p. 221). Within a country like China, where central government tends to withhold information from the public to maintain the status quo, communities created by micro-bloggers offer an alternative information source. Bruns (2008) attributed the expanding micro-blogging community to weblogs lowering the barriers for the dissemination of information and participation in online conversations as well as to the blurring of the roles of the message sender and receiver. The result of this feature of micro-blogs is the blogosphere's collective reporting power and its informal peer-review process (Tremayne, 2007). Micro-bloggers increase the propagation of information by repeatedly posting, reposting, and commenting on the blog articles.

As of 2012, there has been no finalized law dealing with cruelty to animals in China, even though legislation has been drafted to address cruelty. There are no charitable organizations like Royal Society for the Prevention of Cruelty to Animals (RSPCA) in China. The voice of animal welfare activists is largely muted due to the lack of attention from both mass media and the general society. Usually in China, animal cruelty has seldom been brought into media spotlight. Consequently, the general society has little or no awareness of this issue. But micro-blogs have made the propagation of downplayed information possible, as was the case with the attempt to prevent the bear bile farm.

Micro-Blogging's Functional Role

Studies of micro-blogging can be categorized into three schools of exploration. The first school examines micro-blogging as an independent and functional communication platform. From this perspective, scholars have examined popular recommendation channels (Cheng, Sun, Hu, & Zeng, 2010) to understand the prevalent use and structural patterns of micro-blogging (Java, Song, Finin, & Tseng, 2007) and to examine the content of micro-blogging posts. Newly emerging research derived from this functional role of micro-blogging has focused on the role of blogs as a forum of public debate, with consequences for media, politics, and policy (Farrell & Drezner, 2007). Placing, Ward, Peat, and Teixeira (2005) have argued that blogs can be an innovative tool for education. Ho, Li, and Lin (2011) found that the top micro-bloggers have disseminated the concept of the network and displayed multiple kinds of propagation values for users.

A second category of micro-blogging research examines content in organizational blogging activities. For example, branding information was designed and posted by bloggers during a commercial campaign (Jansen, Zhang, Sobel, & Chowdury, 2009). Kaplan and Haenlein (2011) found many commercial companies, such as Starbucks and JetBlue Airways, have tailor-made their brands reinforcing communication through blogs with their potential and current customers. Argüelles, Elsas, Callan, and Carbonell (2008) developed document representation models for recommending blogs in response to a user query.

The third category of micro-blogging research has focused on the view that the majority of blogs deal with personal choices (Bane, Cornish, Erspamer, & Kampman, 2010; Nardi, Schiano, Gumbrecht, & Swartz 2004; White & Winn, 2009): Bloggers write to express their subcultural identities and norms (Hodkinson, 2006; Wei, 2004). Schmidt (2011) argued that codes, rules, and relations frame the situative use of blogs by, for example, suggesting a certain style of writing or providing the technical means to easily link to other content, but the final layout of a micro-blog post is determined by individualized preferences. Code and hyperlinks are subject to change over time, but well-established personal style is relatively stable. How individual bloggers select and represent content online is framed by technology or code, rules (shared routines and expectations), and relations (hyper-textual as well as social connections). Igwe (2008) used content analysis to examine how African

Americans use blogs to create virtual "third place" communities as a means to rebuild aspects of community that are lacking in their "real-world" communities, such as discussion of issues related to HIV/AIDS.

Understanding the functional roles and dynamics of micro-blogs in different social contexts is useful in explaining how some micro-blogging posts become popular and in determining or predicting the influential factors that propagate the information and ideas conveyed by micro-blogging articles. Different perspectives of the animal cruelty campaign that emerged in China's micro-blogging site reflect the three functional roles addressed above. Compared to its counterparts in Western society, micro-blogging is still in its early stage of development in China. Understanding the functions of micro-blogs can help bloggers effectively use the features of blogging posts. Micro-blogs can provide a voice to non-governmental organizations for animal welfare or to grassroots animal activists who have been silenced within Chinese society and who are under-represented in Chinese media. Further examination in the case of the animal cruelty campaign in China can explore how the bloggers and their audiences personalized their choices of presenting and reading micro-blogs while avoiding political sensitivities and responsibilities from the central government.

The Audience of Micro-Blogs

One aspect of social networking research focuses on audience analysis. Due to the particular technical characteristics of micro-blogs, compared to traditional blogs, micro-blog audiences become visible, which means that the audience transforms from silent and passive readers to proactive participants within the virtual community (Scheidt, 2006). Specific features of micro-blogs, such as permalinks, trackbacks, the comment feature on blog postings, and the referencing signals of Twitter, make it possible for the audience to emerge and carry out distributed conversations as asynchronous and non-linear conversations, where multiple authors refer to and discuss a topic on various sites (Efimova, 2009). The class of micro-blogging users and their behaviors is an important domain in audience study (Krishnmaurthy, Gill, & Arlitt, 2008).

Micro-blogging has become a new medium characterized by its fluidity and interactivity as well as its fundamental function of transmitting information. Audience study, as an inseparable part of the process of the interaction, has become a popular domain of micro-blogging research. Based on the characteristics and limitations of online-based communication in general, Boyd (2010) introduced four analytical categories of a blog's audiences: first, the intended audience comprises a blogger's general idea of the audience he or she wants to address, such as friends, colleagues, or those interested in a specific topic. Second, the addressed audience comprises those people that are addressed in a specific blog posting, which may be the same as the intended audience or may be a specific subset, such as when posts directed to a particular group of readers for feedback. Both intended and addressed audiences are an important consideration when deciding what information to disclose online. The third category contains the empirical audience, or those who generally take notice of any given posting. The final category includes the potential audience, which is determined by the technological reach of a blog within the wider context of the medium's network. (Note, however, Farrell and Drezner (2007) argued that there is no ideological consensus for the classification of micro-blog participants or audience. Farrell and Drezner's argument may have its root in the notion that the boundary between participants and audience is blurred.)

One aspect of audience research has examined the congruence and disparities between expectations of privacy and the actual behavior of recipients. Online communities provide a platform for recipients to express their points of views without necessarily exposing their real identity. Thus users can employ the communication tools of micro-blogs while maintaining control over their own personal information and private sphere. Having this ability, micro-blogging users can accurately evaluate audience behavior and effectively disseminate blog information.

Another aspect of studying audiences is inspired by the technological features that provide dynamics for the audience proactive activities in the micro-blogging community. For example, the development of the RSS feed format and the corresponding feed readers from 2000 onwards have allowed users to subscribe to a variety of blogs. Instead of having to regularly and manually visit individual sites of interest, users can aggregate selected sources in their feed reader, which can automatically retrieve new and updated content. In other words, the blogs that the audience follows can determine whether the content is of interest to them. And bloggers can tailor-make their posts based on the message they intend to convey, as well as how likely the audience would follow the information.

A third dimension of research related to audience in the micro-blogging examines the display of public opinions and attitudes, often using sentiment analysis (O'Connor Balasubramanyan, Balasubramanyan, & Smith, 2010). The composition of the audience, as well as the audience's behaviors in the virtual community, needs further critical research. Its theoretical and practical importance is emerging to both social scientists as well as to interested players from various domains, such as politics, business, and media industry. Knowing the unique composition of audiences on Chinese micro-blogging sites could help bloggers understand what kind of audience they are addressing and what type of message would suit the audience best. Furthermore, to solve the fundamental problems regarding animal cruelty in China, understanding the population who are most concerned with the issue could help policymakers evaluate the severity of the problem and work for the best solution.

Framing and Micro-Blogging

In micro-blogging research, framing theory is an effective tool to bridge scholarly concerns about the blogging content and the perception of its audience because the theory embraces both cognitive and sociological elements. Frames may be understood as conceptual tools that media and individuals rely on to convey, interpret, and evaluate information (Neuman, Just, & Crigler, 1992, p. 60). Framing has been applied as an analytic tool in media contexts and as a method of analysis (Entman, 1993). The way an issue is framed is important in determining whether people notice an issue, how they understand the issue, how they remember it, how they evaluate it, and how they choose to act upon the issue (Bullock, 2007; Dimitrova & Connolly- Ahern, 2007; Entman,1993; Gandy & Li, 2005; Iyengar, 1991; Mc-Combs & Ghanem, 2003).

Micro-blogs possess the comparative advantage of speedy publication: They have a first-mover advantage in socially constructing frames for understanding of current events (Farrell & Drezner, 2007, p. 17). Additionally, political commentators rely on blogs as sources of interpretative frames for political developments (Farrell & Drezner, 2007). Brownstein, Freifeld, and Madoff (2009) examined how the information is quickly widespread and adopted through micro-blogs during mass crisis and emergency events.

Although it is the world's largest social-media market, China is vastly different from its counterparts in the West in many ways, but the composition of their social media are virtually identical. Given the ban of Tumblr, Twitter, and YouTube in China, major media moguls in the Western societies have very limited access to China's exploding social-media space. Further, because social media provide important channels for individuals, commercial firms, and political organizations from Western societies to communicate with Chinese, it is useful to understand issues in China's social media space.

Chinese Micro-Blogging Websites

Launched in 2006, Twitter became the largest and most well-known micro-blogging platform in the United States and in many other countries. However, in China, access to Twitter and other social network sites such as Facebook, is banned. In response to the ban, Chinese blogging began in 2002 when the first blogger, Isaac Mao, completed his first post on August 5. Chinese blogging subsequently prospered. There were more than 204 million blogs in China by June 2015. Blogging and reading blogs are among the most popular online activities for Chinese online users (Chinese Internet Network Information Center, 2015). Although blogs have less perceived credibility compared with wired news, they have become an important source for information and an unprecedented way for grassroots activists to express themselves (Chinese Internet Network Information Center, 2007). The blogging's role of pushing the limit of free speech in China has manifested itself in several confrontational scenarios between bloggers and the government (Pan, 2006). China-based micro-blogging sites have inherited many features from their international counterparts, such as the 140-characters limitation and the ability to follow, subscribe, and read other user's posts without permission.

Technology-savvy Chinese urbanites are the major player in Chinese micro-blog community, which has introduced new platforms for posting, viewing, and cross-posting textual-visual-audio contents via digital mobile communication networks (Yu, 2011). The intellectual background of the micro-bloggers and technological development have contributed to the creative energy and talent manifested in the ubiquity of thoughts in the Chinese language-based micro-blogging sites.

A distinctive characteristic of Chinese micro-blogging, compared to the English-based micro-blogging sites, is its prominent role in influencing both political and economic imperatives in the unique social context of contemporary China (Yu, 2011). Yu (2011) described the Chinese blogosphere as a mixture of "emancipation and withdrawal, of the urge to strike a nerve and the instinct to shield oneself in the cocoon of fun and irreverence" (p. 390). Yu accurately characterized the self-marginalization aspect as Chinese bloggers and the general tendency of withholding real identity as a regular blog user, but he has failed to recognize Chinese bloggers' attempts to participate in and influence the policy-making process through the leeway afforded by communication via micro-blogs versus simply withdrawing.

Research has confirmed that the Chinese-language blogosphere provides a growing venue for free speech, that the blogs can create an independent space for discourse, and that this sphere aids the development of a civic culture and civil society in China. For example, Marolt (2008) argued that the Chinese-language blogosphere has become a new type of social space in which free thought has the capacity to form conduits for dynamic dissent. Marolt also pointed out the possible influence of active intellectual bloggers who are known to a wider public, who could become mediators between virtual and physical space, and hence, could be facilitators of social change by turning spaces of dissent into spaces of resistance (p. xii).

The claim of the significant impact of Chinese micro-blogging is countered by the opinion that—compared to other actors in domestic politics, such as the specialized interest groups, political action committees, government bureaucrats, or elected officials—bloggers do not appear to be very powerful (Farrell & Drezner, 2007). However, Farrell and Drezner failed to recognize the interrelation and interaction between bloggers and other actors as well as the blogger's influence upon the general public. In other words, the bloggers may influence the policy-makers indirectly via their influence upon powerful people or the general public when they are mobilized by micro-blogs.

Scholars have argued that blogospheres are quite heterogeneous in terms of information, topics, events selected for discussion, how this content is presented in terms of writing style, illustration, and so on, and how these distributed conversations (Efimova, 2009) within and between blogs are structured (Schmidt, 2011). Therefore, the posts in micro-blogs could be used as prime examples of the contingent and under-determined nature of new media formats (Lievrouw, 2002) that allow for various practices.

MAIN FOCUS

Based on those considerations, this chapter explores the functional role of micro-blogging in framing and reinforcing the concept and awareness of animal-cruelty. The case examined is an environmental event that attracted great public and media attention: the Anti-bile bear farm campaign in China micro-blogging site, which presents the necessary characteristics as a communicational platform, basic function as information provider, and audience composition. To address this purpose, the following research questions were posed:

Research Question 1: What were the audience characteristics of the top-blogging posts regarding the Anti-bile Bear Farm Campaign in China during March 2012?
Research Question 2: What were the most common elements or patterns in the top-blogging posts at various stages in the Anti-bile Bear Farm Campaign?
Research Question 3: How did the audiences in the micro-blogging sites perceive the frames presented in the blogging post?

A Workable Solution: Measuring the Audience

Farrell and Drezner (2007) have argued that the distribution of web-links and traffic is heavily skewed within a micro-blogging site: very often a few bloggers command most of the attention of the audience. Hindman, Tsioutsiouliklis, and Johnson (2003) further stated that the skewed distribution prevails in most of the micro-blogging websites. It is therefore justifiable to say that a few elite blogs can provide summary statistics for the measurements of the blogosphere (Farrell, & Drezner, 2007, p. 17) and represent the size of its audience as a whole.

Measuring the audience size of the top-blogging posts involves two steps. First, the number of people who follow the top-bloggers are counted. Most of the China micro-blogging sites offer features that allow users to follow or pay attention to certain bloggers (e.g., celebrities, government officials, journalists) without permission from the figures followed. Once a blogger builds up his or her following list, micro-blogging sites will automatically disseminate blog entries from the followed to the followers' page as new entries are posted.

The updates are usually in Really Simple Syndication (RSS) feed format. Because the posts regarding the anti-cruelty to animal campaign were automatically delivered into the follower population by the website system, it is reasonable to assume a possible propagation relationship occurred between the senders and the audience.

Second, the frequency of a blogging message receiving replies and re-postings are recorded and calculated. This measurement method was based on Ho et al.'s (2011) rigid-propagation relationship model, which states that if X posts a message that contains Q, and an individual Y replies to the message and also posts another message relevant to Q, then the concept Q is considered to have been propagated from X to Y. Consequently, there is a rigid-propagation relationship between X and Y. In this study, the number of replies (feedback, comments and opinions) that were directly related to the blog post, the number or frequency that the post is shared by the audience (which means the posts are directly linked to a specific post from another blog, either in the format of a whole piece of post or a hyperlink), and the number of relevant posts inspired by the blogging post were counted.

The sample collection process started by using a search engine under the micro-blogging section in www.sina.com.cn, the most populated social networking site in China. The key words included "Guizhentang" (the name of the bile bear farm, which translates to mean the chamber of returning to the truth) and "bile bear farm." Until April 5th, 2012, there were more than half million entries that resulted from each key word. Due to the result limits set by Sina.com.cn, only the top 500 posts archives were accessible to regular users. Among the accessible blogging posts, the number of followers and reposts after the 23rd post dropped dramatically. Additionally, starting at the 45th post, most of the blogging articles were reposted versions of the ones from the top 23. Based on these various considerations, 20 posts were regarded as reasonable size for this research.

Framing the Blog Posts

Following the framing theorists' call for using the defragmented frame typologies, a frame analysis was conducted based on the derived from five traditions of research of media framing and the social construction of environmental news: episodic versus thematic framing, micro-issue salience, audience-based frames, attribution of responsibility, and skepticism towards environmental issues (Xie, 2009). Other elements reinforcing the blog message, such as the sentiment-weighted phrases, images and video links, also were examined. Further, to examine audience perceptions, comments responding to the top blog posts were studied following the same frame analysis approach applied in examining the blog posts.

Findings

Column 1 in Table 1 displays the bloggers' diversified professions or industries. Five of the 20 bloggers described themselves as journalists or representatives of media agencies. For example, the most clicked blogger in this chart is a renowned female journalist who has 3,465,222 followers. Other top bloggers include non-governmental organizations (NGO), pet-owners' websites, movie actress, cartoonist, and citizen bloggers. Some of the bloggers used their popularity to disseminate messages about animal rights through their blog posts. Less known bloggers tailor their appealing messages to increase readership.

Farrell and Drezner (2008) argued that unequal distribution of readership, combined with internal norms and linking practices, allowed interesting news and opinions to rise to the top of the blogosphere. The result directly associated with the top blogosphere, as Farrell and Drezner (2008) have argued, is the [increased] attention of elite actors, whose understanding of politics may be changed by frames from the blogosphere.

To illustrate the frames employed by the top bloggers and the audience perceptions of their frames, four representative micro-blogging posts were selected based on such consideration as formats (text, image, video, and cartoon picture), reporting perspectives, and chronological stages.

Stage I: The TV Documentary on the Bear Bile Farm (Early Stage)

This post, which is representative of Stage I, was published by a user registered under the name connected to an online head-hunting website (@51intern.net_War-

Table 1. Distribution and size of audience of the 20 most popular micro-blogging posts

User ID	Topic	Follower	Reply	Repost
青头一 (GreyHead#1)	Bill of bear farm ban	5537	22960	254945
MaGcheung	Ban bear farm (cartoon)	5915	8887	65251
揭露地球 (DisclosEearth)	Fake media coverage	949481	10219	57125
张泉灵 (ZhangQuanling)	Bear bile substitute	3465222	9235	43702
夜枫晨露 (FountainBlue)	Documentary Moonbear	6923	2179	39678
@英腾网_Warren_Ching (@51intern. net_Warren_Ching)	The cry of bile bear	6634	5406	39322
在西安 (at Xi'an)	Biased media coverage	110754	7334	37758
优酷网 (www.youku.com)	Documentary, moon bear	1071895	3535	21586
奇闻惊天下 (StunningStories)	Torture in bear farm	161006	3612	21471
财经网 (www.caijing.com.cn)	Farm owner statement	2221732	7654	18546
邪恶漫画家 (EvilCartoonist)	Iron vest on bile bear	235152	1428	13257
亚洲动物基金 (AsiaAnimalFoundation)	Documentary Moonbear	101217	2381	10868
世界解密档案 (GlobalConfidentalDocument)	Documentary, moon bear	294682	1414	9605
汽车经典 (Auto Classics)	Torture in bear farm	10355	1067	9004
@引领时尚、女人帮 (@starry sky)	Torture in bear farm	440310	650	6320
@张小海AAF(@ZhangXiaohaiAAF)	Anatomy picture	12328	1097	4923
亚洲动物基金(AFF)	Call for bear farm ban	101212	3749	2203
李小冉(LiXiaoran)	Documentary moon bear	2619667	1038	1590
揭露人性(DiscloseHumanNature)	Iron vest on bile bear	114373	180	1527
可爱宠物中心(MengChongWu)	Documentary moon bear	1647536	284	1386

ren_Ching). Compared to other blogger users, this user had a relatively small and stable audience size (the number of followers=6,634), yet a much bigger audience population (the number of replies and reposts=44,729) were actively involved in reposting or replying to the messages. The unbalanced audience size met the criteria for empirical audience category (Boyd, 2010), which means the audience for this particular post were mainly followers who have general interest in blogging posts based on topics. In other words, the audience was attracted by the topic or the content of the message instead of the influence of the blogger user.

Guizhengtang retrieves, or removes, bile from the living bear. Please watch this video: http://t.cn/zO2Ebjc, and listen to their voices. Please re-post the message after watching.

Do those bile bears sound comfortable and pain-free while being retrieved of bile?
Are they really happy? Do they go out enjoying life after the bile retrieval? We call
for the ban of bear farms by the Government and an end to this inhumane practice!
Guizhengtang, you are extremely cruel! We hope all the micro-blogging users will
repost this message. Please repost as many times as possible!

The above are the translated versions of the micro-blogging posts, which were originally written in Chinese. The format for this text was short length with a hyperlink to the documentary "Moon Bear." At least four themes emerged from this post: empathy, video, political measure, and sentiment. Empathy was stressed in the post by asking questions such as whether the bears were truly happy or pain-free after bile being retrieved out of their gall bladder. The political element was demonstrated by calling on the government to ban the bear farm. Sentiment (mainly anger and concerns of cruelty upon animals) was expressed through strong words such as "inhumane" and "cruel." The blog author had included various elements to make the message more compelling (within the limited length). Additionally, a video link was provided in this blogging post to optimize the message-relay process. For example, the images and soundtracks in the video such as the image of a bleeding moon bear in a cage together with its desperate howling made the message more appealing to the audience.

Daft and Lengel (1986) claimed that the video combined acoustic and visual elements and enriched the amount of the information that can be transmitted in a given time interval (p. 560). However, the perception of the audience to this message may differ from the frames setup by the blogger. There were 5,406 replies to this post up to April 5, 2012, among which words with sentiment (anger, karma) appeared most frequently. The majority (90%) of the replies expressed anger towards the cruelty of the bear farm practice, such as: If I were a black bear, I would find all means to kill those who caged me and tortured me!!! Let us die together (User ID: Bluexu's new home). Another reply was as follows: I am afraid I will die of crying after watching the video (User ID: Miss-Wang Gengen_learn to give up).

About 7% of the replies expressed empathy to the pain experienced by the bile bear. One user (ID: Weiyang Yang) wrote: If you are locked in the iron cage all year around, would you be happy? Another user (ID: Tell the truth) wrote: Imagine that (the bile bear) is your own child (would you still do the same thing?)!! Do not you have nightmare while listening to their howling?

A small proportion of replies indicated that the audience perception was beyond the blog author's initial purpose. For example, some users expressed their distrust towards media report over the animal cruelty. They argued that the bear howling in the video was just an animal instinct instead of the result of being subject to great pain: It is terrible to realize that media is so ignorant that they could not tell the difference between a painful bear and instinctive howling from a wild bear. Some believe the China media lack basic morality (user ID: PT China). Bear bile is reported to contain ursodeoxycholic acid, which could be used to treat hemorrhoids, sore throats, sores, bruising, muscle ailments, sprains, epilepsy, reduce fever, improve eyesight, break down gallstones, act as an anti-inflammatory, reduce the effects of overconsumption of alcohol, and to clear the liver. The concern is that the retrieval process requires different degrees of surgery and leaves a permanent fistula or inserted catheter. A significant proportion of the bears die because of the stress of unskilled surgery or the infections. Other respondents proposed to use marketing measures (boycott the product, promote bear bile substitutes, etc.) to ban the bear farm instead of using the political pressure proposed by the author of the post. Clearly, based on the above analysis, the perception of the audience appeared to be largely divergent from the frames from those initiated by the blog author.

Stage II: Bear Bile Substitute (Second Stage)

During the second stage of the campaign, more debates and discussions regarding bile bear farm were carried out through diverse formats. One of the most visited and responded-to messages were conveyed through a cartoon image (see below), in which a tearful bear cries: *Help me, my bile could be substituted by herbs!* The text inside the cartoon says: *Boycott this cruel bear farm industry. There are 1200 bile bears in Guizhengtang bear farm. Please help the moon bear!* NOTE: The moon bear is also known as the Asian black bear and white-chested bear.

The description of the cartoon in Figure 1 provided supplementary information about the herbal substitutes to the bear bile.

If Guizhentang is listed on stock change, the number of bile bear will be increased from 400 to 1200. Guizhentang claims the bile-retrieving method they used creates no pain to the bear. Isn't it terrible being caged in a tiny space? Isn't it painful if you have a wound in your body which will never heal? Furthermore, the active ingredient in bear bile has been successfully synthesized, and there is no need to hurt those poor moon bear!

The information about the bear bile substitute made the appeal for banning the bear farm more convincing to the audience. Similar to posts in the first stage, in this post, sentiment and empathy remain the major themes intended by the author. A concern for retrieving bile from a living being was the core message. Another

Figure 1. Popular post item

important element in this message was the information about the bear bile substitute. The argument in the message was that if the active ingredient in the bear bile could be found in herbal plants, why does the bear farm need to be maintained, causing pain to the bears?

The author (ZhangQuanling) of this blogging post was a renowned and widely respected woman journalist from China's Central Television (CCTV)--China's only state-run national television station. Her insightful reporting and pleasant commentary style attracted more than three million followers across the country to the micro-blogging site under study. There are 52,937 users who either reposted or replied to this post. However, because the author of the post has a much larger population of followers, the relatively small population of followers who reposted or replied may indicate that the audience of this particular post was a smaller technological audience.

As the Anti-Cruelty to Animal Campaign moved to its second stage, more audience members joined the debate on whether the bear farm industry should be banned as a whole. Consequently, the replies to this post present diverse points of view containing both pro (65%) and con (30%) responses. The audience members against the ban criticized that the postings like this one, especially ones published by famous journalists, lack on-scene observation and examination and were therefore false arguments. For instance, User ID "No eternal distance" responded to the author that *this woman journalist has no courage to investigate the bear farm herself, and she was just "fantasizing" the pain of the bile bear. You have a rich imagination!* Some other users tried to rebut the idea of bile substitute with an expertise tone. User ID "I think of winter rain" left this reply: *To those who have no Chinese medicine background, please do not arrogantly claim that Dahuang (a Chinese herb) can replace bear bile. A lot of Chinese medicines might share similar functions, but it does not mean they can substitute for each other.* One user in the con group related the bile bear to the domesticated livestock and states that livestock and laboratory animals (e.g., white mice) were treated more cruelly, but not many people had voiced concern for their welfare. Some blog users believed that the newly emerged countering opinions were from the think tank and "hired" internet commentators (a typical scenario in the cyber world in China) who were paid to cushion-land or setoff the increasing critiques from the anti-bear farm campaign.

Meanwhile, more and stronger sentiment elements were identified in the pro-ban audience group. Explicit language had been used to express anger. Users addressed questions directly to China's President (which is very unusual in micro-blogging websites due to its political sensitivity) and posted quotations from Buddhist scripts. Some users called for marketing measures to ban the bear farm.

In addition to the con- and pro- groups in the audience, replies containing balanced or neutral replies (5%) towards the bear farm appeared for the first time. User ID "Feng Tao Digest" wrote:

The price as well as the effectiveness of the synthesized bear bile and natural bear bile needs to be compared. Another question is whether the anti-bear farm campaign is targeting Guizhentang or the whole Chinese medicine industry in China. We also should give more consideration to the views from both AFF (Animal Farm Foundation) and medical experts.

This kind of reply provided thoughtful guidance and expert information for other audiences in the comment section. At this stage, discrepancies between the audience's perception and the frames provided by the blogger moved to a higher level. Shaw (1976, in Ellis & Fisher, 1994, p. 4) defined a group as members sharing something in common, such as a common motivation. Ellis and Fisher (1976) have argued that attitudinal similarity is the most frequent reason why people are attracted to other people. In this particular case, the unified perceptions by the audience were largely due to the motivation behind the campaign initiators—ban the bear farm. The attitudinal elements in this post illustrate the reason why certain blog posts are likely to achieve more publicity and attract a wider audience than the others.

Stage III: Disclosing Lies from the Journalism Practitioners (Third Stage)

During the third stage, posts contained only a few words with repeated adverbs and exclamation marks to create a reinforced impact on the audience. Please see below a representative post from Stage III:

Disclose the most most most most most fake coverage!!!!!!!!!!!!!!!! Please repost if you agree!!!

Following the text was a full-sized picture of a journalist, shown in Figure 2, and his statement that the bear appeared to be free from pain while its bile was being retrieved.

The themes identified in the first and second samples failed to emerge in this post. Instead, the author of the post simply presented the journalistic reportage which expressed unfavorable opinions towards ban. The previous two stages of the Anti-Cruelty to Animal Campaign attracted massive attention from the micro-blog users as well as the mass media. At the third stage, thanks to the mainstream media's propagation of the bear farm campaign via different channels, a larger audience took part in the Anti-bile bear farm campaign on the micro-blogging site. Regular micro-blog users were more aware of the possible pain caused to the bear while their bile was harvested directly from their gall bladder. Therefore, any message that contradicted the pre-existing impression would generate resentment among those audiences.

The author (DiscloseEarth) of the above referenced journalist's post had 949,481 followers, which well out-numbered the number of audience members (67,344) who replied to and reposted the message. The audience distribution of this post was another demonstration of intended audience that was composed mainly of the acquaintances of the author of the blog post.

During the third stage of this campaign, the anger from the general blog users had been heightened to its peak level. Not surprisingly, all the replies to this post showed a clear tendency towards banning the bear farm. Comments showing strong resentments, such as furious anger, cursing the bear farm owner, and the use of some

Figure 2. Journalist covering bile retrieval

梁卫浩 V：刚看完取胆引流的过程，约五六分钟。引流针长约十二三厘米，
弯头，有点象为蓝球打气的针。熊爬进箱子里边吃东西，边被取胆汁，一声不
亢，光顾吃了，一点没有痛苦的样子。

extreme swearing words were pervasive and dominant in the comment section. Another prominent phenomenon in this comment section was a large proportion of the blog users copying anti-bear farm statements from their favorite celebrities' blogs and reposted in their own comment section. At this stage, the frames proposed by the initial blogger were perceived and adopted by audience members, reposted under their names, indicating acceptance and agreement.

Stage IV: Vote for the Ban on Bear Farm (Final Stage)

In the fourth stage, typical posts can be illustrated with the following representative short text together with a picture of a healthy and delightful looking Moon Bear.

There is a vote on the Banning of Bear Farm, but few people vote for it. Please go to http://t.cn/h5XtsJ and click the "vote" icon. Please vote and repost. Thanks for your contribution.

The footnote of Figure 3 reads: *Today this fun loving bear has put his terrible past firmly behind him.* The simple combination of text and the image of a normal looking bear (instead of a bleak picture with a tortured bear in pain) aimed to mobilize more blog users to participate in this anti-bear farm campaign. The key elements in this message included appealing, mobilization, image, and hyperlink.

The author (GreyHead#1) of this post had a relatively limited number of followers (5537). But this post attracted a substantial number of replies and was reposted (277,905) the most in this Anti-Cruelty to Animal Campaign, a clear illustration of the empirical audience category. In short, the post achieved the highest viewership based upon its content rather than the blogger's popularity.

Across the four stages of this Anti-Cruelty to Animals Campaign, the number of the participants in this micro-blogging site steadily increased, together with its impact on policy-makers and the society as a whole. At the final stage, the Chinese People's Political Consultative Conference (CPPCC), the highest political consultative organization in China, intended to propose to the government a ban on bear farms in China. Meanwhile, most of the blog users active in this Campaign provided

Figure 3. Moon bear

今天这可爱的月熊已将那恐布的过去抛诸脑后。
Today this fun loving bear has put his terrible past firmly behind him.

support for and consensus with the ban. In the comment section of this particular post, despite the occasional sentiment and empathy elements (5%) found in the replies to the post, the vast majority of the audience simply replied: Already voted. At this final stage, the perception of the message from the audience fully reflected the initial purpose of the blog post. Infante (1975) suggests that people's attitude will be consistent with perceptions of the consequences they believe are most closely associated with the proposal. In the fourth stage, the audience's support to the bear farm ban reflected their belief that by halting the whole industry this animal cruelty could be eliminated for good.

The shortened message at each stage featured conflict and decision modification (Ellis & Fisher, 1976, p. 167), which claimed that the decision-making was modified by little conflict by lowering the level of abstraction of the language phrasing the decision proposal. In the case of the bile bear farm, top bloggers revised their posts at different stages of the campaign based on the conflicts that emerged in the feedback from the audience who were holding different points of view towards the same issue. In other words, how the blogger perceives the receiver and how the receiver is expected to react to the message influence message composition.

CONCLUSION

The analysis of the posts indicates that although the leading blog posts have employed diverse content forms including text, image, video, and cartoons, the elements that appeared to be most appealing to the audience remain the content that included sentiment and empathy appeals. Because the Anti-Cruelty to Animal Campaign was a developing event, the top micro-bloggers adjusted their strategies of presenting messages at different stages, according to the comments from their audience.

One primary value of surfing the internet, including reading blogs, is that users get a real-time picture of what people are considering salient issues. Due to the interactive nature of the micro-blogging site, the response of the audience becomes an important indicator of what is regarded as a top issue among its members. Additionally, as Hargrav (2004) claimed, by monitoring web posts, the researcher could predict if an issue would grow into something to which the mainstream press responds. This study shows that, although micro-blogging posts achieved a certain level of publicity among its audience in the blogosphere, the mainstream media actively included the issue in its own agenda. Because of the impact of the audience and the mass media responses during the first and second stages, the audience at the third and final stages could be more easily mobilized by the brief and short messages published by top bloggers advocating voting for the legislation of laws to ban the bear farm. However, an examination of the message content published by the top bloggers and the comments made by their audiences indicates a discrepancy between the frames set by the top bloggers and the audience perception during the message conveying process at the first and second stages of the campaign.

The study also addressed the composition of the audience on micro-blogging sites in China. Based on the case examined in this research, the micro-blogging audience consists of intended audience (audience that are intentionally targeted by the bloggers) and the empirical audience (audience that expresses interest in general issues in the society).

The case study demonstrates the importance of individual agency in understanding the contested process of shaping behavior and dissent on micro-blogging sites in China. In this campaign, public figures, including movie stars and celebrity journalists, had more influence than ordinary people in shaping an audience's opinion. This finding might help bloggers to decide what kind of strategies can be applied when designing messages and how the message can be disseminated in micro-blogging campaigns to achieve the desired effects.

This study was not without its limitations. When keeping up with the speed of micro-blogging sites, every second counts. The sampled postings and comments from the audience were collected in one fixed time period instead of being followed around the clock. The limitation of this data collection method is that the dynamic information flow could not be traced. Future studies of micro-blogging sites could follow and record around-the-clock updates of the blogging sites to accumulate data with richer information.

FUTURE RESEARCH DIRECTION

This study could be regarded as the first step to understanding the structure of major micro-blogging sites in China and as a supplementary attempt to a global micro-blogging study. The next step in the research may be to map the distribution of the audience in the blogosphere, explore the interactions between the blogs and mainstream media, and follow the moderating role of the mass media influencing a larger population as well as the major policymakers. Other interesting lines of inquiry about micro-blogging in China could include the cognitive process of micro-blogging audiences, especially how their political interest, environmental awareness (knowledge), personal experience, digital skills (interest), and cultural background might influence their perception and the effectiveness of the message reception.

The propagation of the blogging information may be explored as well, exploring how the environment-related information spreads in the blogging and reposting process. Furthermore, this paper is based on data collected from one micro-blogging site in China. Compared to the prevalence of literature rooted in North America culture, more studies focusing on China or Asian society are needed to fill the gap in the literature on diverse social-cultural contexts.

REFERENCES

Arceneaux, N., & Schmitz, W. A. (2010). Seems stupid until you try it: Press coverage of twitter, 2006–9. *New Media & Society*, *12*(8), 1262–1279. doi:10.1177/1461444809360773

Arguello, J., Elsas, J. L., Callan, J., & Carbonell, J. G. (2008). *Document representation and query expansion models for blog recommendation.Second International Conference on Weblogs and Social Media*, Washington, DC.

Bane, C. M., Cornish, M., Erspamer, N., & Kampman, L. (2010). Self-disclosure through weblogs and perceptions of online and real-life friendships among female bloggers. *Cyberpsychology, Behavior, and Social Networking*, *13*(2), 131–139. doi:10.1089/cyber.2009.0174 PMID:20528268

Boyd, D. (2010). Social network sites as networked publics: Affordances, dynamics, and implications. In *Networked self: Identity, community, and culture on social network sites* (pp. 39–58). New York, NY: Routledge.

Brownstein, J. S., Freifeld, C. C., & Madoff, L. C. (2009). Influenza A (H1N1) virus, 2009 – online monitoring. *The New England Journal of Medicine*, *360*(21), 21–56. doi:10.1056/NEJMp0904012 PMID:19423868

Bruns, A. (2008). *Blogs, Wikipedia, second life and beyond: From production to produsage*. New York, NY: Peter Lang.

Bullock, C. (2007). Framing domestic violence fatalities: Coverage by Utah newspapers. *Womens Studies in Communication*, *30*(1), 34–63. doi:10.1080/07491409.2007.10162504

Cheng, J., Sun, A., Hu, D., & Zeng, D. (2010). An information diffusion-based recommendation framework for micro-blogging. *Journal of the Association for Information Systems*, *12*, 463–486.

Chinese Internet Network Information Center. (2007). *Statistical report of Chinese Internet development 2007*. Author.

Chinese Internet Network Information Center. (2015). *The 36th statistical report on Internet development in China*. Author.

Daft, R. L., & Lengel, R. H. (1986). Organizational information requirements, media richness, and structural design. *Management Science*, *32*(5), 554–571. doi:10.1287/mnsc.32.5.554

Dimitrova, D. V., & Connolly-Ahern, C. (2007). A tale of two wars: Framing analysis of online news sites in Coalition countries and the Arab world during the Iraq War. *The Howard Journal of Communications*, *18*(2), 153–168. doi:10.1080/10646170701309973

Efimova, L. (2009). *Passion at work: Blogging practices of knowledge workers.* Enschede, The Netherlands: Novay.

Ehrlich, K., & Shami, N. S. (2010, May). *Microblogging inside and outside the workplace.4th International AAAI Conference on Weblogs and Social Media (IC-WSM)*, Washington, DC.

Entman, R. M. (1993). Framing: Toward a clarification of a fractured paradigm. *Journal of Communication*, *43*(4), 51–58. doi:10.1111/j.1460-2466.1993.tb01304.x

Farrell, H., & Drezner, D. (2008). The power and politics of blogs. *Public Choice*, *134*(1-2), 15–30. doi:10.1007/s11127-007-9198-1

Gandy, O. H. Jr, & Li, Z. (2005). Framing comparative risk: A preliminary analysis. *The Howard Journal of Communications*, *16*(2), 71–86. doi:10.1080/10646170590948956

Giddens, A. (1984). The constitution of society. Cambridge, MA: Polity Press.

Hargrave, S. (2004). *The blog busters.* The Guardians.

Hindman, M., Tsioutsiouliklis, K., & Johnson, J. (2003). *'Googlearchy': How are few heavily-linked sites dominate politics online.* Philadelphia, PA: American Political Science Association.

Ho, C. T., Li, C. T., & Lin, S. D. (2011). *Modeling and visualizing information propagation in a micro-blogging platform.* Kaohsiung, Taiwan: Advances in Social Networks Analysis and Mining. doi:10.1109/ASONAM.2011.37

Hodkinson, P. (2006). Subcultural blogging? Online journals and group involvement among U.K. Goths. In *Uses of blogs* (pp. 187–198). New York, NY: Peter Lang.

Igwe, C. F. (2008). *Beyond the digital divide into computer-mediated communications: A content analysis of the role of community weblogs in building Oldenburg's virtual third places in back America* (Unpublished doctoral dissertation). Pennsylvania State University.

Infante, D. A. (1975). Differential functions of desirable and undesirable consequences in predicting attitude and attitude change toward proposals. *Speech Monographs*, *42*(2), 115–134. doi:10.1080/03637757509375886

Iyengar, S. (1991). Is anyone responsible? How television frames political issues. Chicago, IL: University of Chicago Press. doi:10.7208/chicago/9780226388533.001.0001

Jansen, B. J., Zhang, M., Sobel, K., & Chowdury, A. (2009). Twitter power: Tweets as electronic word of mouth. *Journal of the American Society for Information Science and Technology*, *60*(11), 2169–2188. doi:10.1002/asi.21149

Java, A., Song, X., Finin, T., & Tseng, B. (2007). *Why we twitter: Understanding microblogging usage and communities*. 9th WEBKDD and 1st SNA-KDD Workshop on Web mining and social analysis, San Jose, CA.

Kaplan, A. M., & Haenlein, M. (2011). The early bird catches the news: Nine things you should know about micro-blogging. *Business Horizons*, *54*(2), 105–113. doi:10.1016/j.bushor.2010.09.004

Krishnamurthy, B., Gill, P., & Arlitt, M. (2008). *A few chirps about Twitter*. 1st workshop on online social networks (WOSN'08)., Seattle, WA.

Li, G., Hoi, S. C. H., Chang, K., & Jain, R. (2010). Micro-blogging sentiment detection by collaborative online learning.*IEEE International Conference on Data Mining* (pp. 893-898). doi:10.1109/ICDM.2010.139

Li, Q. (2013). Bile bear IPO halted as opponents cheer. *Global Times*.

Lievrouw, L. (2002). Determination and contingency in new media development: Diffusion of innovations and social shaping of technology perspectives. In *Handbook of new media* (pp. 183–199). London, UK: Sage. doi:10.4135/9781446206904.n14

Marolt, P. W. (2008). *Blogging in China: Individual agency, the production of cyburban 'spaces of dissent' in Beijing, and societal transformation in China* (Unpublished doctoral dissertation). University of Southern California.

McCombs, M., & Ghanem, S. I. (2003). The convergence of agenda setting and framing. In *Framing public life: Perspectives on media and our understanding of the social world* (pp. 67–81). Mahwah, NJ: Lawrence Erlbaum.

Nardi, B., Schiano, D., Gumbrecht, M., & Swartz, L. (2004). Why we blog. *Communications of the ACM*, *47*(12), 41–46. doi:10.1145/1035134.1035163

Neuman, W. R., Just, M. R., & Crigler, A. A. (1992). Common knowledge: News and the construction of political meaning. Chicago, IL: The University of Chicago Press.

O'Connor, B., Balasubramanyan, R., Routledge, B., & Smith, N. (2010). *From tweets to polls: Linking text sentiment to public opinion time series. 4th International AAAI Conference on Weblogs and Social Media (ICWSM)*, Washington, DC.

Pan, P. P. (2006). Bloggers who pursue change confront fear and mistrust. *Washington Post*, p. A01.

Placing, K., Ward, M.-H., Peat, M., & Teixeira, P. T. (2005). A blog on blogging in science education. 2004 National UniServe Science Conference, Sydney, Australia.

Reese, S. D., & Dai, D. (2009). Citizen journalism in the global news arena: China's new media critics. In *Citizen journalism: Global perspectives* (pp. 221–232). New York, NY: Peter Lang.

Scheidt, L. A. (2006). Adolescent diary weblogs and the unseen audience. In *Digital generations: Children, young people, and new media* (pp. 1–25). London, UK: Erlbaum.

Schelling, T. (1960). The strategy of conflict. Cambridge, MA: Harvard University Press.

Schmidt, J. H. (2011). *(Micro)blogs: Practices of privacy management. In Privacy online* (pp. 159–173). New York, NY: Springer. doi:10.1007/978-3-642-21521-6_12

Short, J., Williams, E., & Christie, B. (1976). *The social psychology of telecommunications*. Hoboken, NJ: John Wiley.

Tremayne, M. (2007). Harnessing the active audience: Synthesizing blog research and lessons for the future of media. In *Blogging, citizenship, and the future of media* (pp. 261–272). New York, NY: Routledge.

Wei, C. (2004). Formation of norms in a blog community. In *Into the blogosphere. Rhetoric, community, and culture of weblogs*. Academic Press.

White, D., & Winn, P. (2009). *State of the blogosphere 2008*. Academic Press.

Xie, L. (2009). *Climate change in the changing climate of news media: A comparative analysis of mainstream media and blog coverage of climate change in the United States and the People's Republic of China, 2005-2008* (Unpublished doctoral dissertation). Southern Illinois University.

Yang, Y. (2013). Guizhentang suspends IPO application. *China Daily*.

Yu, H. (2007). Talking, linking, clicking: The politics of SARS and AIDS. *Positions: Positions: East Asia Cultures Critique, 15*(1), 35–63. doi:10.1215/10679847-2006-023

Yu, H. (2011). Beyond gatekeeping J-blogging in China. *Journalism, 12*(4), 379–393. doi:10.1177/1464884910388229

Chapter 6
Using Social Media Tools in Marketing:
Opportunities and Challenges

Nozha Erragcha
Faculty of Law, Economics, and Management, Tunisia

ABSTRACT

Within the new economic and social environment, development of new technologies combined with Internet progress has had a profound impact on consumer lifestyles and, by extension, marketing concepts and practices. Understanding changes in marketing brought by a fast-acting development of digital social networks and Web 2.0 technology has become essential. The purpose of this chapter is to examine the impact of Web 2.0 on marketing and how marketers can use evolving technologies. Our contribution aligns changes in marketing techniques with Internet development and the changes introduced by the transition from Web 1.0 to Web 2.0. The chapter ends with a proposal of about potential implications for managers.

DOI: 10.4018/978-1-5225-1963-8.ch006

INTRODUCTION

In recent years, deep changes have taken place in the field of marketing, especially with regard to the emergence of Internet or digital social networks. With the advent of online social networks, events took a new dimension for both consumers and businesses and therefore for the practice of marketing to provide value to customers.

In response to these developments, marketing as academic discipline and management activity moves from a mass marketing approach via standardized products to a more personalized marketing approach that proposes tailored and specific individual offers. The consumer has changed his/her behaviour. Now, he takes on a new status. The consumer has become more demanding and volatile. Marketing teams should adapt and cope with this new digital media to be closer to their customers and, at the same, time adapt themselves to their needs. If not, they will lose their relevance. A better knowledge of it allows for more targeted marketing campaigns and personalized messages, offers and / or products.

As a result, these changes have significantly affected Marketing as Philip Kotler (Kotler and al., 2012), one of the fathers of marketing, put it. Whereas marketing 1.0 focused on product management, marketing 2.0 is based on the predominance of communitarianism. It became participatory with the advent of tools together under the label Web 2.0. The customer-focused paradigm is based on openness, engagement, cooperation, co-creation, and propensity to help customers rather than control them (Von Hippel & Katz, 2002; Prahalad and Ramaswamy, 2004; Deighton & Konrfeld, 2009). While extending collaborative and participatory Web 2.0, a transition to Web 3.0 is in order. This new age is expressed in the cooperation of participants (Barassi & Trerè, 2012).

The business world was no exception to this revolution. As more and more organizations move into the virtual world, some have considered the potential of using digital social networks in their information systems and with their partners. The purpose is to promote social links to improve human-machine interaction and do more business through e-commerce. This brought about significant changes in the way people work and behave and in human relationships. The changes have also led to improvements in how companies function, resulting in gains in productivity and innovation. This new platform system enables online managers to consider Web 2.0 environment in a different and innovative way. More recently, marketing researchers emphasize the value of the optimal experience (online flow) in the context of understanding consumer behavior on the Web (Bridges and Florsheim, 2008; Thatcher and al., 2008; Chen, 2006; Skadberg et al., 2005; Pace, 2004). These studies suggest that psychological chaos (flow) is similar to exploratory behavior. This behavior expresses the desire of individuals to navigate and interact with the environment. In the context of social media, this behavior is of particular importance in the exploration for the collaborative creation of knowledge and the opportunity to engage in consumer-to-consumer (C2C) communications such as sharing experiences and knowledge through eWOM (electronic word of mouth), seeking information, and meeting people (Raab et al., 2015). Furthermore, prior flow experience literature has recommended flow theory as an appropriate theoretical framework for understanding user behaviors in online environments (Chang & Zhu, 2012; Huang, 2003; Novak et al., 2000), and to keep customers satisfied in the context of social media (Fornerino et al. 2008, Koufaris 2002, Hoffman and Novak, 1996).

In this regard, this paper highlights how companies can make the most of digital technologies that marketers can use to effectively and efficiently devise their internet marketing plans.

Studies on the impact of social media as a marketing tool have shown that opportunities and challenges for firms are also scarce. The potential success of the subject is now being expanded to analyze the kinds of research that needs to be pursued to make additional research progress in the related area of social media marketing. In this paper, we provide a brief overview of Web 2.0, social media, and creative consumers, and explore the challenges and opportunities that these phenomena present to managers generally and to marketers and their strategies in particular.

THE EMERGENCE OF WEB 2.0

The terms Social Media and Web 2.0 are often used as interchangeable; however, some observers associate the term Web 2.0 mainly with online applications and the term Social Media with the social aspects of Web 2.0 applications (participation, openness, conversation, community, connectedness) (Spannerworks, 2007). In this paper, we will use the term Web 2.0 as an umbrella term for web applications fulfilling a number of criteria to be defined further on.

The Web 2.0 is a revolution of the new Web paradigm. The 2.0 does not qualify as a technological revolution but rather an evolution of usages, a cultural and informational evolution (Rayan & Jones, 2009).

The Web 2.0, also known as the Community Web era, was started in 2004 by Tim O'Reilly at a conference organized by O'Reilly and Medialive International (2004). Web 2.0 is a collection of interactive, open source, and user-controlled Internet applications enhancing the experiences, collaboration, knowledge, and market power of the users as participants in business and social processes (Constantinides, 2014). In contrast to the first generation of Web, Web 2.0 is based on a wide variety of active tools that provide true interactivity between users based on pooling of individual knowledge and information sharing with a paradigm shift and changing business models.

Web 2.0 technologies transform broadcast media monologues (one to many) into social media dialogues (many to many) (Berthon et al. 2012). Web 2.0 applications made it possible to find more information, save time, better share information, or to be more visible on the web. In parallel, these applications allow partners to communicate, share, and respond by participating with their comments and expertise in an online process that builds up relationships, communities, and networks within a company.

Web 2.0 technologies cover a dynamic and interactive aspect of content and combine both social and technical aspects as shown in Figure 1 below (Poynter and Lawrence, 2008). Creative consumers are the dynamos of this new media world, hence "social web" (Weber, 2007). This relationship values the power of social context in creating affective, intellectual relationships, membership groups, reference groups, and virtual communities. It is the bidirectionality of information which takes over unidirectionality (Poynter et Lawrence, 2008), symbolised by top-of-the edge applications and publication tools like blogs and collaborative platforms like the Wiki, offering production possibilities, diffusion, and content consumption.

As seen in Figure 1, Web 2.0 can be thought of as the technical infrastructure that enables the social phenomenon of collective media and facilitates consumer-generated content. The latter are distinguished by the difference in focus: social media can be thought of as focusing on content, and consumer generation on the creators of that content. To put it simply, Web 2.0 enables the creation and distribution of the content that is social media.

This new version of the Web rests on social media (Kaplan & Haenlein, 2010). The marketplace often refers to social media as user-generated content (UGC) or consumer-generated media (CGM) (Poynter et Lawrence, 2008). It is important to distinguish between the media and the consumers, based on crowdsourcing processes defined by use of intelligence and innovation of many people to create content. They generate a new continuous and interactive dialogue between users who become true collaborators and producers of goods and services.

This phenomenon uses participation and collaboration architecture between the different users and promotes exchange, creativity, responsiveness, innovation, and flexibility (O'Reilly, 2005). It is through added value of different users' individual actions that collective intelligence "IC" (Levy, 1997) emerges.

Figure 1. Web 2.0 infrastructure
P.R. Berthon et al. 2012.

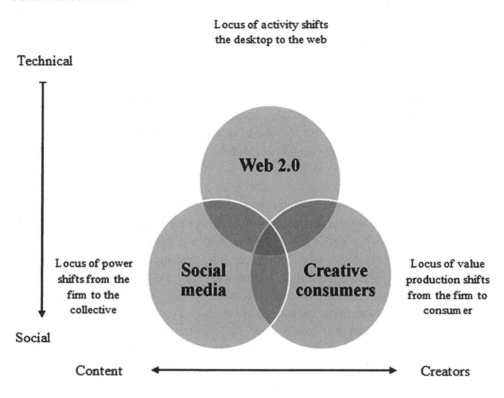

SOCIAL MEDIA AND SOCIAL NETWORKING

Web 2.0 as a new Web paradigm is at the origin of the advent of Social Networks Digital. It is important to note first that this concept is expressed in different ways depending on the perspective taken by authors. Some refer to the term "digital social networks," community sites dedicated to networking (Mercier, 2008), others use the term "socio-digital networks." (Coutant & Stenger, 2009)

According to Berthon et al., (2012), "Social media is the product of Internet-based applications that build on the technological foundations of Web 2.0." Based on the analysis of the relevant literature in the field, Erodgmus and Cicek (2012) define social media as "the activities, practices and behavior met in the communities which gather to share information, knowledge and opinions by means of conversational environments." Besides, as Kaplan & Haenlein (2010, p. 61) emphasize, the definition of Social Media is a group of Internet-based applications that build on the ideological and technological foundations of Web 2.0, and that allow the creation and exchange of User Generated Content. Social media is the product of

Internet-based applications that build on the technological foundations of Web 2.0 (Berthon et al. 2012).

Social media, through the use of new technologies (RSS feeds, blogs, microblogs, wikis, photo and video sharing tools, social networking, mashups-tools to create a new service through the contribution of third sites content, bookmarking-web site links-saving tool), use collective intelligence in an online collaborative mode. Figure 2 gives us an overview.

Social networks are different from social media. Indeed, they are an example of these but they include online activities for social interaction and content sharing, combining indexing and social bookmarking tools, virtual worlds, digital social networks, photo or video sharing sites, wikis, RSS feeds, blogs, and microblogging tools.

Two dimensions reflect social networking sites (Coutant et Stenger, 2009). The first dimension is technological tools relating to information and communication, while the second dimension is the idea that the core value of social networking sites is relational in nature and based on a participation of architecture. At this level, the involvement of stakeholders is paramount.

Web professionals cannot agree on a common definition of "digital social networks." Several definitions have been offered, a summary of them has been proposed by Girard and Fallery (2009). Stenger and Coutant (2010) proposed a definition of RSN that seems to perfectly describe this concept. They consider RSN as web services that allow individuals:

Figure 2. The digital environment

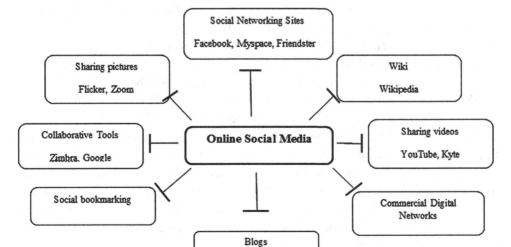

1. To construct a public or semi-public profile within a system,
2. To maintain a list of users with whom they share a link,
3. To view and navigate on their list of connections and those established by others within the system, and
4. To base their attractiveness mainly on the first three points and not on a particular activity.

Digital social networks (RSN) are a tool that allows for the formation of contact networks, and provides users a connection with their online friends with whom they share different content and applications and creates a network of private or professional relationships.

Socialization is the central value of Digital Social Networks. Customers are grouped into virtual communities or tribes around a common interests or passions, identical cultures and ways of life. This leads to self-controlling of their members who constantly discover shared interests or ideas. Digital social networks are an information infrastructure, invisible to users (Zammar, 2012).

Indeed, some Internet-based social networks have become true promotional tools that allow people to login to communicate, connect and play with others. Facebook is a virtual community used by businesses as a communication tool and a buzz platform (Turcotte-Choquette & Parmentier, 2011). Facebook's original purpose was simply to connect people who generally know each other off-line; or at least want to meet. In some ways, Facebook took over for Myspace years ago, evidenced by the finding that 65% of Facebook users also have a Myspace account (Small Business Trends).

Table 1 classifies the different categories of social media outlets in terms of their application and use with reference to the classification provided by Web 2.0 resources.

Several studies suggest that young consumers have already adopted online social media as an integral part of their life. The advent of digital social networks came along a generation change (Kabla and Gourvennec, 2011). Each generation has its own characteristics in their ways of understanding media. Therefore, generational differences offer important insights into the motivators (Krishen et al. 2016).

This young generation is also called "digital natives," (Prensk, 2001)"Internet generation," "Millennium Generation," "Generation Tech," "Generation Y" (compared to the preceding X generation), "Generation Z," the "Echo Boomers Generation" (whose parents are mostly baby boomers), and the "multi-screens generation" (Helme-Guizon & Ottmann, 2010). It is described as immature, flexible, imaginative, and creative (Helme-Guizon & Ottmann, 2010). They have habits in terms of Internet use completely different from the older generation. The young prefer blogging and content diffusion, continuous Internet connection and attendance, and strong communication use.

Table 1. Social media landscape

Classification of Social Media	
Online publication of opinions or information	• Blogs (personal opinion journals or online information) • Wiki (collaboration with an online content through a central web site, Wikipedia) • Citizens journalism portals (sites enabling individuals to publish online articles or blogs judged interesting to be shared with others, e.g. BlogSpot, Blogger, Digg).
Content sharing sites	• Videos (e.g. YouTube) • Photos (Flickr) • Links to other sites (del.icio.us: bookmarking) • Music, diaporamas, product reviews
Tools or sites allowing real time discussions, video-supported or not	• Facebook, Myspace, Bebo • Sites targeted to particular niches (LinkedIn or Boompa) a tool to create social networks (Ning)
Tools for micro-blogging or publishing	Twitter, Pounce, Jaiku, Plurk
• Tools for social networking • Personal 'Live cast' platform	• Friend feed, Socializr, Socialthink • Justin.tv, BlogTV, Yahoo!Live • Mobile version (Qik, Flixwagon, Kyte)
Virtual networking platforms	• SecondLife, Entropia Universe, There • Chats 3D (Habbo, IMVU) • For kids (Club Penguin, Stardoll)
Networked games sites	• Pogo, Kongregate, Cafe, Three Rings • World of Warcraft, etc.

Cazzava, 2008.

WEB 2.0 AND MARKETING: THE SHIFT FROM ACTION TO INTERACTION

Marketing has experienced very rapid development since the advent of the Internet in the way it communicates, in its communication media, and in its very definition. An effort was made to adapt it even at the level of approach. This has resulted in the emergence of the marketing 2.0. By reviewing the relevant literature, it is clear that definitions of social media marketing have a significant relationship with e-marketing. Meanwhile Kaplan and Haenlein (2010) refer to social media as online applications that have a closely aligned.

No doubt the use of social media in business, which has been developing for about ten years, has since been consolidated and is a fully-evolving research field. Indeed, traditional marketing is primarily based on face-to-face interaction and the physical presence of sellers. Therefore, communication is unidirectional. The main function was then supporting the production while taking into account the financial and human resources components. The proposed consumer offer is a combination of a multitude of components: product development, pricing, promotion, and distribution (Goi, 2009). At this stage marketing is only tactical (Vandercammen, 2012). Uncertainty of economic context, scarcity of demand and change in consumer behaviour made it difficult to manage.

Social media marketing makes use of these social media applications as an extension to fulfil traditional marketing. Marketing activities via online applications allow the production of information and collaboration among users (Kaplan and Haenlein, 2010) and web-based technologies to create interactive medium where users and groups member can be found sharing, co-creating, discussing, and modifying are known as user-generated content (Kietzmann et al., 2011).

Marketing 2.0 can be summarized to as combination of three concepts: Web marketing, Web 2.0 and Social Media (Mayol, 2011). Unlike Web 1.0, interfaces of social media tools help facilitate tasks or information exchange between users (Akhras and Akhras, 2013) and the one-way communication paradigm is found replaced by a multi-directional scheme. These tools provide an opportunity for consumers as they offer greater diversification of interactions, particularly those promoting the social aspect made possible thanks to blogs, wikis, tagging and social bookmarking, media sharing, RSS feeds, and syndication (Cych, 2006, Anderson, 2007; Depover et al, 2007). E-collaboration and e-participation are prominent aspects of the use of social media in business. The idea is to effectively use as much collective intelligence as possible because it is the power of collective intelligence that is potentially behind the web.

The fundamental principle of marketing 2.0 is to integrate the consumer at all levels of the marketing process and to consider him/her as an active player in the marketing process, not a single receiver (Bressolles, 2012). These changes require the development of tools allowing consumers to interact in order to improve the management of the relationships with current customers.

Scheid et al. (2012) reported that marketing 2.0 affects traditional marketing in two ways:

1. Enhancing effectively and efficiently the functions of traditional marketing.
2. Transforming marketing strategies: creating new business models.

Similarly, marketing 2.0 has to move away from "transactional marketing" to a new approach that could be characterized as "facilitator marketing." (Pelet, 2011) Such an approach is focused on both sharing knowledge with customers and on enabling knowledge sharing between customers. (Pablo et al, 2006)

The growing influence of Web 2.0 and social media gave birth to a new type of marketing, commonly called "inbound marketing." Its principle is simple: it is to bring the customer rather than go get them. The goal is not to go looking for customers on the Internet, rather to bring them to the brands. It is a move from a "push marketing" or "outbound marketing" approach to a "pull marketing" or "inbound marketing" approach.

Inbound marketing is meant to gain the interest and commitment of customers rather than just make them buy, like the case with outbound marketing. It is not so much about promoting products in a web environment where available information flow is almost endless. It is more about seeking to engage and educate the customer, an approach in which outbound marketing shows its limits. By empowering customers, the Internet changed and redefined the relationship between customers and businesses. The ability to access a huge amount of information about products and services has reduced the existing information asymmetry, while modifying the traditional balance of power.

Electronic word of mouth became an important component of customers' online purchase process (Erkan & Evans, 2016). The user becomes a "consum'actor" also called "prosumer" or "post-consumer." (Cova & Cova, 2009) In short, the customer became a co-developer and co-creator of value. Indeed, brands take into account perceptions of consumers while defining their marketing mix.

The integration of customer in companies' marketing procedures and communication as a key player and in some cases is essential. Consumers can then be active participants in the product design process or improvement. They can even participate in the construction of advertising messages (Mencarelli & Pulh, 2009). Positioning themselves as content creators, connected in networks with other content creators, customers can freely express their opinions about brands and their products. This strategy has now become essential to creating and distributing high quality web content. This is called "earned customers" (client acquired by content) as opposed to "paid customers" (customers bought through advertising or paid search).

This strategy aims to establish a dialogue by rethinking how to communicate with the target audience and establishing an exchange-based relationship. Creating and sharing relevant, useful and qualitative content (through a corporate blog, for example) may attract qualified prospects, thereby generating more traffic to its website and eventually converting them into customers. This involves interacting with them, not inconveniently or intrusively, but more implicitly.

Indeed, we can identify consumers attitudes towards brands through their interaction on the Web: blogs, forums, social networks (Facebook, Twitter), and online citizen media. Therefore, the myth of "customer is king" (Regnault, 2003) becomes a reality on the Web 2.0. Indeed, the customer becomes the true master of the situation. In sum, the major changes that have affected traditional marketing because of the appearance of the marketing 2.0 are:

1. The shift from an action strategy to an interaction strategy.
2. Decentralization of value creation on a network of sites.

Similarly, the consumer is involved in the design of the offer and even becomes active in developing the marketing mix as well as in disseminating advertising messages (thanks to buzz). Web 1.0 and Web 2.0 are compared in Table 2. Accordingly, communication is no longer a matter of persuasion; it becomes a conversation.

OPPORTUNITIES AND CHALLENGES FOR MARKETERS

Some Internet-based social networks have become true promotional tools today. People log in to express themselves, connect, and play with others. Social Media made customers more sophisticated and helped them develop new tactics in searching, evaluating, choosing, and buying goods and services (Albors et al., 2008).

Facebook is also another form of a virtual community adopted by businesses as a communication tool and a buzz platform (Turcotte-Choquette and Parmentier,

Table 2. Marketing characteristics and mutations

Web 1.0 and Web 2.0 Comparisons		
	Web 1.0	**Web 2.0**
Function	Based on documents	Focused on users
Features	Passive	Active
Tools	Groupware database	Social networking sites
Relations and Quality	Read only: static Web	Reading-writing: interactive Web
	Marketing 1.0	Marketing 2.0
Context	Industrial Revolution	Social Media
Center of Interest	Sell products	Satisfaction and loyalty
Communication	Unidirectional	Interactive
Interaction	One to many	Many to many
The Consumer's Role	Passive	Contributor

2011). Nevertheless, it is noteworthy that this new Community approach is not only limited to entertainment (like the iconic example of Myspace), but it also has a professional dimension (LinkedIn). Indeed, digital social networks now enable companies to develop business opportunities and build relationships with customers using objective factors such as knowledge of the customer. This will allow them to gain visibility and credibility (Pelet, 2011).

In sum, five main reasons seem to justify the use of social media to promote small businesses:

1.   Spontaneously expand the targets without incurring significant advertising costs.
2.   Use blogs and social and business networking sites to increase visits to the company's Web site through other social media websites (As a result, positioning the company's web page can improve their visibility in the major search engines and ultimately website traffic increases).
3.   Combine social media-oriented strategy with other marketing strategies.
4.   Build up a strong credibility by participating and engaging in relevant forums.
5.   Understand that social media sites contain information, such as user profiles, that can be used to target a specific group of users for advertising purposes.

Moreover, Mayol (2009) found that social media enable companies to positively influence consumers' views and behaviors. Therefore, because of these important benefits, it seems that the use of social media as a marketing tool will be less risky.

Social networks play an increasingly important role and could very quickly replace the traditional Internet-based media. Table 3 shows the differences between

Table 3. Comparison between traditional networking and online social networks

Traditional	Online Social
Follows a geographic base	No barriers
Based on common interests	Based on common interests
Limited by social class, religion	No limits Sans limits (in principle)
Limited dissemination of information	Online dissemination of information
Powerful leaders are limited to traditional media or personal actions	• Presence of powerful leaders • Online and exponential influence
Diffusion and promotion of innovation and novelties are limited by physical space or by traditional media necessary for communication.	Online diffusion and promotion of innovation and novelties
No or limited personal information about members.	Online availability of personal information about members

traditional networks and web networks. First, the online network is known by immediacy. Furthermore, it demonstrates an openness made possible by the reduced physical limits.

The social media landscape has deeply changed companies' marketing practices. Moreover, it changed the very concept of the market, allowing niche businesses to become much more profitable. Micro-targeting becomes a way to communicate more effectively.

Accordingly, implications and recommendations for businesses are numerous. Marketers can use social media tools to guide their customer targeting strategies, maximize their benefits, and enhance co-production and cooperation of consumers.

If companies want to exploit the potential of social networks to reinvent customer relationships, they need to give a new impetus to CRM while developing strategic and operational programs that ensure both structure and flexibility.

Social CRM is a strategy for customer relationship management, not corporate management. The concept is still in its infancy for many who are challenged by rapid changes. The quicker companies adopt the vital concept that the customer controls the relationship, the more they benefit and exploit the potential of social networks

Social media is a growing reality. Then, it became necessary for business managers to become aware of its impact on their brands and, by extension, to pay more attention to virtual communities.

WEB 2.0 AND FLOW EXPERIENCE

The Web provides opportunities that can easily help people to enter a state of flow. Flow has been conceptualized as an optimal experience or autotelic, which refers to a state of consciousness that is sometimes experienced by individuals fully involved in an enjoyable activity (Csikszentmihalyi, 2004, 1990, 1997; Pace, 2004). It can be described as a psychological state in which people become completely involved in the whole experience within a stimulus when they are fully absorbed. (Gao & Bai, 2014)

Based on the view of Csikszentmihalyi, optimal experience (Weibel et al. 2008; Chen 2006; Pilke 2004; Chen et al., 1999) flow is characterized by new common distinctive aspects (Weibel et al. 2008; Chen 2006; Pilke 2004; Chen et al. 1999):

1. Clear goals,
2. Immediate feedback,
3. Balance between challenges and skills,

4.   Action and awareness merged,
5.   Concentration on the task,
6.   Self-consciousness disappears,
7.   Sense of time becomes distorted,
8.   The activity becomes an end in itself, and
9.   It is an "autotelic" experience.

Flow has been conceptualized as an optimal experience, the best feelings, the most enjoyable experiences possible in human lives that stem from people's perceptions of challenges and skills in given situations (Csikszentmihalyi, 1975; Csikszentmihalyi & LeFevre, 1989). Flow is characterized by a balance between perceived challenges and perceived skills (Csikszentmihalyi, 1975). If challenges begin to exceed skills, one first becomes vigilant and then anxious; if skills begin to exceed challenges, one first relaxes and then becomes bored (Nakamura & Csikszentmihalyi, 2002, p. 90). Thus, "over time, the same activity may make a person feel anxious one moment, bored the next, and in a state of flow immediately afterward." (Chen et al., 1999, p. 588)

However, this concept was developed when marketers began to become interested in the design of commercial, attractive, rich, interactive, user-friendly, and engaging sites. In this context, Hoffman and Novak (2009, 1996) were the first to apply the web flow experiences. They developed an integrative conceptual model that traces the more developed relationship between the flow and consumer online behavior. They argue that the web is a conducive environment to the production of the flow experience. This specific experience emphasizes an uninterrupted sequence of responses facilitated by an interactive, intrinsically enjoyable machine, led by a loss of consciousness and strengthening of the self (Hoffman and Novak, 1996). The different theoretical orientations helped conceptualize the flow in relation to different activities such as sport, work, and human-computer interaction, shopping via the Internet, and recently SNS.

Throughout Web 2.0 applications, individuals are motivated only by virtue of the interest that the subject experiences in the practice of the activity itself (Weibel et al., 2008), without expectation of extrinsic reward to the activity. The inherent pleasure in the activity is the only motivation of the subject. This is as described in 2004 by Csikszentmihalyi in his book *Living Psychology of Happiness* as a "dynamic, spontaneous, wellbeing, wholeness, joy and creativity state."

According to Ding et al (2010), flow experience has been served as a basis to facilitate the creation of a compelling experience. Web 2.0 applications encourage users to participate, hopefully facilitating the unconscious sharing of knowledge, especially tacit knowledge such as experience, technique, and insight. On the Web, "the interactivity between the virtual environment behind the computer screen and human beings provides users with a route to experience flow." (Chen et al., 2000)

CO-PRODUCTION: A PLATFORM FOR PARTICIPATORY MARKETING

Although co-production is devoted to a particular interest by the company and the customer, this concept has not yet been specified. It was founded in the field of services marketing and belonged to the practical experiences of experiential consumption (Holbrook and Hirschman, 1982).

Co-production is an umbrella term to conceptualize customers' physical and mental participation in production and delivery processes (Fisk et al, 1993). Bettencourt et al. (2002) defined co-production as "functional, collaborative involvement in the production of services, which is essential for successful service delivery." Marketing-wise, consumers have become participatory customers who live an experience (Schmitt, 1999). This experience takes place during the interaction between the different participants. Several meetings determine the experience and give it a dynamic and an interactive dimension (Cheung and To, 2011).

Customer participation can be part of a costs strategy, provide a greater productivity (Auh et al, 2007, Lovelock and Young, 1979), and offer a major competitive advantage (Bendapudi & Leone, 2003). This idea is echoed by Prahalad and Ramanswamy (2000) who said that customers' skills can be used in the service of a competitive strategy. It is through the development of the new "Service-Dominant Logic" approach that the collaborative aspect of the customer is considered more and more in marketing research (Vargo & Lusch, 2004a). As opposed to a product-dominant logic (GD Logic) founded on product exchange between consumers and service providers (Grönroos, 2006), this new approach suggests an exchange of skills, knowledge, and processes and is based on the principle of co-creation.

The aim of marketing is, in this case, to engage consumers in the production of content. In this context, the role of the consumer is no longer passive, but it becomes a co-creator of value for the firm (Prahalad & Ramaswamy, 2004) through the tools of digital social networks, the comments they leave in forums, online video files, and the various features offered by the platform. Consumer participation is presented as a way to establish a new balance between consumption and production (Firat &Venkatesh, 1993).

Moreover, from a marketing perspective, the co-creation of value over the Internet rests on texts and tracks. This is a purely informational environment. The

Web allows people to actually shift from a consumption-based model to a model advocating co-creation or prosumption (production / consumption) (Tapscott & Williams, 2008). The purpose of co-production is the creation of a new power balance between the consumer and the producer, drawing its arguments on theories of "consumer empowerment" (Wathieu et al. 2002) and reinforced by manipulating various Web 2.0 features and tools. It is no longer about marketing to consumers; it is rather about marketing with consumers.

In an effort to increase productivity, it is interesting to encourage consumers to take an active role in the production of goods and services (Bendapudi & Leone 2003) through consumer characteristics (e.g. personality, self-esteem, and demographic characteristics), motivation, preferences, commitments, and skills considered factors affecting co-production. (Meuter et al 2005)

Thus, the consumer goes from being a "target" to being a partner. His/her purpose is not to inform about the offer but to participate in the offer. Good examples of the latest trends in crowdsourcing (Brabham, 2008) (public assessment of a new product / service) are co-creation (innovation with the public) and mass customization (personalized product series).

According to Tapscott and Williams (2008), the web offers individuals the opportunity to substitute the classical model of consumption by another of co-production or prosumption (production / consumption), which allows them to participate in the design and consumption of goods. Thus, communities are formed on different parts of the Web in order to share information about products, to discuss them, or to exchange them. Networking site "Second Life" is an example of online community where users themselves are content creators (Tapscott & Williams, 2008).

Co-creation via the Web is an upcoming trend. It can also be defined as crowdsourcing processes (use of intelligence and innovation of many people to create content). They generate a new continuous and interactive dialogue between users who become real collaborators and producers of goods and services, since firms use their consumers to find new solutions or improve existing products or services (Lorenzo-Romero et al., 2014). This phenomenon uses participation and collaboration architecture between the different users and promotes exchange, creativity, responsiveness, innovation, and flexibility (O'Reilly, 2005).

CONCLUSION

In order to be more competitive and creative, marketers can no longer ignore this new development when defining their marketing strategy. Social media is a growing reality and it becomes necessary for business managers to be aware of their impact on their brands and, by extension, to pay more attention to virtual communities.

It is therefore no surprise that one might assume that in front of these changes in consumption practices and enormous changes of consumers and markets, the structure of companies' boundaries and the necessary skills and expertise for the development of new projects are further modified. However, it is here seen in its socio-technical context and leads to consider marketing increasingly a management perspective of the value created by users.

One of the potential solutions to the challenges of marketing for business is the use of social media. Social media allows businesses to conduct marketing activities effectively despite limited financial resources, lack of expertise, and competition with larger business organizations.

This article proposes a literature review, consisting of a presentation of recent developments in Web and parallel generations. These new developments suggest new opportunities. We stressed first the importance of the impact of Web 2.0 on the definition of corporate marketing strategies by identifying characteristic and strategies of marketing 2.0. Even if Web 2.0 has not yet exhausted its potential as a marketing approach, the new challenge is no longer dominantly reach customers or to conduct work in the marketing process of companies, but it is to study their intentions and desires by analyzing their activities on the Web. This can already point to a new generation of marketing based on a pervasive and intelligent network (Mayol, 2011): the 3.0 marketing behind Web 3.0.

In the marketing 3.0 era, consumers have changed. They become more sensitive to the concerns of society. In such context, companies should anticipate or adapt themselves to new trends to meet this new context, finally abandoning the limits of marketing 1.0 and 2.0 and launching themselves into a new era of Marketing 3.0. In a digital world, interconnected and open, we should develop new techniques. To achieve their objectives, companies should focus primarily on improving their core business and making it coherent with the values sought by the community.

Managerial Implications

The Web can be an extremely useful tool for marketers in creating strong brands and gaining competitive advantages. To effectively utilize the advantages offered by the Internet, though, firms must adopt social media as a channel for providing information to customers and connecting with stakeholders. As marketing communications become increasingly integrated with the digital space, marketers can use social media to create digital linkages with customers. Tiago and Verıssimo (2014) propose two main methods for developing these linkages:

1. Perform as a digital or interactive firm, thereby maintaining or reinforcing the high levels of digital marketing usage, or
2. Adopt various kinds of social media interaction to increase usage of digital marketing.

All efforts in the area of media and technology can be used to help marketers to increased engagement, stronger social interaction between individuals, the community and society, and subsequent customer engagement.

REFERENCES

Akhras, A., & Akhras, C. (2013). Interactive, Asynchronous, Face-to-Face: Does It Really Make a Difference? *Procedia: Social and Behavioral Sciences, 83*, 337–341. doi:10.1016/j.sbspro.2013.06.066

Albors, J., Ramos, J. C., & Hervas, J. L. (2008). New learning network paradigms: Communities of objectives, crowdsourcing, wikis and open source. *International Journal of Information Management, 28*(3), 194–202. doi:10.1016/j.ijinfomgt.2007.09.006

Anderson, P. (2007). *What is Web 2.0? Ideas, technologies and implications for education*. Bristol: JISC.

Auh, S., Bell, S. J., McLeod, C. S., & Shih, E. (2007). Co-production and customer loyalty in financial services. *Journal of Retailing, 83*(3), 359–370. doi:10.1016/j.jretai.2007.03.001

Barassi, V., & Treré, E. (2012). Does Web 3.0 come after Web 2.0? Deconstructing theoretical assumptions through practice. *New Media & Society, 0*(0), 1–17.

Berthon, P. R., Pitt, L. F., Plangger, K., & Shapiro, D. (2012). Marketing meets Web 2.0, social media, and creative consumers: Implications for international marketing strategy. *Business Horizons, 55*(3), 261–271. doi:10.1016/j.bushor.2012.01.007

Bettencourt, L. A., Ostrom, A. L., Brown, S. W., & Roundtree, R. I. (2002). Client Co-Production in Knowledge-Intensive Business Services. *California Management Review, 44*(4), 100–128. doi:10.2307/41166145

Brabham, D. C. (2008). Crowdsourcing as a Model for Problem Solving an Introduction and 87 Cases. *The International Journal of Research into New Media Technologies*.

Bressolles, G. (2012). *L'e-marketing*. Dunod.

Cavazza, F. (2008). *Panorama des médias sociaux*. FredCavazza.net.

Chang, Y. O., & Zhu, D. H. (2012). The role of perceived social capital and flow experience in building users continuance intention to social networking sites in China. *Computers in Human Behavior, 28*(3), 995–1001. doi:10.1016/j.chb.2012.01.001

Chen, H. (2006). Flow on the net: Detecting web users positive affects and their flow states. *Computers in Human Behavior, 22*(2), 221–223. doi:10.1016/j.chb.2004.07.001

Chen, H., Wigand, R., & Nilan, M. S. (1999). Optimal Experience of Web Activities. *Computers in Human Behavior, 15*(5), 585–608. doi:10.1016/S0747-5632(99)00038-2

Cheung, M. F. Y., & To, W. M. (2011). Customer involvement and perceptions: The moderating role of customer co-production. *Journal of Retailing and Consumer Services, 18*(4), 271–277. doi:10.1016/j.jretconser.2010.12.011

Constantinides, E. (2014). Foundations of Social Media Marketing. *Procedia: Social and Behavioral Sciences, 148*, 40–57. doi:10.1016/j.sbspro.2014.07.016

Coutant, A., & Stenger, Th. (2009). Les configurations sociotechniques sur le Web et leurs usages: le cas des réseaux sociaux numériques. 7ème Colloque du chapitre français de l'ISKO 27-34.

Cova, B., & Cova, V. (2009). Les figures du nouveau consommateur: Une genèse de la gouvernementalité du consommateur. *Recherche et Applications en Marketing, 24*(3), 3. doi:10.1177/076737010902400305

Csikszentmihalyi, M. (1975). Beyond boredom and anxiety. San Francisco, CA: Jossey-Bass.

Csikszentmihalyi, M. (1990). *Flow*. New York, NY: Harper and Row.

Csikszentmihalyi, M. (1997). *Finding flow*. New York, NY: Basic.

Csikszentmihalyi, M. (2004). *Vivre la psychologie du Bonheur*. Paris: Edition Robert Laffont.

Csikszentmihalyi, M., & LeFevre, J. (1989). Optimal experience in work and leisure. *Journal of Personality and Social Psychology, 56*(5), 815–822. doi:10.1037/0022-3514.56.5.815 PMID:2724069

Deighton, J., & Kornfeld, L. (2009). Interactivitys Unanticipated Consequences for Markets and Marketing. *Journal of Interactive Marketing, 23*(1), 1, 2–12. doi:10.1016/j.intmar.2008.10.001

Depover, C., Karsenti, T., & Komis, V. (2007). *Enseigner avec les technologies, Favoriser les apprentissages, développer des compétences*. Presses de l'Université du Québec.

Ding, D. X., Hu, P. J., Verma, R., & Wardell, D. (2010). The Impact of Service System Design and Flow Experience on Customer Satisfaction in Online Financial Services. *Journal of Service Research, 13*, 1.

Erdoğmuş, İ., & Çiçek, M. (2012). The impact of social media marketing on brand loyalty. *Procedia: Social and Behavioral Sciences*, *58*, 1353–1360. doi:10.1016/j.sbspro.2012.09.1119

Erkan, I., & Evans, C. H. (2016). The influence of eWOM in social media on consumers purchase intentions: An extended approach to information adoption. *Computers in Human Behavior*, *61*, 47–55. doi:10.1016/j.chb.2016.03.003

Firat, A. F., & Venkatesh, A. (1993). Postmodernity: The Age of Marketing. *International Journal of Research in Marketing*, *10*(3), 227–249. doi:10.1016/0167-8116(93)90009-N

Fisk, R. P., Brown, S. W., & Bitner, M. J. (1993). Tracking the evolution of the services marketing literature. *Journal of Retailing*, *69*(1), 61–103. doi:10.1016/S0022-4359(05)80004-1

Fornerino, M., Helme-Guizon, A., & Gotteland, D. (2008). Expériences cinématographiques en état dimmersion: Effets sur la satisfaction. *Recherche et Applications en Marketing*, *23*(3), 93–111. doi:10.1177/205157070802300306

Gao, L., & Bai, X. (2014). Online consumer behaviour and its relationship to website atmospheric induced flow: Insights into online travel agencies in China. *Journal of Retailing and Consumer Services*, *21*(4), 653–665. doi:10.1016/j.jretconser.2014.01.001

Girard, A., & Fallery B. (2009). *Réseaux Sociaux Numériques: revue de littérature et perspectives de recherche*. Academic Press.

Goi, C. L. (2009). A Review of Marketing Mix: 4Ps or More? Internation. *Journal of Marketing Studies*, *1*(1), 1–15.

Grönroos, C. (2006). *What Can a Service Logic Offer Marketing Theory?* Academic Press.

Hoffman, D. L., & Novak, T. H. P. (2009). Flow Online: Lessons Learned and Future Prospects. *Journal of Interactive Marketing*, *23*(1), 23–34. doi:10.1016/j.intmar.2008.10.003

Hoffman, D. L., & Novak, T. P. (1996). Marketing in Hypermedia Computer-Mediated Environments: Conceptual Foundations. *Journal of Marketing*, *60*(3), 50–68. doi:10.2307/1251841

Holbrook, M. B., & Hirschman, E. C. (1982). The experiential aspects of consumption: Consumer fantasies, feeling, and fun. *The Journal of Consumer Research*, *9*(2), 132–14.

Huang, M.-H. (2003). Designing Website Attributes to Induce Experiential Encounters. *Computers in Human Behavior, 19*(4), 425–442. doi:10.1016/S0747-5632(02)00080-8

Kaplan, A., & Haenlein, M. (2010). Users of the world, unite! The challenges and opportunities of Social Media. *Business Horizons, 53*(1), 59–68. doi:10.1016/j.bushor.2009.09.003

Kietzmann, J. H., Hermkens, K., McCarthy, I. P., & Silvestre, B. S. (2011). Social Media? Get Serious! Understanding the Functional Building Blocks of Social Media. *Business Horizons, 54*(1), 241–251. doi:10.1016/j.bushor.2011.01.005

Kotler, P., Kartajaya, H., & Setiawan, I. (2012). *Marketing 3.0: produits, clients, facteurs humains*. Edition De Boeck.

Krishen, A. S., Berezan, O., Agarwal, S., & Kachroo, P. (2016). The generation of virtual needs: Recipes for satisfaction in social media networking. *Journal of Business Research, 69*(11), 5248–5254. doi:10.1016/j.jbusres.2016.04.120

Lévy, P. (1997). *L'intelligence collective: pour une anthropologie du cyberspace*. La Découverte.

Lorenzo-Romeroa, C. L., Constantinides, E., & Brüninkc, L. A. (2014). Co-Creation: Customer Integration in Social Media Based Product and Service Development. *Procedia: Social and Behavioral Sciences, 148*, 383–396. doi:10.1016/j.sbspro.2014.07.057

Lovelock, C. H., & Young, R. F. (1979). Look to Consumers to Increase Productivity. *Harvard Business Review, 57*, 168–178.

Mayol, S. (2011). *Le marketing 3.0*. Editions Duno.

Mencarelli, R., & Pulh, M. (2009). La communication 2.0: Un dialogue sous conditions. *Décisions Marketing, 54*, 71–75.

Mercier, P.A. (2008). Liens faibles sur courants faibles: Réseaux sociaux et technologies de communication. *Informations sociales, 147*, 20-31.

Meuter, M. L., Bitner, M. J., Ostrom, A. L., & Brown, S. W. (2005). Choosing Among Alternative Service Delivery Modes: An Investigation of Customer Trial of Self-Service Technologies. *Journal of Marketing, 69*(2), 61–83. doi:10.1509/jmkg.69.2.61.60759

Nakamura, J., & Csikszentmihalyi, M. (2002). The concept of flow. In *Handbook of positive psychology* (pp. 89–105). New York, NY: Oxford University Press.

Novak, T. P., Hoffman, D. L., & Yung, Y.-F. (2000). Measuring the customer experience in online environments: A structural modeling approach. *Marketing Science*, *19*(1), 22–42. doi:10.1287/mksc.19.1.22.15184

O'Reilly, T. (2005). *What is Web 2.0: Design patterns and business models for the next generation of software*. Academic Press.

Pablo, E., Desouza, K. C., Schäfer-Jugel, A., & Kurzawa, M. (2006). Business customer communities and knowledge sharing: Exploratory study of critical issue. *European Journal of Information Systems*, *15*(5), 511–524. doi:10.1057/palgrave. ejis.3000643

Pace, S. (2004). A Grounded Theory of the Flow Experiences of Web User. *International Journal of Human-Computer Studies*, *60*(3), 327–363. doi:10.1016/j. ijhcs.2003.08.005

Pelet, J.E. (2011). *Le e-commerce renforcé par les réseaux sociaux numériques: résultats d'une application expérimentale de la méthode Delphi*. Academic Press.

Pilke, E. M. (2004). Flow Experiences in Information Technology Use. *International Journal of Human-Computer Studies*, *61*(3), 347–357. doi:10.1016/j. ijhcs.2004.01.004

Poynter, R. & Lawrence, G. (2008). Insight 2.0: Nouveaux médias, nouvelles règles, nouvelle vision approfondie. *Revue Française du Marketing*, 25 – 38.

Prahalad, C. K. (2004). "The Cocreation of Value," in Invited Commentaries on "Evolving to a New Dominant Logic for Marketing". *Journal of Marketing*, 68.

Prahalad, C. K., & Ramaswamy, V. (2000). Co-opting Customer Competence. *Harvard Business Review*, *78*, 79–87.

Prahalad, C. K., & Ramaswamy, V. (2004a). Co-creation Experiences: The Next Practice in Value Creation. *Journal of Interactive Marketing*, *18*(3), 3, 5–14. doi:10.1002/dir.20015

Raab, C., Berezan, O., Krishen, A., & Tanford, S. (2015). What's in a word? Building program loyalty through social media communication. *Cornell Hospitality Quarterly*.

Rayan, D. & Jones C. (2009). *Understanding Digital Marketing, Marketing strategies for engaging the digital generation*. Kogan.

Regnaud, D. (2003). Le trompe-l'oeil du client roi, pour une vraie relation de service dans les services grand public. *Lettre de CISTE*, *35*, 1–6.

Scheid, F., Vaillant, R., & De Montaigu, G. (2012). *Le marketing digital: dévelop-per sa stratégie à l'ère numérique*. Ed Eyrolle.

Schmitt, B. H. (1999). *Experiential Marketing: How to get customers to sense, feel, think, act, and to relate to your company and brands*. New York, NY: Free Press.

SpannerWorks. (2007). *What is social media*. Retrieved from www.spannerworks.com/ebooks

Tapscott, D., & Williams, D. A. (2008). *Wikinomics – How Mass Collaboration Changes Everything*. Portfolio.

Taylor, I. (2008). *Why Social Media Should Be a Key Ingredient in Your Marketing Mix*. Academic Press.

Tiago, M. T., & Verissimo, J. M. (2014). Digital Marketing and Social Media: Why Bother? *Business Horizons, 57*(6), 703–708. doi:10.1016/j.bushor.2014.07.002

Turcotte-choquette, A. & Parmentier, M-A. (2011). Le web 2.0: mieux le comprendre pour mieux l'utiliser. *Cahier de recherche, 11*(2).

Vandercammen, M. (2012). *Marketing: l'essentiel pour comprendre, décider, agir*. Deboeck.

Vargo, S. L., & Lusch, R. F. (2004a). Evolving to a New Dominant Logic for Marketing. *Journal of Marketing, 68*(1), 1–17. doi:10.1509/jmkg.68.1.1.24036

Von Hippel & Katz. (2002). Shifting innovation to users via toolkits. *Management Science, 48*(7), 821-833.

Wathieu, L., Brenner, L., Carmon, Z., Chattopadhay, A., Wetenbroch, K., Drolet, A., & Wu, G. et al. (2002). Consumer control and Empowerment: A Primer. *Marketing Letters, 13*(3), 297–305. doi:10.1023/A:1020311914022

Weber, L. (2007). *Marketing to the social web: how digital customer communities build your business*. Hoboken, NJ: Wiley & Sons.

Weibel, D., Wissmath, B., Habegger, S., Steiner, Y., & Groner, R. (2008). Playing online games against computer- vs. human-controlled opponents: Effects on presence, flow and enjoyment. *Computers in Human Behavior, 24*(5), 2274–2291. doi:10.1016/j.chb.2007.11.002

Zammar, N. (2012). *Réseaux sociaux numériques: essai de catégorisation et de cartographie des controverses*. Université Rennes 2.

Chapter 7
Social Networking Engagement and Crisis Communication Considerations

Mitchell Marovitz
University of Maryland University College, USA

ABSTRACT

This chapter covers crisis communication, focusing on the crucial activities before, during, and after a crisis occurs. An environmental scan identifies risks an organization may encounter. Prioritizing these risks informs the creation of crisis communications plans for each risk. These plans include a strategy to guide all organizational communications efforts. Timeline, budget, products, digital resources, and formative measurement all must be considered. Practice is essential. These actions can prepare an organization and its people to manage high-pressure, high-speed activities in real time. Once the crisis is controlled, it is time to evaluate the plan and institute adjustments as required.

DOI: 10.4018/978-1-5225-1963-8.ch007

INTRODUCTION

When I was asked to write this chapter, I couldn't stop thinking about what new insight I could offer. I have spent much of my career dealing with crises, or potential crises, from personal tragedies as a public affairs officer in Germany during 1982-1985 to the 2004 prisoner abuse scandal that took place at Abu Ghraib in Iraq. It occurs to me that I have planned for crises, implemented others' plans, and have adjusted both to account for the realities that faced us on the ground as the crises unfolded. One thing my experience has shown me is certain: no plan, as the old Army saying goes, survives first contact with the enemy. Yet, I am just as certain that without a plan, you are doomed to fail to achieve your objectives. Planning affords you the opportunity to think things through in the comfort of your office. It allows you to get to know the people you will be working with in a real crisis. And, it permits you to have something to practice.

What I was able to see over the years is that while our understanding of crises and the communications tools we have at our disposal have gotten better, the basics have not changed much. Crisis managers must be able to envision what can happen, prioritize potential crises, identify the resources necessary to resolve the crisis, and lead and manage those resources when a crisis strikes. The goal, of course, is to return the organization to normal operations as quickly as possible. While it goes without saying that operational excellence gets an organization back to normal, an active, creative, and well implemented crisis communications campaign cuts through the fog of crisis, informs employees about what needs to be—and is being—done, displays empathy on behalf of the organization to those affected, and demonstrates professionalism in resolving the problem. A well implemented crisis communications effort can determine whether the organization can survive the crisis after the crisis ends.

In this chapter, we will take a journey to explain the role of communications in crises. We will briefly examine theories of crisis communication and focus on the important role digital and social media strategies have assumed over the last 20 years. We will also examine the latest thinking on how best to measure social media activities so that your work can indeed help your organization accomplish its goals.

CRISIS MANAGEMENT AND CRISIS COMMUNICATION

Imagine a world without Twitter, without Facebook, without Instagram. Imagine a world without the internet. Well, let us not go back that far! Let us just go back to the world of Windows 3.1, when the internet was for nerds only, the stuff of the Defense Department and college professors. Amazon.com had not gone online yet.

The Rodney King Riots

On April 29, 1992, four police officers from the Los Angeles Police Department were acquitted in a state court of an assault on Mr. Rodney King. Disturbances began that evening and lasted through the morning of May 4th. By the time the riots were over, 54 persons were killed, 2,383 injured (221 critically), and 13,212 arrested. There were 11,113 fires, and damage was estimated at $717 million for Los Angeles County (Mendel, 1996). James Delk, the California National Guard's deputy adjutant general at the time, said in a 1996 Rand corporation PowerPoint presentation, "I did not have a good handle on public affairs. You need an 800-pound gorilla running that show for you (slide 51)." He cited his inability to quell the rumor that his soldiers only had one bullet each: the Barney Fife rule. He said, "The trouble with poor public affairs is that it creates the environment in which we operate and it can get soldiers killed (slide 51)." Mendel (1996) notes that by 1992, planning and exercising for this kind of crisis was allowed to deteriorate. Interagency cooperation was ineffective and the civilian command and control system was "was sometimes slow to respond with coherent direction to the supporting military (p.6)."

I arrived in Los Angeles on September 2, 1992. It was a beautiful day, as most days in LA are, though the radio complained about the high humidity: 20%. My wife and I laughed because we had just come from our assignment in Panama, where we had not seen (or felt) humidity as low as 20% in our entire time there!

I was the new chief of the Army's public affairs office there. I was the Army liaison officer to the entertainment industry. I was also responsible for Army community relations in the Greater Los Angeles area. In that capacity, my office took Mendel's (1996) observation to heart and we decided to establish a better public relations relationship between the military and civilian public sector public affairs offices.

My community relations officer, Kathy Ross, connected with local, county, and state police and emergency service offices. As the new guy on the block, and senior active duty public affairs officer in the region, she took this initiative as an opportunity to introduce me to the military public affairs officers in the region. Together, we used the telephone and held face-to-face meetings with our counterparts and persuaded many of them to attend a two-day symposium on crisis communications planning that we hosted in the Wilshire Federal Building.

The results were gratifying by the standards of those days. People came, listened, and got to know one another. Over the next year and a half, we hosted two additional symposia, which led to other meetings, which led to the offices coordinating amongst themselves and with their organizational counterparts to create plans.

For me, I knew we had succeeded when, during the 1994 Northridge earthquake, I was literally "out of the net," stuck at my home with no communications for two days, yet public affairs coordination went on: messages got out to affected publics and the national guard was not federalized (Komchenko, 1997). In hindsight, we were lucky. We had a little technology (mostly fax and some email) and a year and a half to get to know one another, to meet and to plan and to practice.

Hurricane Katrina

By 2005, technology improved. The internet got better. It was faster and more ubiquitous. It was mostly an entertainment medium, however, and it proved too fragile a channel to communicate survival messages (Piper, P. and Ramos, M. 2006).

Hurricane Katrina hit the southern US coast on August 29, 2005. This category 3 storm, although not the strongest to hit the US, brought devastation to vast swaths of Florida, Mississippi, and Alabama. It was in New Orleans, Louisiana, however, that crisis management activities unraveled and communications played a significant role in the unraveling:

We had never considered that there would not be a way to communicate. All of our resources were wiped out. We could occasionally call out on a landline in the power company's command center. I got a few SOS messages to someone on my staff and those messages were released to the news media.
Another call was to a local AM radio station. I was only able to form a Joint Information Bureau (JIB) once the military arrived and provided support. – Sally Forman, Director of Communications for Mayor of New Orleans (Fearn-Banks, 2007, p 112)

Instead of radio and television, helicopters with bullhorns flew over housing areas, looking for and directing survivors. Thankfully, radio station WWL stayed on the air "throughout the crucial periods of the disaster (Fearn-Banks, 2007, p. 123)."

Another communications failure revolved around people looking for people. Two-way communication in and out of the area was severely restricted. Cell phones were intermittent, and it was difficult even for ham radio operators to get through (Fearn-Banks, 2007, p. 127). Piper and Ramos (2006) note that text messaging was more reliable than voice circuits for communications.

To be sure, blogging went on (Fearn-Banks, 2007, p. 130), but from far-away locations and related to news coverage provided by broadcasters and print journalists. The Pew Research Center (2005) notes that the internet was used to coordinate relief from outside the area. Pew Internet Project director, Lee Rainie said, "I think people have a sense that the Internet is a tremendously powerful and useful tool for them to provide human aid and comfort. You can do it from anywhere on the planet where there is a modem. You do not have to be living in the vicinity in order to make a difference or show your concern." (Pew Research Center, 2005)

In the end, however, the population was largely uninformed during Hurricane Katrina as few had access to electricity and mass communications receivers. People relied on face-to-face exchanges for truly local news and information.

Hurricane Sandy

Seven years later, Hurricane Sandy devastated the Eastern seaboard of the United States, killing 48 Americans and hundreds of citizens from other nations from the Caribbean to Canada. But something was different. There was no huge outcry from citizens about not knowing what to do or where to go. Further, emergency services were largely where they said they would be. Also, neighborhoods shared information about what stores were open and what services could be found where. Cohen (2013) notes, "Hurricane Sandy marked a shift in the use of social media in disasters. More than ever before, government agencies turned to mobile and online technologies. Before, during, and after Sandy made landfall, government agencies throughout the Northeast used social media to communicate with the public and response partners, share information, maintain awareness of community actions and needs, and more."

WHAT HAVE WE LEARNED?

One thing we know: although things were far from perfect in these disasters, people coped and society persevered. As horrible as the Superstorm was, the use of high technology, including social media, became integrated into the communications management process. As importantly, private-public partnerships sprang up to create technology support structures to permit electronic devices to operate during a crisis.

Crisis Management and the Role of Crisis Communication

Coombs (2007), in his situational crisis communications theory, says, "A crisis is a sudden and unexpected event that threatens to disrupt an organization's operations and poses both a financial and a reputational threat." (p. 164) Can we plan for a crisis? What should we do? How can we measure our success supporting our organizations? To understand that, we need to look into the processes of crisis management and learn the role of crisis communications in managing crises and the role of digital channels in the overall crisis communications effort.

Crisis management, according to Fearn-Banks is "a process of strategic planning for a crisis or negative turning point, a process that removes some of the risk and uncertainty from the negative occurrence and thereby allows the organization to be in greater control of its own destiny." (2011, p. 2) Crisis management involves identifying a strategy to get the organization back to normal, communicating that strategy to internal and external stakeholders, and managing crisis planning and operations efforts before, during, and after the crisis. It involves bringing to bear all of the tools available to the corporation or entity to get the organization "back to normal."

There are several approaches to describing the crisis management process. Crandall et al cite Smith (1990) and Richardson (1994) suggesting a three-step framework that breaks down into pre-crisis, crisis, and post-crisis activities.

He also cites Myers (1993) and Fink (1996) who offer four-stage frameworks. Myers breaks-down the "crisis" phase into an "emergency response" phase during the first hours of a crisis and "interim processing" during the remainder of the crisis. Fink breaks down the crisis stage into "acute" and "chronic" stages. Both include pre-crisis activities, Myers calling it "normal operations" and Fink calling it "prodromal." Both also offer a "Restoration" stage where the organization returns to normal operations.

Crandall, Parnell and Spillan (2014) suggest a 2 x 4 framework consisting of a landscape survey, strategic planning, crisis management, and organizational learning phases for managing crises both internal and external to the organization. The landscape survey is an environmental scan inside and outside the organization. It is designed to identify strengths and weaknesses, which could indicate vulnerabilities to crises. Internally, the authors advise us to consider the organization's "enthusiasm" for crisis planning, its ethical culture, and the diligence with which the organization enforces safety procedures. Externally, consider industry vulnerability, political stability, and macroeconomic trends, including effects of technology advancements. Strategic planning requires a management team led by a top executive. Crandall et al (2014) recommend the crisis management team be led by a senior executive and have the following characteristics:

- Ability to work in a team environment,
- Ability to think under pressure,
- Ambiguity tolerance,
- Good listening skills,
- Verbal skills,
- Critical thinking skills.

The authors reiterate the importance of planning, organizing, and practicing so that when a crisis happens, the organization is ready to act. Organizational learning occurs after the event. It is akin to a summative evaluation.

Fearn-Banks (2011) identifies five stages in the life cycle of crises: detection or identification, prevention/preparation, containment, recovery, and learning/evaluation. Detection or identification focus on the conditions that can result in a crisis. Prevention and preparation address planning and practicing for potential crises. The idea here is that through preparation, relationships can develop, some crises can be averted, and people can practice to recognize prodromes or act on situations they may face. Prodromes are foreshadowing events; non-crisis activities that happen to let you know a crisis may be coming.

Containment is responding to the exigency. Containment" may be a poor choice of words in today's vernacular. Fearn-Banks (2011) actually means that the activities in this stage are "designed to limit the duration of the crisis or to keep it from spreading to other areas affecting the organization." (p. 7) Recovery is getting back to normal after the immediate crisis has ended, and learning is evaluating what happened and thinking about how to get better for next time.

Detecting and preparation can seem like daunting and expensive tasks. There are so many things that can go wrong. Which should you plan for first? Fearn-Banks (2011) suggests the use of crisis inventory. She provides a list of common crises (p. 301) to get the planner started. Once the types of crises are identified, she suggests prioritizing them based on the answers to two questions:

1. How likely is this crisis to occur? and
2. What is the potential damage to the organization should the crisis occur?

By reducing the answers to a numerical score from 1 to 5, you can prioritize the order in which to begin planning. This is an important decision because there is only so much money to go around and it is important to plan for the right crises. Once you have established the priority of the crises you may face, plan for each crisis. Identify spokespeople, gather your resources, and practice, practice, practice.

González-Herrero and Smith (2008) focus exclusively on the digital domain. They note that audiences today are highly fragmented and use their own voices to express their opinions through peer media such as blogs and social networks (p. 144). They offer a four-step model for crisis management in the virtual world that is explained in Table 1.

Why Crisis Communication?

If crisis management is about identifying potential crises and planning actions to get organizations functioning normally as quickly as possible, crisis communications, then, "is the dialog between the organization and its public(s) prior to, during,

Table 1. Crisis management considerations

González-Herrero and Smith Crisis Management Model	
Issues Management	Activities are similar to Fearn-Banks' detection stage but include activities like starting a corporate blog and monitoring tone and language to help recognize prodromes.
Planning/ Prevention	In the digital arena, this suggests not only placing a crisis planning manual online but also to identify what the organization can "proactively do in advance of a possible crisis" (González-Herrero and Smith, 2008, p. 149). Some suggested activities include building a dark website, identifying potential third-party allies, and practicing.
Crisis	Normally occurs only after traditional media pick up the story, activities focus on the speed of reaction and real-time monitoring.
Post-Crisis	Activities require the organization to continue monitoring online activity, defining strategies to rebuild the organization's reputation, and conduct a summative evaluation.

and after the negative occurrence." (Fearn-Banks, 2011, p. 2) Communications is a responsibility of the crisis manager. Communications allows the manager to accomplish her tasks.

At an interpersonal level, communication facilitates these efforts by allowing responders—those actually delivering services that will end the crisis—to communicate with each other and with the crisis headquarters to coordinate activities, verify efforts are working, and to inform and calm the organization's stakeholders and other audience segments.

Second, the internal audience, arguably the most important audience during a crisis, must be kept appraised of what is going on for safety reasons: They must know what they are expected to do. But there is more. To mass media covering a crisis, a firm's employees are more believable than the executive team. Employees are the people reporters go for "the truth." Employees also talk to family and friends who engage their networks and spread what they've heard. If they have good information and have practiced their roles, and if they understand and support organizational goals, they will be able to mitigate the negative effects of the crisis.

Third, the organization's stakeholders need to know the organization is well-managed and in capable hands and that it will emerge from the crisis quickly and, hopefully, stronger than before.

Fourth, consumers and other audience members listen, watch, and make decisions about the organization, either positively or negatively, about the nature or fabric of an organization. How an organization reacts in a crisis could very well sway audience members to come back...or not. A fifth audience is the intervening audience of the media. Although last in this list, they are far from the least important audience in a crisis. This group includes traditional media representatives as well as bloggers and website representatives. These people reach directly into the homes of consumers and other audience members. They act as a filter for those not participating directly in the crisis and their opinions spread through interpersonal and shared media channels.

Crisis Communications Theory

Crisis communications theories provide the theoretical basis for developing crisis communications plans and for the inclusion of multiple communications strategies in the planning process. Mass media channels such as print, radio, and television combined with a strong and continuing media relations strategy have been the strategies of choice in the bulwark of crisis communications planning and implementation efforts throughout the modern era. Traditional media do have limitations, however. In the waning days of the Hurricane Katrina crisis, we saw, for the first time, the promise of digital technology in crisis communication when the New Orleans IT team was able to establish communications using a hotel internet connection (Crandall, 2014). Internally, organizations today have also turned to digital technology, especially intranets, to communicate with employees.

Coombs (2007), in his situational crisis communications theory, defines a crisis as "a sudden and unexpected event that threatens to disrupt an organization's operations and poses both a financial and a reputational threat." (p. 164) He notes that the responsibility of the communicator is to address the physical and psychological concerns of the audience segments first, then focus on the reputation of the organization. He groups crises into three clusters: victim, accidental, preventable. He then suggests a two-step process to assess reputational threat: (1) determine the initial crisis responsibility attached to the crisis and (2) consider prior history and prior relationship reputation, which can intensify the effect of the crisis on the audience segments. The reputational threat will determine the appropriate crisis response strategy.

Coombs (2007) holds that as the reputational threat and negative affect increases (both are functions of situational factors), crisis managers should utilize crisis response strategies with the requisite level of accepting crisis responsibility.

While Fearn-Banks (2011) and Crandall et al (2014) acknowledge that a digital strategy is important to successful crisis communication today, González-Herrero and Smith (2008), zero-in on the digital domain, saying that organizations "need to plan and determine how the company will use the Internet to interact and exchange information with its constituencies should a more 'traditional' crisis occur." (p. 146) Their four-step crisis management model includes a prescriptive approach to identifying, planning, implementing, and analyzing communications in the digital domain.

Fern-Banks (2011), too, offers a highly prescriptive approach to crisis communications in general, including a planning template, checklists, guidelines for spokespeople, guidelines for writing social media messages, briefing formats, news release formats, and even suggestions for staffing and equipping an emergency operations center.

Digital Communications Channels during Crises

When we think about using digital communications channels for crisis communications, what platforms or tools should we be thinking about? Also, what is the role of search engine optimization and search engine marketing in driving audiences to the content they need? The literature is rich in such discussion.

First, let us examine what we mean by digital channels. Television and radio long ago completed their transition from analog to digital technologies. In doing so, they have become more mobile and interactive. Still, they remain an essentially mass medium best suited for disseminating information to large swaths of audiences rather than as a platform for focusing micro-targeted messages to specific groups. Having said that, do not dismiss the importance of a strong media relations component to your crisis communications effort (Utz, Schultz and Glocka, 2013). Everyone will be watching TV, listening to the radio, and reading the newspaper (or digital equivalent) in the ramp-up to, during, and even after a crisis event.

Perhaps the most important digital platform is your organization's website. And not just your main website: consider building a "dark site." This platform remains invisible until you need it. Thus, you can pre-populate it with fact sheets and backgrounders about the organization, points of contact, a telephone number for friends and relatives to call for information about employees, contractors, and family members who may be affected by the crisis. As the dark site becomes live, the communications staff can populate it with crisis-specific information and context. Updates are easy and because the site shares the organization's URL, stakeholders will already know how to access it, and you can cross-promote the site across traditional and other digital channels for other audience members. Also, remember to build your website with SEO/SEM in mind: research search terms and include them in your headlines and stories. Make it easy for the audience to find you when they need you.

The website is important, but is it social? Lon Safko (2012) defines social media as, "the media we use to be social (p. 3)." This is a simple concept, but there are hundreds of technologies that drive social media and new platforms go online every day. I would name the ones I know, but they will be out of date by the time this chapter is published. Safko (2012) categorizes them twelve different ways. Nowhere in his list do you see the word, "website." He does include "microblogging," but not "blogging."

Although websites and blogs can be interactive, they tend to be one-way, from the blogger or the organization to the audience member. We call them "social media," but users typically engage the blogger or organization via a "comment" button on the website or blog. As I said, it is "social" and "engaging," but not in the same way as platforms like Facebook or micro-blog sites like Twitter.

Facebook, YouTube, and Twitter are highly popular platforms. Facebook, however, increasingly reaches older audiences. Still, it is highly popular and, odds are, your organization has Facebook friends with whom you already have established relationships. I am convinced there is virtually nothing you cannot find on YouTube. Twitter is used by media reporters and bloggers. During a crisis, pre-approved messages can inform your followers and drive them to your website or link directly to organizational fact sheets, talking papers, and emergency information as news occurs. It is an excellent platform to reach out to them. Instagram reaches a younger demographic, as do Tumblr and Foursquare. As I said, new platforms seem to come online every day. It is actually difficult to keep track of them, which is another challenge for the digital communications team.

Gao, Barbier and Goolsby (2011) discuss the power of crowdsourcing over social media channels to engender support for disaster relief efforts, funding, and information exchange. They cite research that shows it is possible to generate "community crisis maps" that allow organizations to share information "as well as collaborate, plan, and execute shared missions." (p. 10) Crowdsourcing tools, they say, "collect data from emails, forms, tweets, and other unstructured methods." (p. 11) An analysis of the data can yield insight into materiel requirements and where those materials are needed. The authors note that the technologies are not mature and do have some drawbacks. For example, there is no provision for collaboration among the different NGOs, which means several may act to the same requests.

With the plethora of platforms, how can one create a digital strategy that will rise above the noise to mitigate issues (risks that have happened—a crisis) and achieve the organizational goal to get back to a state of normalcy as quickly as possible?

Schultz, Utz and Göritz (2011) examined the value and use of social media in crisis communication. Their work suggests that the medium used is actually more important than the messages distributed when the goal is to have viewers forward messages: Twitter users are more likely to share than blog users, who in turn are more likely to share than non-users of blogs or Twitter. The authors say "For all three dependent measures—reputation, secondary crisis communication and reactions—main effects of medium occurred, whereas the message had only a significant effect on secondary crisis reactions." (p. 25) Interestingly, however, the authors note that secondary crisis communication, that is, the willingness to pass along a message, was highest when the original content came from a newspaper article. The authors believe this may be because people talk more about newspaper articles than blogs or tweets.

Utz, Schultz, and Glocka (2013) found that the use of social media in a crisis is important because it "…influences the effectiveness of the crisis communication, as it is now seen as a cue for the willingness of the organization to quickly inform its stakeholders and to engage in dialog with them." (p. 45) They go on to suggest that traditional media, especially given the higher credibility of online newspaper articles, still play an important role in crisis communications and that it is important to spread consistent messaging across channels. Further, they assert the importance of addressing emotions in addition to providing information or rationalizations in communications.

Implementing Digital Media Strategy

Richard Edelman (in Caywood, 2012) suggests one avenue to pursue: understanding the new-media ecosystem. He describes a media environment divided into four segments or "cloverleafs": mainstream media, tra-digital, social media, and owned media. (p. 258) The Tra-digital segment consists of mainstream brands that provide content across platforms and includes subject-specific platforms like Mashable. Also, do not forget owned media like Yammer, a popular microblogging platform usually found behind the firewalls of organizations. Yammer is designed to let employees engage among themselves and with organizational leadership. It is a great tool help identify prodromal activities before they become crises.

Edelman charges communications managers to do several things. Start with thinking like a media company to drive the conversation in your organizational business space. Actively listen, solicit customer comments, and then create compelling, entertaining and relevant content. In a crisis, entertainment may not be appropriate, but compelling content will keep the target audience engaged and willing to listen. It is the first step to creating brand ambassadors before a crisis. Next, engage continuously for the obvious benefits it can bring. Finally, activate influentials, harkening back to Rogers' *Diffusion of Innovations* (2003) which tells us to identify those individuals who have your audience's attention. Engage them. Earn their support.

Arnold and Ewing (2012) note how difficult it is to "[align] stakeholders with the interests of a company, [find] common ground and [build] a lasting relationship…[in] the incredible 24/7 hot media environment that has revolutionized communications and facilitated building online communities of interest since 1997." (p. 345) They reinforce our belief that while our communication revolution has made instantaneous news a reality, cultural differences impact how messages are interpreted and understood. They cite Peter Himler in offering insight into the value of social media:

- The ability to detect and neutralize a problem before it becomes an issue thanks to monitoring tools.
- The ability to create one's own content.

Similarly, Englehart (2012) notes significant changes in the way social media has impacted crisis communications. News cycles no longer exist. Triggers for crises exist on everyone's cell phone, many of which are internet connected. In such a light, he offers two suggestions:

- Plan for the unplanned.
- Weigh the cost to survival of not preparing for a crisis.

I find this second suggestion of particular import. I cannot begin to count how many times I have been brought into a crisis situation only to learn that no preparations have been made. No practice has been done. No one knows what to say or who should say it. Deeper analysis often indicates no one had time, or it was too expansive to plan and practice, but there was plenty of time and money to fix the problem after it happened. Go figure.

Langley (2014) cites Wikipedia as the first "social" site, opening to visitors in 2001. LinkedIn, founded in 2003, actually predates Facebook, which did not come online until the next year (retrieved from http://www.businessinsider.com/how-facebook-was-founded-2010-3, May 8, 2016). YouTube came online in 2005 (Langley, 2014).

With this revolution in communication going on, it is wise to ask about social media's relationship to other digital technologies and how it has changed the way we plan for crisis communications. Langley (2014) provides some insight: "As a means of communication…the internet in general and social media in particular bring key changes to organizations. The key features of the digital age can be summarized as: speed, globalization, emerging technologies, disintermediation (or the ability of an organization to reach directly to its audience), lack of regulation, data democratization, and interactivity." (p. 25)

He identifies nine categories of digital crises, which he calls "brandjacks." He takes apart 136 cases to examine what worked and what did not for each one. He surmises that: (1) volume does not necessarily indicate success, (2) you should keep your staff motivated, engaged, and loyal and asked them to post their thoughts on their favorite social media platforms, and (3) keep your employees knowledgeable about the law and what they legally can say and cannot say when posting, and ask them to post their thoughts on their favorite social media platforms (Langley, 2014).

Langley (2014) does admit that letting employees speak their minds is a radical change for most organizations. But as he goes on to say, "For years, organizations have sought to maintain the idea that their reputation can be manipulated by strict control of who is allowed to speak and the messages they deliver. If it ever worked, it does not work now." (p. 300)

Goldstein (2015), citing Ann Marie van den Hurk, principal of Mind The Gap Public Relations, PR News work in the Book of Crisis Management Strategies & Tactics, Vol. 8, offers these considerations for integrating social media (Table 2) into every crisis scenario your brand or client might face.

All of this is not to say crisis communications planners should drop media relations activities. On the contrary, media relations is a vital component of any crisis communications plan. The media is an excellent and efficient way to provide information about what is going on and what the organization is doing about it for masses of people at once. What you do with the media will naturally find its way onto digital platforms, including social media platforms. By embracing a digital strategy that complements the media relations strategy, crisis communicators can effectively and efficiently tell the organization's story. In this way, you can abide by the old (and very true) adage: "Tell the truth, tell it fast." We have heard how fast social media spreads the word. If the publics perceive the organization is honest in its dealings and is solving its problems, the impact of the crisis can be mitigated.

Table 2. Social media integration techniques

Integrating Social Media in Crisis Situations
Criticism: Do not censor criticism on your blog, Facebook account, or YouTube channel unless it violates your stated community guidelines. This is a difficult concept for organizations to get accustomed to in the age of social media. Removing the offending comments may lead to more, harsher comments.
Tone: Social media is not the space for corporate tone. When responding, be personal, polite, and professional. Never respond in a dismissive or impolite manner. It will only add fuel to the fire.
Order: Many organizations are afraid to stand up for themselves on social media. It is OK to bring order to the organization's online space, which will allow for concerns to be addressed
Listen: Listen to and try to understand what the negative commenter wants. Respond directly to the person when possible. Respond publicly and have an open conversation or acknowledge the concern and then take it offline. How an organization handles a particular situation depends on the factors involved.
Channel: Different social media channels have unique tones because they target different audiences. Each channel needs to communicate the same message, but that message needs to conform to the style of a particular channel. What works in a media release, on a website, or in a brochure will not necessarily work on Twitter or Facebook.
Update: Websites and social media platforms need to be updated 24/7. During a crisis, people will be expecting current information. They will be expecting interaction on social media platforms.

Source: van den Hurk, A. (in Goldstein, 2015)

I know you've heard this before, but let me reiterate one key to success in the digital world, as it is with traditional media, is to know your audience. Go where they are. Tailor your messages based on the media channels used and cultural needs of the various audience segments (especially in foreign locations, but even in our diverse land). The idea is to facilitate understanding without disseminating contradictory messages. Keep your employees informed, engaged, and loyal...they are your best spokespeople. Come out from underneath the silo of communications and interact with the rest of the crisis management team. Get smart about what the operators do in a crisis. Let them know you are thinking about messaging, timelines, platforms, and the all-important technology support structures (e.g., strategically placed battery charging stations) needed to support the crisis communications effort, especially the digital effort.

In the end, communicators dismiss the impact of digital technology in a crisis at their own peril. It is not a lot of extra work, though there is an extra cost, to include these channels in a crisis management strategy or in the crisis communications plan.

Staffing for the Digital Effort

During the pre-crisis phase, normal staffing of the digital team should be sufficient. However, you should consider retainer contracts for some skills because once a crisis erupts, you will require additional IT and communications resources quickly. Depending on the size of your organization and the degree to which you use social media, you should account for IT support for the website and various platforms, digital content development, video and audio production, measurement monitoring, analysis, summative evaluation, and management. Talk to your IT, production and digital content personnel. Explain the extra workload and timelines to them; get their sense of the extra staffing and equipment required, and of the costs involved.

Measuring the Digital Effort

What should we measure and how should we measure it? Okay, so you have put together a digital strategy that incorporates social media platforms that your audiences go to. How are you going to measure how you are doing? Are your messages getting through? Are they being understood? What is the audience doing with those messages? Is the communications climate helping to (1) resolve the crisis and (2) mitigate the reaction in the eyes of your stakeholders and other audiences?

Basic questions include: How many people are coming to the website? Where on the site are they going? How long are they staying there? Where are they going and what are they saying (and doing) afterwards? Certainly, Google Analytics, http://www.analytics.google.com is a great place to go for basic measurement...and some of it is free! After a relatively painless account setup process, you'll get a tracking ID. For free you can use the services listed in Table 3.

And, of course, Google sells subscription services such as Google Analytics 360 Suite, which is designed to help marketers understand consumer behavior and then provide them with more engaging brand experiences (Google, Inc., 2016a). Other companies that do work similar to Google Analytics include WebTrends and Omniture. Will these products work for public relations professionals planning for or in the middle of a crisis? At some level, yes they will. But for insight into whether messages are being understood and affecting behaviors, you may want to check into proprietary products from companies such as Cision or Zignal.

Cision tools allow you to access its media database, distribute press releases, manage influencer outreach, measure social media activities and analyze the effectiveness of campaigns. Social media analysis includes sentiment analysis, social reporting that include conversion analytics, impressions, share of voice, and customer engagement as well as brand analysis. Cision's solution also offers media analysis that quantifies the reach and impact of your public relations efforts.

Radian 6 is another popular tool. It focuses on social media monitoring specifically. While it can be used in a brand protection capacity, the Web Analytics world website suggests it is highly useful in a proactive sales and marketing capacity, searching the "social web for sales and marketing opportunities." (Radian 6

Table 3. Free analytics capability

Using Google Analytics
Data Collection & Management: Collection and Configuration APIs help you collect data and manage your account in custom, scalable ways. With the Collection APIs and SDKs, you can measure how users interact with your content and marketing initiatives on any device or platform. The Configuration APIs let you explore flexible and programmatic ways to manage your Google Analytics account. Data collection and management with Google Analytics provides a single, accurate view of the customer that can be customized to your needs and shared across the organization.
Cross Device Data: The multi-screen, multi-device world is the new normal. Google Analytics' Measurement Protocol measures digital platforms beyond web and apps, so you can connect offline conversions with online activity.
Event Tracking: How do visitors actually interact with your pages and/or your mobile app? Use Event Tracking to measure activities like downloads, video plays, and mobile ad clicks.
Mobile SDKs: Our native iOS and Android SDKs make it easy for you to measure user interaction with your app by tracking key events and activities.
User Permissions: User Permissions let you choose the right levels of access for different users of your Google Analytics account. You can let some people manage your entire account, while others can simply view and analyze.

Source: Google, Inc., 2016b.

Overview, n.d.) Zignal Labs provides a software solution it says will allow you to "interpret data to report and take action on trends, activities, and conversations in real time." (Zignal Labs, n.d.)

Criticalmention.com, Carma.com, Symscio.com, and IBM also offer social media measurement services. This is not an exhaustive list. Many companies offer such services and you will need to research costs and capabilities among them to find the best fit for your organization.

To help you organize your media measurement, the International Association for the Measurement and Evaluation of Communications offers social media measurement frameworks that will help you decide what you want to measure and provide a matrix for visualizing the effects of paid, owned and earned social media; program, business and channel social media (International Association for the Measurement and Evaluation of Communications, 2014).

I want to reiterate that as technology changes, so do the platforms various audience segments use. Thus, communicators need to be vigilant for new platforms and to have established their relationships with crisis management leadership to permit flexibility in messaging and rapid response to product development.

Paine (2011) argues that from a measurement perspective "the locale may have shifted, but the rules and tools really aren't all that different." (p. 77) She divides social media into two worlds: the one you control and the one you do not. You control your own website, your YouTube channel, your blog, etc. You do not control everything else. You can measure what you control easily enough with Google analytics, WebTrends, and Omniture. If you do not control the site, you will have to go to each site and get that data. (p. 78)

Paine explains that what is important is not how many people have the potential to view your site but what they are doing once they get to your site. If the idea is to establish a deepening relationship with a visitor to your site, Paine (2011) suggests five levels of engagement:

- **Lurking:** Click throughs, unique visitors, likes.
- **Casual:** Repeat visitors, Twitter followers, comments.
- **Active:** Retweets, repeat comments, reposts, shares, use of hashtags, @ messages.
- **Committed:** Registration, positive sentiment, net promoter score.
- **Loyalist:** Trial, purchase, advocacy.

Focusing on measurement during crises, Paine (2011) suggests that a key measure is *trust*. Use Table 4 to work through the process of measurement.

Table 4. Crisis measurement skills

Managing the Measurement Process
Questions to Ask
• Have the behaviors, programs, and activities we implemented changed what people know, think, and feel about the organization, and how they actually act? • Have the actions or behaviors of our organization had an effect on the trust that our constituencies feel toward our organization? • Have the public relations and communications efforts that were initiated to build trust had an effect?
Tips for Answering Questions
• Define a specific desired outcome from the crisis (this should be done during the pre-crisis phase) • Define your audiences and what you want your relationship to be with each one (Note: I'd recommend this be done during the pre-crisis phase as well) • Define your benchmark • Define your measurement criteria • Select a measurement tool • Analyze results, glean insight, and make actionable recommendations • Make the changes and measure again
Dr. Jenn Davis, co-founder of Union Metrics, a Twitter provider, suggests the following information to ensure success.
• If you want to measure awareness, then use metrics like volume, reach, exposure, and amplification. How far is your message spreading? • If you want to measure engagement, then look for metrics around retweets, comments, replies, and participants. How many people are participating, how often are they participating, and in what forms are they participating? • If your goal is to drive traffic to your website, then track URL shares, clicks, and conversions. Are people moving through social media to your external site and what do they do once they're on your site? • If your goal is to find advocates and fans, then track contributors and influence. Who is participating and what kind of impact do they have? • If your goal is to increase your brand's share of voice, then track your volume relative to your closest competitors. How much of the overall conversation around your industry or product category is about your brand

These quantitative results are surely helpful, but they do not tell the whole story. What is the tone of the conversation? Do stakeholders seem to understand the causes and appreciate what you are doing to resolve the issue? Is there a difference in sentiment between stakeholders and other audience members? These kinds of qualitative differences require deeper analysis. Paine (2011) recommends a media monitoring capability that covers print, television, radio, online news sources, blogs, Facebook threads, tweets, YouTube videos, Flickr sets, social bookmarks, bulletin boards, forums, communities, and other sources of information that exist in your marketplace. (p. 165) To measure how your social media strategy is working, first identify your goals and benchmarks, or key performance indicators. And then, select the tool. As we mentioned earlier, there is no shortage of tools. To some extent, your budget will help in the selection process.

Many crisis management and crisis communications plans talk about "learning" and the importance of evaluating your effort after an actual crisis. I do not dispute the importance such summative evaluation. Honest and frank analysis of what went right and what went wrong will inform you for future events and form the basis of formative research for future plans. I cannot emphasize enough, however, that planning needs to be done and manpower needs to be assigned to monitoring media during the crisis as well. Broom and Sha (2013, p. 324) explain that during implementation, key questions to be answered focus on distribution, placement, the potential audience, and the attentive audience. You may also want to measure "impact," or knowledge gained, opinions, attitudes, or behaviors changed. After the crisis, as a part of summative evaluation, you may want to measure repeated changed behavior or even social and cultural change resulting from the crisis. Like Paine (2011), Broom and Sha (2013) also suggest monitoring content position and prominence, share of voice, the detail given to issues important to you, the messages disseminated by the content aggregator, and visuals included in the media story.

Broom and Sha (2013) also differentiate between delivered audiences and effective audiences. (p. 325) The delivered audience includes everyone receiving the communication. The effective audience, however, includes only those in the target audience. The attentive audience includes those who pay attention to your messages and is smaller yet. Broom and Sha (2013) say readership, listenership, and viewership studies are best at measuring attention. These results come slower, as they tend to depend on surveys, diaries, and interviews. The telephone interview is one way around this, although with the proliferation of cell phones, getting data this way is increasingly more difficult.

IN REVIEW

Crisis communications is a critical component of the crisis management process. Crisis managers use communications to transfer sometimes lifesaving knowledge, attitudes, and skills to the people who need them before, during, and after a crisis occurs. As such, crisis communications plans are a natural part of the crisis management planning effort. Traditionally, crisis communications plans have focused on media relations. More recently, the internal audience has been considered a key audience as well.

Today, we include digital communications as an important strategy for good reasons: they work, even when other channels of communication do not, and key members of the audience use those channels. Further, digital media use affects stakeholder reactions and secondary communications. A sound digital strategy, then, includes developing content for all the platforms your audiences use. You

Table 5. Organizing a digital strategy for crisis communications

	Crisis Communications Digital Strategy Checklist	
	Requirements	**Actions**
Pre-Crisis	Conduct an environmental scan of your organization to identify risks.	✓ Determine the likelihood of the risk becoming an issue
		✓ Determine the amount of damage that can occur to the organization should the risk become an issue
		✓ Prioritize the risks
	Develop a crisis communications plan for each of the potential risks in order of priority. **NOTE:***At this point the plan is a general crisis communications plan. No decisions have been made as to whether or not digital channels will be used.*	✓ Provide a short background paragraph explaining the rationale for creating the communications plan
		✓ Explain the goals of the plan and how the world will look when the plan is successful
		✓ Determine objectives
		✓ Determine the measureable steps you will take to ensure success of the plan
		✓ Determine how you will know when you are moving toward your goal
		✓ Identify your audiences
		✓ Develop messages for the audiences;
		✓ Determine what you want to say to each audience segment
	Develop a communications strategy that describes how you will achieve your communications objectives. **NOTE:***It is when devising the communications strategy that you should consider whether or not the digital domain has a role in the plan.*	✓ Do you want to position your organization in some way? ✓ Do you want to draw or back away from attention? ✓ How will you disseminate information (e.g., via media relations activities, broadcast video or audio, digital, face-to-face encounters)?
	Determine if a digital strategy can help achieve crisis communications objectives.	✓ Where do your audience members, including intervening audiences (e.g., media representatives), go for information? ✓ Do you want to create buzz about the organization? ✓ Do you want to involve your supporters or stakeholders and encourage them to take actions intended to affect outcomes? ✓ Do you want to engage audiences and move them from being detractors to neutral positions or move them to be advocates and activists on behalf of the organization?

continued on following page

149

Table 5. Continued

Crisis Communications Digital Strategy Checklist	
Requirements	**Actions**
If you answer yes to step 4, develop a digital annex to the Crisis Communications Plan.	✓ Determine the objectives of the strategy in terms of what you want people to talk about (Do you wish to inform? Engage? Drive traffic? Create advocates? Drive to action?) ✓ Write your objectives as SMART objectives (Specific, Measurable, Attainable, Relevant, Time-bound)
Determine which digital platforms are most appropriate to reach your audiences and allow them to interact in a way that facilitates information flow or engagement.	✓ Where is your audience and how do they interact with those platforms? ✓ Will "how they interact" with the platforms match what you say you want them to do in your objectives statements?
Develop a timeline that supports the basic crisis communications plan timeline	✓ Publish the timeline for all to see/use
Develop products and content	✓ Consider dark sites, pre-approved tweets, blogs, posts, FAQs, Fact Sheets ✓ Refer to messaging to insert calls for action and the identification of places to go for more information ✓ Identify all equipment needs, including back-up power and IT equipment ✓ Remember to coordinate with operations staff for recharging stations, if necessary
Create a budget	✓ As required: Consider costs for: manpower; management, web and IT services (e.g., contract support, extra bandwidth, briefing space, cell phones, etc.); production (e.g., dark website, news briefings, paid content, etc.); equipment (e.g., fly-away kits with laptops, batteries, paper, pens, blank log sheets, etc.); and measurement activities
Consider SEO/SEM tools and techniques to help drive traffic to important sites (e.g., dark sites) during the crisis	✓ As required
Develop a formative and summative evaluation plan that measures movement toward accomplishing the objectives along the timeline.	✓ Determine what you want to measure ✓ Establish measurement benchmarks ✓ Determine how you will gather the data ✓ Determine how you will analyze the data ✓ Determine how you will report and disseminate your findings

continued on following page

Table 5. Continued

	Requirements	Crisis Communications Digital Strategy Checklist
		Actions
	Practice, Practice, Practice	✓ Consider separate digital domain practice sessions ✓ Participate in practice sessions with the rest of the crisis communications and crisis management teams. ✓ Adjust content based on your results ✓ Practice some more
Crisis	Implement the plan, including the digital strategy, conduct constant formative evaluation and, above all, BE FLEXIBLE.	✓ Make sure equipment is available and operational ✓ Monitor SM; Respond immediately; Keep a log; Activate the dark site, as required; Disseminate reports as indicated in the basic crisis communications plan. ✓ Coordinate digital activities with internal and media relations activities ✓ Consider streaming news conferences ✓ Conduct formative evaluation and adjust messaging, products and platforms accordingly
Post-Crisis	Conduct Summative Evaluation	✓ What went right ✓ What went wrong ✓ What changes should be made ✓ What is the best way to disseminate the report
	Makes changes to Plan/Strategy	✓ As required
	Practice some more!	✓ As required

may also consider building a dark website ready for deployment at the flick of a switch. Once the crisis begins and you begin to implement the crisis communications plan, it becomes crucial to conduct formative evaluation to learn if you are reaching your audiences, how effective your messages are, and what you can do to make them more effective. Finally, after the crisis is over and the organization is back to normal operations, summative evaluation will afford you an opportunity to learn what worked, what did not work, and how you can be an even more effective communicator the next time.

The Table 5 checklist will help you organize a digital strategy for the crisis communications effort in relevant stages. Please note that the table uses the three-step framework in organizing actions. The checklist is applicable even if you use four- or five-stage frameworks, although the groupings of the actions may change.

REFERENCES

Arnold, J., & Ewing, R. (2012). Issues management methods for reputational management. In *The handbook of strategic public relations and integrated marketing communications New York* (pp. 335–352). McGraw Hill.

Broom, C., & Sha, B. (2013). Effective public relations (11th ed.). Boston, MA: Pearson Education, Inc.

Cohen, S. (2013, March 7). Sandy marked a shift for social media use in disasters. *Emergency Management*. Retrieved from http://www.emergencymgmt.com/disaster/Sandy-Social-Media-Use-in-Disasters.html

Coombs, W. (2007). Protecting Organization Reputations During a Crisis: The Development and Application of Situational Crisis Communication Theory. *Corporate Reputation Review*, *10*(3), 163–176. doi:10.1057/palgrave.crr.1550049

Crandall, W., Parnell, J., & Spillan, J. (2014). Crisis management. Los Angeles, CA: Sage Publications, Inc.

Davis, J. (2012, April 24). *The 5 Easy Steps To Measure Your Social Media Campaigns*. Retrieved from https://blog.kissmetrics.com/social-media-measurement/

Delk, J. (1995). *MOUT: A domestic case study*. Los Angeles, CA: Rand Corporation. Retrieved from https://www.rand.org/content/dam/rand/pubs/conf_proceedings/CF148/CF148.appd.pdf

Edelman, R. (2012). PR and the media cloverleaf. In *The handbook of strategic public relations and integrated marketing communications* (pp. 258–261). McGraw Hill.

Englehart, H. (2012). *Crisis communications: brand new channels, same old static. The handbook of strategic public relations and integrated marketing communications* (pp. 401–413). McGraw Hill.

Fearn-Banks, K. (2007). *Crisis communications: a casebook approach* (3rd ed.). Mahwah, NJ: Lawrence Erlbaum Associates, Inc.

Fearn-Banks, K. (2011). *Crisis communications: a casebook approach* (4th ed.). New York, NY: Routledge.

Gao, H., Barbier, G., & Goolsby, R. (2011). *Harnessing the crowdsourcing power of social media for disaster relief. In IEEE Intelligent Systems* (pp. 10–14). IEEE Computer Society.

Goldstein, S. (2015, November 4). A social media checklist for your crisis communications plan. *PR News Online*. Retrieved from http://www.prnewsonline.com/water-cooler/2015/11/04/how-to-integrate-social-media-into-your-crisis-plan/

González-Herreo, A., & Smith, S. (2008). Crisis communications management on the web: How internet-based technologies are changing the way public relations professionals handle business crises. *Journal of Contingencies and Crisis Management, 16*(3), 143–153. doi:10.1111/j.1468-5973.2008.00543.x

Google, Inc. (2016a). *Google analytics solutions website*. Retrieved from https://www.google.com/analytics/#?modal_active=none

Google, Inc. (2016b). *Google analytics features website*. Retrieved from: http://www.google.com/analytics/standard/features/

International Association for the Measurement and Evaluation of Communications. (2014). *Program and Business Channel Social media* [artwork]. Retrieved from http://amecorg.com/wp-content/uploads/2014/06/Program-Business-and-Channel-Social-Media-Measurement-Framework.pdf

Komchenko, S. (1997). *Civil-military relations in domestic support operations. The California national guard in Los Angeles 1992 riots and Northridge earthquake of 1994* (Master's thesis). Monterey, CA: Naval Postgraduate School.

Kumar, K. (2015, October 20). The beginner's checklist to planning your social and digital media strategy. *Social Media Week*. Retrieved from http://socialmediaweek.org/blog/2015/10/beginners-checklist-planning-social-digital-media-strategy/

Langley, Q. (2014). *Brandjack*. New York, NY: Palgrave Macmillan. doi:10.1057/9781137375360

Madden, M. (2005). *Hurricane Katrina: In the face of disaster and chaos, people use the internet to coordinate relief*. Pew Research Center. Retrieved on May 22, 2016 from http://www.pewinternet.org/2005/09/07/hurricane-katrina-in-the-face-of-disaster-and-chaos-people-use-the-internet-to-coordinate-relief/

Mendel, W. (1996). *Combat in cities: The LA riots and operation Rio*. Foreign Military Studies Office.

Paine, K. (2011). *Measure what matters*. Hoboken, NJ: John Wiley & Sons, Inc.

Piper, P., & Ramos, M. (2006, June). A Failure to Communicate Politics, Scams, and Information Flow During Hurricane Katrina. *Searcher Magazine, 14*(6). Retrieved on from http://www.infotoday.com/searcher/jun06/Piper_Ramos.shtml

Radian 6 Overview. (n.d.). Retrieved from http://www.webanalyticsworld.net/ analytics-measurement-and-management-tools/radian-6-overview, May 9, 2016.

Rogers, E. (2003). *Diffusion of innovations* (5th ed.). New York, NY: Free Press.

Safko, L. (2012). *The social media bible*. Hoboken, NJ: John Wiley & Sons, Inc.

Schultz, F., Utz, S., & Göritz, A. (2011). Is the medium the message? Perceptions of and reactions to crisis communication via twitter, blogs and traditional media. *Public Relations Review*, *37*(1), 20–27. doi:10.1016/j.pubrev.2010.12.001

Utz, S., Schultz, F., & Glocka, S. (2013). Crisis communication online: How medium, crisis type and emotions affected public reactions in the fukushima daiichi nuclear disaster. *Public Relations Review*, *39*(1), 40–46. doi:10.1016/j.pubrev.2012.09.010

Zignal Labs. (n.d.). *Make intelligence central to your business* [website]. Retrieved from http://zignallabs.com

Section 3
Examining Social Media Effectiveness

As the magnifying glass in Figure 1 illustrates, this section addresses a closer look at the challenge of analyzing online activities to get a sense of the effectiveness of online interactions. We take a broad view of measurement in an attempt to open the door to conversations, discovery, and research in this area. We cover two non-profit situations to evaluate return on investment. Models of participation in social networks and social media use in election campaigns are also examined. This broad sampling of activity is an important step in starting a conversation about social media implications in these areas.

Figure 1. Examining effectiveness

Chapter 8
CHOICES:
Measuring Return on Investment in a Nonprofit Organization

Leigh Nanney Hersey
University of Louisiana – Monroe, USA

ABSTRACT

Social media is increasing becoming a prominent tool in today's nonprofit sector. By 2010, the largest 200 nonprofit organizations in the United States used social media as a tool to meet their goals (Barnes, n.d.). According to those surveyed the top reason for using social media is for increasing awareness of the organization's mission (90%). In studying the American Red Cross' use of social media, Briones, et al. (2011) found that the use of social media built relationships with the public. This chapter explores the success of a mid-sized nonprofit organization, CHOICES: Memphis Center for Reproductive Health, as it develops a strategic social media plan to increase awareness and support for the organization. Through this case study, we will address how this organization has used social media to advance its mission and the process used to develop performance metrics along the way.

DOI: 10.4018/978-1-5225-1963-8.ch008

INTRODUCTION

Social media is becoming an increasingly prominent tool for today's nonprofit sector. By 2010, the largest 200 nonprofit organizations in the United States were using social media as a tool to meet their missions (Barnes, n.d.). According to those surveyed, most nonprofit organizations use social media to increase awareness of the organization's mission (90%). In studying the American Red Cross' use of social media, Briones, et al. (2011) found that the use of social media built relationships with the public. Social media can be especially important in smaller nonprofit organizations with small marketing budgets and few staff members.

This chapter explores the success of a mid-sized nonprofit organization, CHOICES: Memphis Center for Reproductive Health, as it develops a strategic social media plan to increase awareness and support in the community. Through this case study, the authors will address how CHOICES used social media to advance its mission and the process used to develop performance metrics along the way. Nonprofit organizations need to improve their ability to measure the effectiveness of their social networking strategies (Barnes, as cited in West, 2011).

This case study explores the success a nonprofit organization has had with its strategic use of social media. It will add to the literature on how nonprofit organizations can measure their effective use of social media. Unfortunately, too many nonprofit organizations begin using social media tools without a clear plan or understanding of how to use these tools strategically (Wymer & Grau 2011). From this case study, nonprofit leaders can learn the importance of developing a clear plan and measuring the return of investment of their own social media use to develop a better networking platform.

BACKGROUND: SOCIAL MEDIA USE BY NONPROFIT ORGANIZATIONS

In the past decade, social media has become a more important tool for nonprofit organizations. Transformational social media communication tools have significantly increased audience access to nonprofit organizations engaged in cause marketing and advocacy. While often thought of as primarily a communications tool, when used effectively, social media can help nonprofit organizations better meet their missions. Social media has provided increased ability not only for outreach and advocacy, but also for education, collaboration, service provision, volunteer recruitment, and financial support (Shirky, 2008; Pynes, 2009). The new tools have also resulted in greater expectations from the public for organizational communication leadership and technology skills. There are four critical areas to evaluate when surveying the current landscape of nonprofit social media utilization: *Usage, Coordination, and Responsibility, Strategy,* and *Organizational Capacity.*

Usage

Nonprofit leaders realize that traditional methods of communication are no longer adequate for today's supporters (Wymer & Grau, 2011) and therefore are expanding use of social media. Once, e-mail was the common tool, providing a quick and inexpensive way to reach supporters. Some considered email a "revolutionary tool for opening up new ways to communicate with donors and colleagues, alerting activists, and distributing information" (Wymer & Grau, 2011; p. 3). However, some question the effectiveness of email as the percentage of people who open the emails from nonprofit organizations continue to drop (M+R, 2014). Wymer and Grau (2011) suggest that social media and internet-based communications should not replace traditional forms of communication, but should instead offer more effective opportunities for reaching people, particularly during times of economic stress. M+R (2014) found that only 0.07% of fundraising emails sent from 53 U.S.-based national nonprofit organizations were opened in 2013. At the same time, the nonprofit organizations in the study saw an increase in social media numbers, with Facebook fans increasing by 37% and Twitter followers by 46% from the previous year.

Nonprofit organizations use social media for a wide range of activities, including increasing accountability and transparency, fundraising, cyber volunteering (Waters 2010), engaging others in conversation, strengthening media relations (Eyrich, et al 2008), attracting new customers, raising awareness, sharing information, fostering community (Handley & Chapman, 2011), and advocacy (Guo & Saxton, 2013). Schaefer and Hersey (2015) found the integration of social media positively impacted the marketing efforts, brand awareness, stakeholder support, and the promotion of events and fundraising for a mid-sized animal welfare organization. The Humane Society of the United States found a number of tangible and intangible benefits to their social media strategy. The organization saw its email database increase, obtained new content for posts, garnered free PSA's, raised money, recruited new donors, and recruited members, fans, and friends (Kanter, 2010). In addition, the organization also saw intangible results, particularly in raising awareness about animal welfare issues. Once aware of the issues, people generated discussions and participated in these issues. The organization also received recognition and media attention through its social media use (Kanter, 2010). Identifying and measuring intangible successes is also an important part of using social media, particularly after early adoption when the more tangible elements are harder to realize (Kanter, 2010).

One of the greatest benefits of using social media is the ability to have two-way conversations with those that are interested in the nonprofit organization. Unlike traditional methods of marketing which push information out, social media allows for the "deepening of relations with their clients and supporters and increases the frequency of exposure of their message" (Levinson, Adkins, & Forbes, 2010, p. 195). Unfortunately, many nonprofit organizations do not take advantage of the ability to build relationships and are more likely to engage in one-way communications through social media platforms (Waters & Jamal, 2011).

Coordination and Responsibility

Nonprofit leaders must address whether social media should be managed by communications officers or by information technology (IT) departments. Nonprofit organizations with public relations departments are more likely to adopt social media practices than those without (Curtis, et al, 2010). On the other hand, many smaller nonprofit organizations have neither multiple departments nor specialists on staff. Little has changed since Orlikowski and Scott (2008) reported minimal direction on how to formalize technological responsibility structures in the organization studies literature. The authors recommend research into reframing conventional organization structures in favor of shared connections and responsibilities across department boundaries.

Technological advances have been a wildcard for everyone in the nonprofit sector (Salamon, 2003). Although organization leaders may have been quick to see the benefits of social networking, many still lack the human resources and knowledge needed to put it to best use (Pope, Isely, & Asamoa-TuTu, 2009). Collaborative structures and open dialogue, rather than fixed IT solutions, encourage such adaptation (Dawes, Cresswell & Pardopublic, 2009). Integration of new online communication technologies to institutionalize collaboration between stakeholders leads to greater creativity, as well as more loosely connected communities of interest (Linden, 2010). Successful integration and utilization is contingent, however, on an organization's leadership.

The speed of communications innovation and the associated organizational culture shock have left many agencies struggling to keep up because of outdated or underutilized technology, restrictive cultures, and vague policies (Greene, 2011). Munnukka and Järvi (2013) found that while procedural controls and policy focus could manage these risks, knowledge was the key. Integrating such a large change calls for the development of new governance and strategic communication cultures within organizations that embrace the new normal of constant training and feedback.

The public now expects organizations to maintain communications that require comment moderation, timely feedback, and information curation while maintaining system security, interoperability, and information protection (Howard, 2011). Accordingly, in a survey of 53 national advocacy groups, Obar, Zube, and Lampe (2011) found that leaders believe the new mediums play an essential and cost effective advocacy role by strengthening communication speed, outreach, and feedback. Understanding the value of social media and providing structure and professional development support leads to more successful integration (Leighninger, 2011).

Ojoa, Esteveza, and Janowskia (2010) further note that successful implementation of the technological sea-change depends on each organization. The long range benefits of adoption of new technology often exceeds initial expectations, therefore organizations should consider reframing cultures to support a flexible innovation process, constant communication, experimentation, and training (Atkinson & McCay, 2007).

Strategy

The quantitative study by Zerfass, Fink, and Linke (2011) indicates that despite strong interest in social media among public relations and communication practitioners, the lack of strategy, policy, guidelines, training, monitoring, and evaluation suggests skill in strategic utilization and oversight is lacking even in the corporate sector. While they found many organizations claiming to have strategies for social media, nine out of 10 had no explicit policy frameworks to oversee organization use. Their research indicates a need for focus on developing basic structures for social media communications strategy and that the concept of governance may be used in order to analyze the dynamics of introducing these modes of communication.

Kanter and Paine (2012) note that approximately 70 percent of attendees at networked nonprofit seminars admitted to using social media but not evaluating their efforts with analytics tools. The reasons given for this obvious oversight in professionalized communications strategy and responsibility included: consequences, difficulty of setting measurable objectives, the data dump, and that measurement is too much work or requires too much oversight.

Thus, education of communications and public relations outreach staff in social media practices, not just technology, and the formation of governance strategy are crucial steps needed to achieve the best outcomes of social media engagement and utilization. Dawes, Cresswell, and Pardopublic (2009) promote knowledge networking as a new solution for external and interagency management problems that often plague the nonprofit sector, and this may provide insight into how the sector can quickly leap the learning curve by sharing communications-based knowledge.

Organizations can no longer be one-way communicators (Shirky, 2008; Leighninger, 2011) relying on static websites or even comment-free posts on social sites.

Strategies to successfully adapt to the interactive communications culture can be used by organizations large and small. Management strategies include identification and communication of the need, an implementation plan, internal support, stakeholder participation, management commitment, external support from key stakeholders, sufficient resources, institutionalized change, honest capacity assessment, measuring the success, and comprehensive integration (Fernandez & Rainey, 2006; Kanter, 2010; Menzel, 2010).

In their review of two surveys in Australasia and Europe, McNamara and Zerfass (2012) speak to these strategies. Noting that optimistic views of social media's potential fail to account for the conflict between the open, uncontrolled practice and traditional organizational strategy, their findings identify a need for a strategic focus and integration. Demonstrating that the use of social media for organizational communication was shown to be mostly experimental, rather than strategic, the authors note that social media is most often incorrectly used without clear objectives, consistent integration, or evaluation with Key Performance Indicators.

Heller Baird and Parasnis (2011) note that customer relationship management (CRM) strategies must be updated to adapt to the communications change. Rather than the traditional idea of customer, or client/supporter for nonprofits, relationship management serves as a means for extracting the greatest value for the organization. Social media has put the client in a position of influence to trump carefully-managed campaigns with immediate viral networks. The authors identify a new strategy, social customer relationship management (Social CRM), as a way to navigate traditional communication strategies toward an organizational facilitation of collaborative experience and dialogue (Heller Baird and Parasnis, 2011).

Organizations looking for frameworks to connect in natural, organic, and deeper ways with supporters, colleagues, and communities should look toward shared, participatory approaches to social media as a format for utilizing and enhancing strategic communication efforts (Hallahan et al., 2007; Falkheimer & Heide, 2010; King, 2010; Torp, 2011, and Zerfass et al, 2010). Organizations are starting conversations with potential supporters/clients using search engine optimized (SEO) blogs, hash-tagged Twitter posts, and eye-catching YouTube informational videos. Adept organization leaders are following those initial connections up with online social collaboration using Google groups and wikis. However, the network builders such as Facebook, LinkedIn, and Twitter have virtually remade brand awareness and community outreach strategies on a cyber-sized scale.

Many nonprofit organizations, similar to for-profit brands, have found that incorporating social media into existing outreach efforts engages stakeholders in new and expanded ways. Even for such client and/or cause-focused organizations, the introduction of social media presents one of the most disruptive forces facing professional communicators today. The mildly interested become more involved with cause organization brands as information is shared. A sense of community is formed among individual supporters who might never have otherwise crossed paths. New supporters are attracted. Brand management is now possible on a scale previously quite rarely plausible for small to mid-sized organizations as an effective direct communication channel to supporters and members of the media have been made available free of external charge.

Heller Baird and Parasnis (2011) suggest that companies, and by extension non-profit organizations, would be wise to reinvent relationship management strategy. Their suggestions, adapted for the nonprofit sector, include: thinking of stakeholders holistically, understanding that the public is now a key part if not the major player in the online conversation integrating initiatives across outreach channels, allowing community intimacy to form organically through service provision rather than debating the merits of social media, surveying followers to invest them in the outcome, and making social commerce campaigns seamless with fresh content and incentives to capitalize on the community platform's viral benefits.

Since the audience expects better service provision and crisis communications with better resource deployment using social mediums, organizations should implement new communications strategies before the onset of a need or crisis (Sherman, 2011; Walker, 2011). Aaker and Smith (2010) recommend storytelling across the variety of web platforms to emotionally engage stakeholders with such calls to action.

Organizational Capacity

Many nonprofit organizations have the desire to make an impact on their passion. However, few have the organizational capacity to achieve their goals. Limited finances often prevent nonprofit organizations from carrying out their missions (Waters, 2010). Social media can assist with building organizational capacity by reaching more people with fewer dollars (Wymer & Grau, 2011). Communications barriers have been largely leveled with the new technologies (Palotta, 2008; Leighninger, 2011). While the external cost may be zero, the internal costs associated with salaries and training must be recognized and accounted for.

In reviewing the literature, several challenges related to the nonprofit organizational capacity begin to surface. One of the most common problems nonprofit organizations face when taking on social media is being unable to dedicate staff and time to maintain an active presence (Munnukka & Järvi, 2013; Waters, 2010). Even large organizations such as the American Red Cross see the availability of human resources as the largest barrier for social media usage (Briones, et al., 2011). Similarly, nonprofit leaders are also concerned about the budgetary resource requirements for training and maintaining social media sites (Briones, et al., 2011; Kanter & Fine, 2010; Waters, et al., 2009). Despite the low financial investment associated with getting started in social media, a larger cost in human resources is often realized.

Despite a steady increase of staff time dedicated to social media activities, only 21% of nonprofit organizations have at least one full-time staff member assigned predominantly to maintaining the organization's social media presence (Barry, 2012). With this change, new job descriptions must be developed to incorporate social media responsibilities. For example, an animal welfare organization in Florida hired additional staff after realizing the media relations manager was dedicating 15 percent of her time to social media, duties not listed in her initial job description (Schaefer and Hersey, 2015).

Return on Investment

While there are many benefits to using social media, including cost effectiveness, relationship building, and the ability to reach large numbers of people quickly, challenges also exist. In reviewing the literature on social media, several challenges for nonprofit organizations surface. These include leaders' fear of giving up control (Kanter 2010; Kanter & Fine, 2010), lack of a strategic plan (Wymer & Grau, 2011), human and budgetary resource requirements for training and maintaining social media sites (Briones, et al., 2011; Kanter & Fine, 2010; Waters, et al., 2009), and measuring effectiveness (West, 2011). Concerns about the Return of Investment cross the sector boundaries with 36% of responding Fortune 500 companies also expressing ROI as a major concern, behind only time spent on social media (Barnes & Lescault, n.d.). This section reviews the literature on these areas, bringing a better understanding to the issues and why nonprofit organizations face these challenges.

Many in the business community use the standard of ROI, or Return on Investment, when measuring effectiveness. Kanter (2010) suggests a different application of measuring ROI, measuring Return on *Insight* or *Impact* instead. While nonprofit leaders often want tangible results immediately, Kanter stresses that success in the early stages of social media strategy is often intangible, considering measurements like the number of conversations and relationships generated by having a social media presence.

One of the most beneficial ways to approach measuring effectiveness is to establish the objectives while developing the social media plan (Wymer & Grau, 2011). General goals they suggest include listening and learning, building relationships and issues awareness, reputation management, content generation and education, taking action and fundraising, and building a community (p. 82). Handley & Chapman (2011) suggest four primary objectives for social media use:

1. To attract new customers,
2. To raise awareness about the organization,
3. To share information about the organization, and
4. To nurture relationships and encourage people to tell others about you.

The authors further elaborate by encouraging organizations to set clear goals that can be objectively measured. For example, rather than the broad brand awareness goal "to generate a lot of buzz about the organization," a more measureable goal would be to "generate 100 new likes for the Facebook page" within a certain time frame. Brigida and Colman (2010) suggest four measurement categories for social media: awareness, sentiment, engagement and depth, and conversion.

At the heart of social media investment is the idea of building relationships (Handley & Chapman, 2011; Levinson, Adkins, & Forbes, 2010). "You do that ... over time, but repeatedly and consistently creating content they care about and want to share freely with their friends or colleagues, and by encouraging them to engage with you and to sign up for things you publish..." (Handley & Chapman, 2011, p. 7). MacLaughlin (2010) suggests a three-step framework for measuring online metrics. The first step is to *identify the audience* and know what you want to learn about them. Once you know who you want to analyze, then you are able to *measure the behavior* of these people. Lastly, once the who and the what is determined, you are able to measure the *conversion* or call to action that the target audience takes.

Tools are constantly being developed and refined to help with the measurement task. Web analytics are online software based tools that track various patterns based on the social media platform. The data can be stored and compared over time to help improve the effectiveness of the platform (Kent, Carr, Husted & Pop, 2011). Although based on numbers, it is important to critically analyze the data. "The key to using analytics effectively is to think creatively and strategically. Numbers, and data, do not speak for themselves" (Kent et al., 2011, p. 537). In addition to technology tools, a successful metrics program must also include an organizational culture that understands and embraces the role evaluation plays in reaching goals (MacLaughlin, 2010).

The Organization

CHOICES, an independent, nonprofit community health agency (formerly known as Memphis Center for Reproductive Health) was founded in 1974 in Memphis, TN. The agency's mission is to empower individuals in the Mid-South community to make informed choices for and about their reproductive health. Its vision is to completely transform the way reproductive health care is perceived and provided in the Memphis community. From the beginning, the agency provided innovative services including free pregnancy testing, first trimester abortion care, and counseling that was specifically focused on the needs of the partners of abortion patients. In addition, CHOICES helped establish the first program in the United States to provide counseling, gynecology, and forensics services around the clock to victims of sexual assault. CHOICES is now a comprehensive reproductive medical practice that provides a range of sexual and reproductive health services for more than 3,000 women, men, and teens each year. CHOICES offers a new model for community-based, comprehensive, reproductive health care. The organization hosts and presents medical provider trainings in multiple reproductive health topics. It also partners with local stakeholders to connect young people with affordable, accessible care.

The organization has deep feminist roots that have fostered a deep commitment to its patient-centered model of care that prioritizes trust among the organization's clients and their choices. Today, the organization is continuing to work towards the integration of a broad range of reproductive health services into a comprehensive and cohesive practice that reflects the life-long needs and experiences of women, men, families, and LGBTQ individuals, and the entire community in achieving and maintaining reproductive health. According to its IRS Form 990, the organization brought in $1.8 million in 2013. Approximately 16% of this revenue came from private donations. As the organization looks to the possibility of future expansion, leaders realize the importance of expanding its donor database.

Measuring ROI at CHOICES

CHOICES realized that an important factor in reaching more people includes strategically using social media networks. The organization uses Facebook, Twitter, Google+, and Instagram for promotion. Supporters of the organization tend to be younger and possess an activist nature. Social media seemed like an effective way to reach this population. The organization brought onboard a new staff member in the spring of 2015 to develop a social media plan and measure the results. This person started as an intern, but was kept on staff following her internship to continue this work.

Developing a strategic social media plan and creating effectiveness measurements can help a nonprofit organization improve its online engagement (Schaefer & Hersey, 2015). The social media plan was incorporated into the larger financial development and communications plan and coordinated with the organization's Fundraising and Infrastructure Development Plan. CHOICES felt that social media could be a tool in helping the organization reach its overall development goals of:

1. Building a fundraising infrastructure,
2. Increasing overall donations by 43%, and
3. Expanding and diversifying the organization's base of donors, supporters, and fundraising sources.

The organization realized the importance of including performance management and data analysis when developing any kind of program and included data collection and performance evaluation tasks from the start of the project.

Measurement and Results

Although the development plan included a variety of objectives and tasks, for the purposes of this case study, only the ones related to social media are included. This section identifies the different objectives of the development plan, the tasks used to meet these objectives, how they were measured, and their results as of spring 2016, approximately 10 months after the initiation of the plan.

Infrastructure Development

CHOICES realized early on that the infrastructure was not in place to fully support its development plan. Therefore, several goals were identified to help increase the organization's capacity. Capacity building can be defined as "the ability of nonprofit organizations to fulfill their missions in an effective manner" (McPhee and Bare, 2001, p. 1). Three overall goals were established for the infrastructure development:

1. Develop strategic marketing plan to increase visibility,
2. Develop fundraising infrastructure and culture, and
3. Develop intentional and active roles for volunteers.

Many of the objectives focused on board development and the creation of systematic efforts to address marketing, advertising, and other promotional outlets. However, several objectives incorporated tasks that were related to social media strategy. Table 1 identifies all of these strategies. Through these strategies, CHOICES would develop two keys areas of its infrastructure: stories generation and volunteer development.

Fundraising Development

In order to build its network of support, CHOICES identified four primary fundraising development goals. The first goal was to diversify donor base/revenue sources

Table 1. Social media activities: infrastructure development key strategies

Develop Strategic Marketing Plan to Increase Visibility			
Objective	**Task**	**Measurement Tool**	**Results**
Create "CHOICES/ Community Stories" bank	Post and promote "call for stories" on social media sites	Number of stories collected	16 total stories
Develop Intentional and Active Roles for Volunteers			
Objective	**Task**	**Measurement Tool**	**Results**
Develop program and processes that allow the community assistant to facilitate meaningful engagement for all interested volunteers	Develop and implement procedures for recruiting volunteers through social media	Number of posts	Two posts, one in June 2015 and one in September 2015, across Facebook, Twitter, and Instagram
		Number of visits to the CHOICES volunteer webpage from social media sites	*June*: 181 total clicks originated from social media sites, 77 (43%) opened the volunteer application, and 27 (35% of those that opened the application) completed the application *September*: 116 total clicks originated from social media sites, 48 (41%) opened the volunteer application, and 16 (33% of those that opened the application) completed the application

and increase annual donations by 43%. Many nonprofit organizations look to have diversified funding streams. While having a variety of funding sources can prevent a nonprofit organization from depending too much on one source, it also can give nonprofit organizations less ability to control their revenue streams than government or for-profit organizations have (Grønbjerg, 1991).

The second goal was to maintain an impactful online/social media presence, something the organization struggled with before the implementation of this plan. The third goal was to maintain and effectively manage existing grant funding. As grants make up approximately 83% of the organization's private funding, it plays an important role in the fundraising development plan. However, social media did not play a role in achieving this goal; therefore, it will not be explored further in this chapter.

The fourth goal was to produce effective fundraising events and increase event revenue by 5%. The organization's annual public awareness and signature fundraising special event is CONDOMONIUM. Held each spring, this event supports the Patient Assistance Fund for un- and underinsured patients. The event features fashion and costume designs out of condoms, as well as food, music, and entertainment. Attendees pay their age for admission to the event. Strategic use of special fundraising events can support an organization not only through the funds raised through the event, but also through the strengthening of relationships with new donors and the introduction of the organization to potential donors (Davis, 2013).

CHOICES staff developed a number of objectives and tasks to help them meet these goals. Table 2 shows those related to social media. Tasks included the development of databases as well as direct ways to use social media to meet these goals. Measurement tools were indicated at the beginning of implementation to help

Table 2. Social media activities: fundraising development key strategies

Diversify Donor/Supporter Base and Increase Donation by 43%			
Objective	**Task**	**Measurement Tool**	**Results**
Gain a minimum of 50 new donors during social media driven fundraising campaign	Gather database of usable templates and documents for launching a social media campaign driven fundraising campaign	Was database created?	Yes. The database consisted of 30 graphic images to be shared on social media sites throughout the campaign and accompanying verbiage for each platform.
	Develop strategic plan and formal procedures for managing social media giving campaign	Was plan developed?	Yes. All posts were scheduled in advance and times were chosen based on analytics of when followers were most active. Staff also developed a plan for using small amounts of money to boost posts strategically throughout the campaign.
	Promote event via email, website, and social media	Were segmented email groups created?	Yes. Donors were segmented according to interests based on their tags and self-identified interests.
		Number of emails sent to segmented groups	Two emails were sent to all contacts (kick-off and final appeal); two emails were sent to each targeted group throughout the campaign with targeted appeals
		Was campaign specific donation page established?	Yes. This page contained information about each giving level and donor incentives
	Implement campaign during designated time span	Was campaign implemented?	Yes
	Maintain detailed records of social media and donor activity before, during, and after the campaign	Was data stored from Facebook, Google, and Twitter analytics?	Yes

continued on following page

Table 2. Continued

Increase Online Visibility and Maintain an Impactful Online/Social Media Presence			
Objective	**Task**	**Measurement Tool**	**Results**
Create and maintain a CHOICES blog with a minimum of 100 views per post.	Develop formal plan, schedule, and processes for CHOICES' blog.	Was plan developed?	Yes
	Implement and maintain blog using ModX platform	Was blog developed? -Number of posts	Yes, 11 posts as of 5/1/2016
	Develop and implement matrix for review of blog content to ensure it is on brand and tells a consistent story	Was matrix developed?	Yes. All posts must be related to the following topics: reproductive and sexual freedom, health, justice, and rights; sexual and/or gender identity; racial and social justice; personal stories related to any of the above topics
	Develop and implement process to track and store data related to blog traffic	Was data collected from google analytics?	Yes.
Increase social media followers by 20% (over entire fundraising year) and increase monthly interactions by 10%	Using social media templates and guides from Hootsuite and the National Coalition for Sexual Health (NCSH), develop and implement schedule and procedure for posting content on social media sites.	n/a	CHOICES decided not use a third party service
	Develop and implement matrix to ensure all social media posts are on brand and telling consistent story	Was matrix created?	Yes
	Determine ad budget for promotion of posts on social media sites	Was budget developed?	Yes, $250 per year used to promote mission-critical posts, fundraising posts, and special event posts
	Develop and implement strategic schedule for the use of ad budget to promote social media content	Was schedule developed?	Yes.

continued on following page

Table 2. Continued

Increase page visits to CHOICES' website by 10% during fundraising year	Establish procedure for tracking webpage visit data and ensure Development Staff has access to this data	Was procedure developed?	Yes. Data is stored and reported in Google analytics and reviewed by community partnerships team and website developer at monthly meetings.
	Employ strategic keywords and small portion of ad budget to increase CHOICES' position on Google searches	n/a	This was not yet implemented because the web developer recommended waiting until the new website was functional.
Produce Effective Fundraising Events and Increase Event Revenue by 5%			
Objective	**Task**	**Measurement Tool**	**Results**
Increase CONDOMONIUM revenue by 5%	Request that community partners and other stakeholders promote the event via social media	Did community partners share event?	Yes. Focus Magazine, The Unleashed Voice media group, Healthy & Free TN, MGLCC, and many board members, staff, and volunteers shared the event.
Launch *CHOICES Presents* ... Happy Hour series with a minimum of three events	Promote event via signage, CiviCRM, email blasts, and social media posts	n/a	CHOICES discontinued the happy hour series after one event because it cost more to produce than was earned.

determine if the tasks were having the desired effect. The results were reviewed periodically throughout the year in order to make adjustments if needed.

In addition to measuring the results of the different tasks, CHOICES staff members also measured the results of the overall objectives. Table 3 lists all of the objectives and their results. During the ten months the plan has been implemented, CHOICES has met or surpassed almost all of the social media oriented objectives of the plan. Not only has the organization seen more interactions with its social media posts, but also an increase in funds raised from long-term donors as well as new friends. The only goal that has not shown significant improvement is website visits. The organization hopes that a forthcoming website update and corresponding strategies will help reach this goal in the next two quarters. While some may suggest that ten months is not a long enough time to determine success, Kent (2011) suggests it only takes three to six months for organizations to see meaning in their analytic data.

Table 3. Objectives and results

CHOICES Outcomes	
Objective	**Results**
Gain a minimum of 50 new donors during social media driven fundraising campaign (goal $5,000)	Between Oct. 14, 2015 and May 5, 2016, CHOICES has a total of 90 first time donors. The organization raised $9,000 during the Fall 2015 campaign, 80% more than goal.
Increase social media followers by 20% (over entire fundraising year) and increase monthly interactions by 10%	From June 2015 to May 2016, the number of followers to the CHOICES Facebook page increased by 44%. In the period from June 1, 2015 to December 31, 2015, CHOICES average organic FB post reach was 265. For the period from January, 2016 to May 1, 2016, it was 837, an increase of 215%.
Increase page visits to CHOICES' website by 10% during fundraising year	CHOICES did not meet this goal. Pageviews, sessions, and new visit percentages remained stagnant. The organization hopes the launch of the new website and the launch of its Google Ad Words profile, this will change for the next two quarters.
Increase CONDOMONIUM revenue by 5%	CHOICES exceeded this goal in 2016 by raising $9,000 more than the previous year, an increase of 53% more than the previous year.
Create and maintain a CHOICES blog with a minimum of 100 views per post	8 of the 11 blog posts have between 100 and 480 unique views.

CHALLENGES

As this was the first time creating such a detailed development plan and incorporating social media as a critical part of building organizational awareness and support, it is not surprising that staff met some challenges along the way. Several of these challenges stemmed from changes in the organization's overall plans. For example, the initial plan indicated using social media for an advocacy event. However, a joint grant that was awarded changed the direction of the event and related social media objectives.

Other challenges arose when proposed strategies were not working and were either discontinued or modified. For example, the organization wanted to create a story bank with personal experiences that could be shared to help promote the organization. While 16 stories were collected through social media posts, the format changed to a blog, incorporating a written patient story collection. In addition, a donor cultivation event promoted through social media was discontinued after one time due to high expenses.

Despite these challenges, CHOICES was able to see much success with its strategic use of social media. Although the staff and leadership stayed true to the intent of the plan, they also realized the importance of staying flexible to help meet the broader mission of the organization.

OPPORTUNITIES

Staff members were also able to take advantage of new opportunities through its focus on strategic social media use. For example, the organization created a CHOICES volunteers Facebook group to facilitate better communication with existing volunteers. This opportunity tied closely to the infrastructure goal of developing intentional and active roles for volunteers. However, it was not a task that was created at the beginning of the plan. The organization is now taking advantage of another opportunity by incorporating social media strategy into its sponsorship packages to leverage these relationships. Part of the sponsorship packages now state social media mentions and sharing opportunities for both partners.

CONCLUSION

This chapter demonstrates how a mid-sized nonprofit organization was able to develop and implement a strategic development plan that incorporated social media as a key element of the plan. CHOICES benefitted from hiring a new staff member dedicated to social media that took the time to research social media strategy before implementing a plan. As noted in the literature, it is important for a nonprofit organization to acknowledge that the strategic use of social media includes having a staff member dedicated to the coordination of the tool (Barry, 2012).

The success of the plan was in large part due to a few key features. First of all, the organization created a plan and fully incorporated social media. While this may seem like an obvious task to some, too many nonprofit organizations begin using social media tools without a clear plan or understanding of how to use these tools strategically (Wymer and Grau (2011). By having a clear plan, the organization was able to strategically use social media rather than use it in a haphazard way. Second, the organization identified goals and measurement tools from the beginning, then collected data along the way to analyze the results. Wymer and Grau (2011) state that having these things in place at the beginning is key to measuring effectiveness of social media. The goals should be clear and something that can be measured

(Handley & Chapman, 2011). While CHOICES did use some less specific objectives that were tied to the development of new initiatives, it also identified very specific objectives such as gaining a minimum of 50 new donors. Goals such as these are easy to measure and determine the level of success.

Throughout its plan, CHOICES addressed the four critical areas of social media evaluation. First of all, the organization's leaders realized the importance of using social media. As an organization with younger, socially motivated supporters, it is important for CHOICES to look to social media to reinforce current relationships and initiate new support. While a single person was hired with the main responsibility of creating and implementing the social media plan, she coordinated with a number of people throughout the organization's different departments to integrate stories, events, and news into the social media platforms. Most importantly, the organization embraced the idea of creating not only a social media plan but one that allowed for measurable results, while still allowing room for adjustments. As noted in the literature, organization leaders and staff are often deterred from evaluating their social media plans due to a fear of consequences if the goals are not met (Kanter & Paine, 2012). Instead of fearing consequences, the organization created a culture that used the measurement tools to learn and adapt. Lastly, the organization realized early on they needed to increase their capacity to organize a successful social media strategy. In addition to hiring a person dedicated to the task, the organization also incorporated an improved website and fundraising tools.

When looking at the organization's ROI for its social media usage, initial results appear promising. CHOICES achieved tangible results such as an increase in special event revenue and new donors. In addition, CHOICES also achieved intangible results such as increasing the number of followers and reaching more people via posts on Facebook. As noted by Kanter (2010), it is important that nonprofit leaders keep in mind both the tangible and intangible returns of impact. While the intangible impacts may not be felt immediately, they are part of the relationship building aspect of social media that can lead to long-term impact. As the organization continues to expand its reach, it now has a larger base of supporters that can help share its message.

As a case study, the results that CHOICES had cannot be generalizable to the larger nonprofit sector. Each organization must identify its own audience and the best way to reach them. However, nonprofit leaders can take a lesson from CHOICES and how it incorporated a social media plan into its larger development plan, created measurable objectives from the beginning, and collected data along the way. Through these activities, CHOICES was able to successfully increase its fundraising efforts, allowing the organization to better meet its mission.

REFERENCES

Aaker, J., & Smith, A. (2010). The dragonfly effect: Quick, effective, and powerful ways to use social media to drive social change. San Francisco, CA: Jossey-Bass.

Atkinson, R. D., & McKay, A. S. (2007). *Digital prosperity: Understanding the economic benefits of the information technology revolution.* The Information Technology and Innovation Foundation.

Barnes, N. G. (n.d.). Social Media Usage Now Ubiquitous Among US Top Charities, Ahead of All Other Sectors. Center for Marketing Research. *University of Massachusetts.*

Barnes, N. G., & Lescault, A. M. (n.d.). Executives Concerned about ROI, Name Facebook Most Effective, Blogs Continue Decline: The 2015 Inc. 500 and Social Media. Center for Marketing Research. *University of Massachusetts.*

Barry, F. (2012). *2012 Nonprofit social networking benchmark report.* Academic Press.

Brigida, D., & Colman, J. D. (2010). How successful are your social media efforts? In *Internet Management for Nonprofits: Strategies, Tools, & Trade Secrets. (181 – 202).* Hoboken, NJ: John Wiley & Sons.

Briones, R. L., Kuch, B., Liu, F., & Jin, Y. (2011). Keeping up with the digital age: How the American Red Cross uses social media to build relationships. *Public Relations Review, 37*(1), 37–43. doi:10.1016/j.pubrev.2010.12.006

Curtis, L., Edwards, C., Fraser, K. L., Gudelsky, S., Holmquist, J., Thornston, K., & Sweetser, K. (2010). Adoption of social media for public relations by nonprofit organizations. *Public Relations Review, 36*(1), 90–92. doi:10.1016/j.pubrev.2009.10.003

Davis, C. (2013). *An Analysis of Financially Successful Special Fundraising Events* (Master's Thesis). University of Akron.

Dawes, S., Cresswell, A., & Pardopublic, T. (2009). From need to know to need to share: Tangled problems, information boundaries, and the building of public sector knowledge networks. *Public Administration Review, 69*(3), 63–84. doi:10.1111/j.1540-6210.2009.01987_2.x

Eyrich, N., Padman, M. L., & Sweetser, K. D. (2008). PR practitioners use of social media tools and communication technology. *Public Relations Review, 34*(4), 412–414. doi:10.1016/j.pubrev.2008.09.010

Falkheimer, J., & Heide, M. (2010). Crisis communicators in change: From plans to improvisations. In Handbook of crisis communication (pp. 511-526). Academic Press.

Fernandez, S., & Rainey, H. (2006). Managing successful organizational change in the public sector. *Public Administration Review*, *66*(2), 168–176. doi:10.1111/j.1540-6210.2006.00570.x

Greene, S. (2001). Astride the digital divide. *The Chronicle of Philanthropy*, *13*(6), 18–19.

Grønbjerg, K. (1991). Managing grants and contracts: The case of four nonprofit social service organizations [Electronic version]. *Nonprofit and Voluntary Sector Quarterly*, *20*(1), 5–24. doi:10.1177/089976409102000103

Guo, C., & Saxton, G. D. (2013). Tweeting social change: How social media are changing nonprofit advocacy. *Nonprofit and Voluntary Sector Quarterly*.

Hallahan, K., Holtzhausen, D., Van Ruler, B., Verčič, D., & Sriramesh, K. (2007). Defining strategic communication. *International Journal of Strategic Communication*, *1*(1), 3–35. doi:10.1080/15531180701285244

Handley, A., & Chapman, C. C. (2011). *Content Rules: How to Create Killer Blogs, Webinars, (and More) that Engage Customers and Ignite Your Business*. Hoboken, NJ: John Wiley & Sons, Inc.

Heller Baird, C., & Parasnis, G. (2011). From social media to social customer relationship management. *Strategy and Leadership*, *39*(5), 30–37. doi:10.1108/10878571111161507

Howard, A. (2011). 2011 Gov 2.0 year in review: A look at the Gov 2.0 themes, moments and achievements that made an impact in 2011. *O'Reilly Radar*. Retrieved from http://radar.oreilly.com/2011/12/2011-gov2-year-in-review.html

Kanter, B. (2010). The ROI of Social Media: The "I" stands for insight and impact. In T. Hart, S. MacLaughlin, J. M. Greenfield, & P. H. Greier Jr., (Eds.), *Internet Management for Nonprofits: Strategies, Tools, & Trade Secrets*. Hoboken, NJ: John Wiley & Sons.

Kanter, B., & Paine, K. D. (2012). *Measuring the networked nonprofit: Using data to change the world*. John Wiley & Sons.

Kent, M. L., Carr, B. J., Husted, R. A., & Pop, R. A. (2011). Learning web analytics: A tool for strategic communication. *Public Relations Review*, *37*(5), 563–543. doi:10.1016/j.pubrev.2011.09.011

King, C. (2010). Emergent communication strategies. *International Journal of Strategic Communication, 4*(1), 19–38. doi:10.1080/15531180903415814

Leighninger, M. (2011). Citizenship and governance in a wild, wired world: How should citizens and public managers use online tools to improve democracy? *National Civic Review, 100*(2), 20–29. doi:10.1002/ncr.20056

Levinson, J. C., Adkins, F., & Forbes, C. (2010). *Guerrilla Marketing for Nonprofits. 250 Tactics to Promote, Recruit, Motivate, and Raise More Money.* Entrepreneur Press.

Linden, R. (2010). *Leading across boundaries: Creating collaborative agencies in a networked world.* San Francisco, CA: Jossey-Bass.

MacLaughlin, S. (2010). Demystifying online metrics: Understanding the hits, clicks, and errors. In T. Hart, S. MacLaughlin, J. M. Greenfield, & P. H. Greier Jr., (Eds.), *Internet Management for Nonprofits: Strategies, Tools, & Trade Secrets.* Hoboken, NJ: John Wiley & Sons.

MacNamara, J., & Zerfass, A. (2012). Social media communication in organizations: The challenges of balancing openness, strategy, and management. *International Journal of Strategic Communication, 6*(4), 287–308. doi:10.1080/155311 8X.2012.711402

McPhee, P., & Bare, J. (2001). Introduction. In C. J. De Vita & C. Fleming (Eds.), *Building Capacity in Nonprofit Organizations* (pp. 1–4). Washington, DC: Urban Institute.

Menzel, D. (2010). Ethics moments in government: Cases and controversies. Boca Raton, FL: Taylor & Francis.

M+R. (2014). *2014 M+R Benchmarks.* Available from http://www.mrbenchmarks.com

Munnukka, J., & Järvi, P. (2013). *Perceived risks and risk management of social media in an organizational context.* Institute of Information Management, University of St. Gallen.

Obar, J., Zube, P., & Lampe, C. (2011). *Advocacy 2.0: An analysis of how advocacy groups in the United States perceive and use social media as tools for facilitating civic engagement and collective action.* Social Science Research Network. Retrieved from: http://ssrn.com/abstract=1956352

Ojoa, A., Esteveza, E., & Janowskia, T. (2010). Semantic interoperability architecture for governance 2.0. *Information Polity, 15,* 105–123.

Orlikowski, W., & Scott, S. (2009). Sociomateriality: Challenging the separation of technology, work and organization. *The Academy of Management Annals, 2*(1), 433–474. doi:10.1080/19416520802211644

Pallotta, D. (2008). Uncharitable. Medford, MA: Tufts University Press.

Pope, J., Isely, A., & Asamoa-Tutu, F. (2009, April). Developing a marketing strategy for nonprofit organizations: An exploratory study. *Journal of Nonprofit & Public Sector Marketing, 21*(2), 184–201. doi:10.1080/10495140802529532

Pynes, J. (2009). Human resources management for public and nonprofit organizations. San Francisco, CA: Jossey-Bass.

Salamon, L. (2003). *The resilient sector.* Washington, DC: Brookings Institution Press.

Schaefer, G., & Hersey, L. N. (2015). Enhancing Organizational Capacity and Strategic Planning Through the Use of Social Media. In Cases on Strategic Social Media Utilization. Hershey, PA: IGI Global.

Sherman, A. (2011). How law enforcement agencies are using social media to better serve the public. *Mashable.* Retrieved from: http://mashable.com/2011/08/31/law-enforcement- social-media-use/

Shirky, C. (2008). *Here comes everybody: the power of organizing without organizations.* New York, N.Y.: Penguin Books.

Torp, S. (2011). *The strategic turn: On the history and broadening of the strategy concept in communication.* Paper presented at the International Communication Association 2011 pre-conference, Strategic communication: A concept at the Center of Applied Communications, Boston, MA.

Walker, M. (2011). *Disaster response increasingly linked to social media.* Fierce-GovernmentIT.

Waters, R. D. (2010). The Use of Social Media by Nonprofit Organizations: An Examination from the Diffusion of Innovations Perspective. In T. Dumova, & R. Fiordo (Eds.), Handbook of Research on Social Interaction Technologies and Collaboration Software: Concepts and Trends (pp. 473-485). Hershey, PA: Information Science Reference.

Waters, R. D., & Jamal, J. Y. (2011). Tweet, tweet, tweet: A content analysis of nonprofit organizations Twitter updates. *Public Relations Review, 37*(3), 321–324. doi:10.1016/j.pubrev.2011.03.002

West, M. (2011, February 20). How nonprofits can use social media to spark change. *The Chronicle of Philanthropy.*

Wymer, W., & Grau, S. (2011). *Connected Causes: Online Marketing Strategies for Nonprofit Organizations.* Chicago, IL: Lyceum Books.

Zerfass, A., Fink, S., & Linke, A. (2011, March). Social Media Governance: Regulatory frameworks as drivers of success in online communications. In *Pushing the envelope in public relations theory and research and advancing practice,14th International Public Relations Research Conference* (pp. 1026-1047). Gainesville, FL: Institute for Public Relations.

Zerfass, A., Tench, R., Verhoeven, P., Verčič, D., & Moreno, A. (2010). *European communication monitor 2010. Status quo and challenges for public relations in Europe. Results of an empirical survey in 46 countries.* Helios Media.

Chapter 9

Nonprofit Organizations and Social Media Use:
An Analysis of Nonprofit Organizations' Effective Use of Social Media Tools

Aminata Sillah
Towson University, USA

ABSTRACT

The use of social media technologies such as Facebook, Twitter, Instagram, and LinkedIn has enhanced and increased the communication and engagement strategies available to nonprofit organizations. This chapter focuses on and addresses the question of nonprofit use of social media by examining the main objectives for using social media, and whether social media has been effective in meeting these objectives. Existing research on nonprofit social media use tends to focus on finding out which social media tools nonprofit organizations are using and which one of these yields the most impact. To answer these questions, descriptive analysis is conducted on social media technologies and their usage to identify associations between effectiveness of social media in meeting objectives. These questions go beyond asking why nonprofit organizations use social media and analyzes how they meet their objectives using various social media tools.

DOI: 10.4018/978-1-5225-1963-8.ch009

INTRODUCTION

For many organizations, "social media" is a buzzword that signals the organization's ability to reach its audience. In the nonprofit sector, the use of social-media technologies such as Facebook, Twitter, and LinkedIn has enhanced and increased communication and engagement strategies. Social media is a generic term for a collection of tools and platforms with which users can communicate, connect, and share content (Kanter & Fine, 2008). The rapid increase in social-media applications has made it difficult for most nonprofit organizations to keep pace, thus creating a knowledge gap for nonprofit organizations that want to integrate social media into their operations.

Most nonprofit organizations provide resources to strengthen communities and connect people to resources within their communities. Social media may make it easier to engage with stakeholders and recruit new supporters of the organization. Stakeholders are those with any interest in the organization, including volunteers, donors, and users of its services. Despite the growing use of social-media applications, what has not been explored is how nonprofit organizations have used social media, the main objectives they hope to achieve by using them, and how effectively they use those tools to achieve those objectives.

This research focuses on nonprofit organizations' use of social media and how various social-media tools affect the organization's mission. The purpose of this research is to better understand the main objective of using social media, and how effectively social media help nonprofit organizations meet their larger objectives. In a practical sense, understanding these insights is critically important. For nonprofit executives and directors, it is essential to understand how to reach, activate, and mobilize various stakeholders.

BACKGROUND

Extant literature on what motivates nonprofit organizations to utilize social media includes studies of how they use those applications, with their inherently interactive and decentralized structure, as a strategic tool to communicate and coordinate with important stakeholders, conduct advocacy, raise funds, and engage with the public (Edwards & Hoefer, 2010; Lovejoy & Saxton, 2012; MacAulay, 2009; Waters & Jamal, 2011). Other research on nonprofit organizations' use of social media has examined frequency of usage (Guo & Saxton, 2012), and the degree and breadth of nonprofit use of online content (Saxton, Guo, & Brown, 2007).

For example, Guo and Saxton (2012) examined the prevalence and frequency of advocacy messages in tweets from nonprofits to followers. Other studies suggest that social media applications can influence how nonprofit organizations conduct fundraising, communicate with stakeholders, and build networks (Briones, Kuch, Liu, & Jin, 2011; Guo & Saxton, 2013; Saxton & Wang, 2013). Yet, there is limited systematic empirical study on the main objectives for nonprofit organizations' use of social media, and whether or not social media have been effective in achieving the objectives of nonprofit organizations. With rare exceptions (Saurez, 2010; Saxton, Guo, & Brown, 2007), the understanding of nonprofits' social-media use relies on static collection of information displayed on some of the nonprofit organizations' websites. The literature has not yet examined objectives of social-media use, and nonprofits' perception of the effectiveness of social media in accomplishing their missions in a systematic manner.

This research seeks to fill that gap by examining the current use of social media by nonprofit organizations, in terms of the main objectives for using social media, the effectiveness of diverse social-media tools, and how effective social media is in enabling organizations to serve beneficiaries, communicate and collaborate with stakeholders, and manage their internal processes. To answer these questions, this research analyzes data from a survey entitled *Use and Effectiveness of Social Media among Nonprofit Organizations*, conducted by the Bridgespan Group (2014).

The descriptive analysis resulting from this research contributes to the current literature on nonprofit use of social media. It will help nonprofit organizations understand why they use social media, and more effectively plan how to use it. Furthermore, the results may help nonprofit organizations link their current use of social media to their objectives for using it more efficiently.

Nonprofits and Social-Media Use

Nonprofit organizations are critically involved in the social, political, and economic fabric of society. They provide a channel through which individuals can participate in the democratic process, connect with their communities, deliver and receive needed services, and fund projects, along with making a difference through volunteerism. They differ significantly from the for-profit sector in terms of mission orientation, sources of funding, governance structure, stakeholders, measures of success, and the environments in which they operate. As nonprofit organizations seek to continue to be relevant and competitive in the provision of crucial services for society, they must recognize and adopt innovative strategies to help them deal with challenges they encounter (Saxton & Guo, 2011; Hackler & Saxton; 2007; Kanter & Fine,

2010). Thus, many nonprofit organizations see social media as innovative tools that will give them a competitive edge and help in engaging with stakeholders, funders, and volunteers (Waters et al., 2009; Kanter & Fine, 2010). Understanding the main objectives for nonprofit organizations' use of social media and the effectiveness of social media in meeting those objectives can help nonprofit professionals understand the positive impact of social media, build strategies to better use social media, and possibly lead to more active engagement of stakeholders and donors (Reddick & Ponomariov, 2013).

What motivates nonprofit organizations to adopt and utilize social media is not exactly clear. However, recent studies suggest that social-media applications create leverage for core nonprofit functions, including stakeholder communication and advocacy, building networks (collaboration), communicating with the public, service delivery, and fundraising and donor engagement (Briones, Kuch, Liu, & Jin, 2011; Guo & Saxton, 2013; Saxton & Wang, 2013; Johns Hopkins, 2010; Idealware, 2011). The goal of most nonprofit organizations is to fulfill their social mission by adding some form of public value. One way nonprofit organizations go about meeting this objective is through making some strategic choices related to communication that they will utilize to create mission awareness (Hackler & Saxton, 2007). Furthermore, Waters (2010) indicates that increasing awareness of the purpose of a nonprofit organization will benefit the organization by increasing donations, volunteers, and the number of program participants. Thus, social media provide nonprofit organizations with the necessary platform to spread the word about their mission and goals. As technology proliferate every aspect of doing business, the necessity of social media in reaching a large audience cannot be overstated. As baby boomers retire and millennials – a generation known as the "sharing generation," it behooves nonprofit organizations to reach this audience with the mission and objectives and provide them the platform to raise awareness of the mission of the nonprofit.

Many nonprofit organizations have adopted social media as an effective tool to advocate for social change, promoting their cause by encouraging their supporters to use Facebook and Twitter to "spread the word." Social-media networks have the ability to expand nonprofit advocacy efforts by extending their reach into partners' advocacy networks, identifying new networks of community stakeholders, and mobilizing those individuals to take action (Guo & Saxton, 2012).

One strategy that nonprofits employ to fulfill their social mission is fundraising and donor engagement. Kanter and Fine (2010) suggest that nonprofit advocacy might benefit from leveraging social media to recruit new donors, communicate more effectively with established stakeholders, and develop partnerships with like-minded organizations to more effectively influence public policy. A recent study by Reddick and Ponomariov (2013) revealed that social media are functioning as potential means of increasing levels of participation in the organization, which may influence charitable giving. In his essay, Flandez (2010) described how the March of Dimes implemented a two-year social-media strategy to drive community involvement and donations.

Social media have provided nonprofit organizations with new platforms for communicating with supporters. Social media allow nonprofits to determine their form of communication, frequency of communication, and level of interaction. Waters and Jamal (2011) examined how 501(c)3 philanthropic organizations communicate on Twitter, and found that although large numbers of nonprofit organizations were using Twitter as a tool, they used it only to disseminate information, rather than to open up a new line of two-way communication between them and their stakeholders and followers. Social media can affect how nonprofit organizations not only communicate with stakeholders, but also interact with their peers. In their book *The Dragonfly Effect*, Aaker et al. (2010) demonstrate how the use of social media can help accomplish certain social changes. One of the individuals whose case the authors profiled was a young Stanford University student suffering from leukemia, whose friends used social media to solicit bone-marrow donors. In an attempt to help one individual, social media made it possible for hundreds of people to benefit from the social media activities of the student and his friends. Saxton et al. (2007) note that nonprofit organizations have the ability to connect their stakeholders to their mission, and that smart use of social media may lead to higher levels of public trust and accountability. That research examined 117 community foundations, and found that they were targeting online communications only toward grant seekers, donors, and their community. Extending their understanding of social media use by nonprofit organizations, Waters et al. (2009) conducted a content analysis of 275 nonprofit organizations' Facebook pages, and indicated that although these organizations sought transparency, they often failed to utilize the full benefit and potential of social media.

Nonprofit service-delivery processes should make it easy for service beneficiaries to access and use services offered by the organization. According to a Johns Hopkins report (2010), nearly all nonprofit organizations use some form of technology to deliver services to clients. This may take the form of tracking numbers of clients in a database, having an updated website, or emailing notifications to clients on new programs and services. Integrating social media into nonprofit service delivery provides an opportunity to increase service delivery and achieve better outreach (Johns Hopkins, 2010).

Though the use of social media is on the rise, there are costs associated with the adoption of social media. Even before using social media, nonprofit organizations have to take stock of their resources and capacity, choose the type of social media in which to engage, and decide how frequently they will engage with stakeholders for matters of maintenance and update. Extant research has shown that organizational size is an important factor in determining access to technology and the technological capacity of nonprofit organizations (Hackler & Saxton, 2007; Schneider, 2003). Thus, the size of the organization and its resources (human and financial) may affect how the organization uses social media.

While there is no doubt that social media have been transforming the nonprofit sector, recent research suggests that, compared to the for-profit sector, nonprofit organizations are using social media less frequently over time. Moreover, only a few nonprofits are successfully using social media to accomplish their missions (Saurez, 2010). Understanding the potential of social media and having the resources and capacity to realize their full benefit may help nonprofit organizations align their organizational objectives, processes, and practices. While social media hold significant promise, nonprofit organizations should use them in focused and intentional ways that have been shown to be effective.

The following section describes the data and methodology of research into the current use of social media by nonprofit organizations, and the main objectives of that use. Data is from a survey entitled Use *and Effectiveness of Social Media among Nonprofit Organizations*, conducted by the Bridgespan Group (2014).

METHODS AND DATA

This research was descriptive. The purpose was not to formally test any hypotheses, but to generate directions for future research into nonprofits and social-media use. Descriptive analysis allows the researcher to summarize, organize, and describe quantitative data (Vogt, 1999). This study is based on an online survey of nonprofit organizations on use of social media. The Bridgespan Group, a 501c(3) nonprofit capacity-building organization, conducted descriptive analysis to explore the research questions. The survey, *Use and Effectiveness of Social Media among Nonprofit Organizations*, produced the sample for this research, which consisted of 264 nonprofit organizations. We found that the majority of the responding nonprofit organizations in the sample (84%) are 501(c)(3) charitable organizations. That is, of the 264 organizations surveyed, 84% identified as being 501(c)(3) charitable organizations Nonprofit organizations in our sample vary in scope, size, and budget, ranging from organizations operated by volunteers to those with budgets over $25 million. The average budget of these organizations was $3 million. Organizations in the sample covered a wide range of missions in the areas of education, health, arts/culture, the environment, and civil society. The survey consisted of four areas of inquiry related to responders' experience with social media, and perceived effectiveness of social media in meeting their expectations and achieving their objectives for use of social media.

Findings

Based on responses, we found 8.3% of nonprofit organizations answering the survey did not use any social media tools. Among nonprofit organizations that used social media for some functions, 242 responded that they utilize social media mainly for information sharing and for social and professional networks. The distribution of the ways nonprofit organizations use social media is shown in Table 1.

The survey asked questions regarding how nonprofit organizations were currently using social media tools and platforms—blogs, Twitter, YouTube, GIS, Facebook, Myspace, wikis, interactive online games, Google Docs, among others. These tools and platform usage were broken down into five categories: information sharing (Twitter, YouTube), social and professional networks (Facebook, LinkedIn), collaboration and coordinating platforms (Google Docs), virtual interaction platforms (Online Games), information management (news feeds) and data analysis tools (GIS). In the category related to information sharing, 79% of the organizations indicated that social media as an information-sharing tool was used either fully or consistently in their work. Of that 79%, nearly 13% described their current usage of social media as an information-sharing tool that was fully integrated in their work.

We realized that these 13% use Twitter, YouTube, and blogs as a means of disseminating information to stakeholders. This finding was surprising, since

Table 1. Current use of social media

How Would You Describe Your Organization's Current Usage of Following Social Media Tools?	Percentage	Number of Responses
Information sharing (Twitter and YouTube)	79%	263
Social and professional networks (Facebook and LinkedIn)	81%	263
Collaboration and coordinating platforms (Google Docs)	56%	263
Virtual interaction platforms (Online Games)	8%	259
Information management (News Feed)	41%	252
Data analysis tools (GIS)	35%	256

Facebook, which is considered the most popular social-media platform, was used in a consistent manner by less than half (48%) of respondents. We also found that 81% of nonprofits that responded to the survey answered that they use social media for social and professional network purposes, either fully or consistently in their organizations. Nonprofit organizations were also using social media as a tool for collaborating and coordinating with stakeholders. Of the respondents surveyed within this category, 56% were using collaboration platforms such as Google Docs, Evite, and message boards at least "a little bit" in their work. However, nearly 45% were not currently using collaboration and coordinating platforms in their work. This finding is noteworthy when we consider that nonprofit organizations tend to collaborate on and coordinate many of their activities to support their social cause. The findings regarding information management (news feeds) were interesting, because only 41% of nonprofit organizations were currently using social media for information management. This finding seems to indicate that there is a disconnect between the current use of social media and how nonprofit organizations are getting information out to their stakeholders. Social media has been cited as important to improving external communication and stakeholder engagement (Waters and Jamal, 2011). By not using social media as information management platforms, nonprofit organizations run the risk of isolating important stakeholders such as donors, volunteers, and program recipients.

Of the nonprofit organizations surveyed, all those that stated they were using at least one social media tool or platform were asked what their main objectives were for using social media. Nearly 62% of all respondents stated that the main objective for using social media was to build awareness of their organization or mission. This finding is consistent with the literature, because most nonprofit organizations use social media for engaging with stakeholders and furthering their mission. Fifty-three percent responded that their main objective was to enhance communications/relationships with their beneficiaries/audiences.

This finding is also consistent with the literature, because social media provide nonprofit organizations with new platforms for communicating with supporters (Waters and Jamal, 2011). Less than 41% stated that they were using social media to better collaborate with supporters, influencers, volunteers, and peer organizations. Only 17% stated that their main objective for using social media was to deliver programs and services. This finding was interesting, because the delivery of programs and services via social media, covered in the literature, suggests that nearly all nonprofit organizations use some form of technology to deliver services to clients, either through email or their website (Johns Hopkins, 2010). Another interesting finding was that 19% of the respondents indicated that their main objective in using social media was to make their internal work processes more effective. This finding could be a link to the issue of capacity. According to Hackler and Saxton (2007), most nonprofit organizations lack the capacity to effectively make strategic use of technology. On the other hand, 25% considered fundraising as their main objective for using social media. It is interesting that only 25% of respondents saw fundraising as one of the main objectives of using social media, since a vast majority of them (81%) identified themselves as using social and professional networks. This finding supports the literature that nonprofit organizations have not incorporated all the benefits of Facebook applications in social networking (Waters, Burnett, Lamm, & Lucas, 2009). Social media provide a platform for nonprofit organizations to fundraise, but without the right capacity, no matter the number of "likes" on Facebook, they would not translate into money for meeting the social mission of the organization, nor add public value.

While research on nonprofit fundraising and community involvement documents the initial successes of using social media, the literature suggests that nonprofit organizations have historically had difficulty implementing successful social-media strategies to impact their mission (Yang and Callahan 2007). Thus, for social media to help nonprofit organizations further their goals, the organizations must tie social media into their broader mission. Table 2 represents the distribution of these responses.

Respondents were asked about the effectiveness of social media tools such as YouTube, Facebook, GIS, Google Docs, and news feeds in achieving the objectives of their organizations. Four options were given to respondents to rate the effectiveness of social media in achieving organizational objectives, ranging from "extremely effective" to "not at all effective." Of the 168 respondents using social media tools such as Twitter and YouTube as an information-sharing tool to meet organizational objectives, 22% found it "extremely effective," while 28% found these tools "somewhat effective." Respondents using Facebook and LinkedIn as professional networking tools to meet objectives (27%, N=172) also found that

Table 2. Main objective of using social media

What Are Your Organization's Main Objective(s) for Using Social Media?	Percentage	Number of Responses
Communications	53%	107
Build Awareness of Organization	62%	163
Collaboration	41%	107
Fundraiser	25%	67
Program and Service Delivery	17%	46

social media were "extremely effective" in meeting the objectives of the organization. Most of the respondents using social media in the capacities listed below found social media to be "effective" in meeting the objectives of the organization. Table 3 provides the breakdown of the effectiveness of social-media usage. It is interesting that while 81% of the nonprofit organizations currently use social media tools (Twitter and Facebook), only 22% found these tools effective in meeting the objectives of their organization. Furthermore, while 84% (N=184) of respondents found online interactive games (virtual social media interaction tools) "effective" in meeting their objectives, less than 8% are currently using these tools.

The survey included questions related to how social media allow nonprofit organizations to serve their beneficiaries (individuals or entities that directly or indirectly benefit from the work of the organization). Of those who responded to this question, 88% (N=140) agreed that social media allowed them to more effectively communicate with existing beneficiaries. Nearly 84% (N=138) agreed that social media allowed them to more effectively identify and reach new beneficiaries. A total of 72% (N=130) agreed that social media was effective in allowing them to effectively deliver programs and services to their beneficiaries. On the other hand, 28% (N= 132) disagreed that social media allowed them to gain better understanding of the characteristics and/or needs of their beneficiaries. Table 4 describes the respondents' answers. A high proportion of respondents in each category agreed

Table 3. Evaluating social media tools

How Effective Have Each of the Following Social Media Tools Been in Achieving Your Main Objectives Indicated Above? (1 = Not at All Effective; 5 = Extremely Effective)				
Social Media Tool/Platform	**Extremely Effective**	**Effective**	**Somewhat Effective**	**Not at all Effective**
Twitter, YouTube, (Information-sharing tools)	22%	43%	28%	7%
Facebook, LinkedIn, (Social and professional networks tools)	27%	38%	28%	6%
Message boards, Google Docs (Collaboration and coordination platforms)	10%	62%	21%	7%
Interactive online games (Virtual interaction platforms)	1%	84%	6%	9%
News feeds (Information management tools)	5%	70%	17%	8%
GIS/mapping tools (Data analysis tools)	13%	67%	13%	7%

Table 4. Evaluating beneficiary outcomes

Important Social Media Interaction							
In Working to Serve Our Beneficiaries Social Media Allow Us to...	Strongly Agree	Agree	Disagree	Strongly Disagree	Proportion of:		N
					Agree	Disagree	
Better understand the characteristics and/or needs of our beneficiaries	27	68	34	3	72%	28%	132
More effectively identify and reach new beneficiaries	39	77	20	2	84%	16%	138
More effectively communicate with existing beneficiaries	50	73	16	1	88%	12%	140
More effectively deliver programs and services to our beneficiaries	25	68	33	4	72%	28%	130

that social media was effective in communicating with beneficiaries, identifying and reaching new beneficiaries, delivering program and services, and understanding the characteristics of beneficiaries. This reiterates how social media has permeated the nonprofit sector.

Six options were given to respondents regarding how social media allow non-profit organizations to communicate and collaborate with their stakeholders (influencers, supporters, volunteers, peer organizations). Most of the respondents (96%, N=140) agreed that social media allowed them to effectively communicate and stay connected with stakeholders. This was followed by 92% of respondents (N=140) indicating that social media allowed them to engage stakeholders as active participants in the work of the organization. Respondents (92%, N= 137) further noted that social media effectively allowed them to identify and connect with new stakeholders. Table 5 further describes the breakdown.

Respondents were asked about how social media allowed them to manage their internal processes and operations. A large proportion of the respondents (74%, N= 99) agreed that social media allowed them to effectively collaborate on their work, using collaboration tools such as Google Documents. Most respondents (71%, N=112) agreed that social media allowed them to effectively share information within their organization, while 63% (N=106) indicated that social media allowed them to better manage and coordinate projects. Table 6 provides a description of responses.

Table 5. Evaluating stakeholder outcomes

In Communicating and Collaborating with Our Stakeholders Social Media Allow Us to...	Strongly Agree	Agree	Disagree	Strongly Disagree	Proportion of:		N
					Agree	Disagree	
Better understand who our stakeholders are and their perspectives on our work	28	82	22	4	81%	19%	136
More effectively communicate and stay connected with stakeholders	48	87	3	2	96%	4%	140
More effectively identify and connect with new stakeholders	43	83	10	1	92%	8%	137
Better engage stakeholders as active participants in our work	42	87	11		92%	8%	140
More effectively understand what our stakeholders are doing and coordinate with their work	22	83	29	4	76%	24%	138
More effectively gather support and/or spur action for a cause	42	78	14	2	88%	12%	16

Organizations in the sample covered a wide range of mission areas, including education, health, arts/culture, the environment, and civil society. Of 155 respondents answering questions related to their organization classification, nearly 18% represented nonprofit organizations that classified themselves as working within the education sector. Only one percent of the respondents classified themselves as a nonprofit organization working within the employment-related sector. Most of the respondents (16%) were classified as human services and community improvement (10%). The distribution of the characteristics of the respondents is found in Table 7.

The average budget of the responding nonprofit organizations was $3 million. Nearly 27% of all respondents had a budget of less than a million dollars. Three percent of respondents reported that they were from an all-volunteer organization

Table 6. Understanding network evaluation

In Managing Our Internal Works Processes and Operations, Social Media Allow Us to...	Strongly Agree	Agree	Disagree	Strongly Disagree	Proportion of:		N
					Agree	Disagree	
More effectively reach internal alignment and/or make decisions (e.g., gather broad staff input and spur internal dialogue on key issues)	10	2	48	5	11%	49%	109
More effectively share information within our organization (e.g., allow everyone to access information anytime, anywhere)	27	53	27	5	71%	29%	112
More effectively collaborate in our work (e.g., use Google documents or wikis)	27	46	22	4	74%	26%	99
More effectively coordinate and manage projects (e.g., keep better track of each other's work)	14	53	34	5	63%	37%	106
Better track and/or manage data in our programs (e.g., gather beneficiaries' outcome data, track website activity).	23	32	28	5	49%	29%	112

and had no budget. This indicates that organizations of various sizes are using social media despite disparities in budget and capacity. Table 8 gives more detail on organizational budget.

FUTURE RESEARCH DIRECTION

Certainly, the ability of nonprofit organizations to engage with social media differs based on their funding, organizational structure and mission. For example, it would

Table 7. Examining organizations

How Would You Classify Your Organization?	Percentage of Organization (N = 155)	Responses
Foundation	5%	8
Arts/culture	8%	13
Education	18%	28
Youth services	6%	10
Health	9%	14
Human services	16%	25
Housing and shelter	6%	9
Philanthropy support	6%	10
Global	5%	7
Community improvement	10%	15
Civil Rights	3%	5
Employment	1%	1
Environment	6%	10

Table 8. Organization resources

Organizational Budget		
What Is the Approximate Annual Budget of Your Organization?	Proportion of Organization (N =172)	Responses
Below $100,000	10%	17
$100,000 – less than $1 Million	27%	46
$1 Million – less than $3 Million	19%	33
$3 Million – less than $5 Million	10%	17
$5 Million – less than $10 Million	10%	17
$10 Million – less than $25 Million	7%	12
$25 Million or more	14%	24
None - all volunteer	3%	6

be interesting to see how budget or the lack thereof relates to the use of social media. Further, future research could also explore whether investing in social media websites for fundraising such as e-marketing would attract new donors or increase the online community of a nonprofit organization. Future research could also explore where social media enhances accountability and in which direction – performance, transparency, or responsiveness.

CONCLUSION

This research aimed to better understand and explain nonprofit organizations' objectives in using social media and whether social media has been effective in meeting stated objectives. The results indicate directions for future research.

REFERENCES

Aaker, J., & Smith, A. (2010). The Dragonfly Effect: Quick, Effective, and Powerful Ways to Use Social Media to Drive Social Change. San Francisco, CA: Jossey-Bass.

Briones, R., Kuch, B., Liu, B., & Jin, Y. (2011). Keeping up with the digital age: How the American Red Cross uses social media to build relationships. *Public Relations Review*, *37*(1), 37–43. doi:10.1016/j.pubrev.2010.12.006

Flandez, R. (2010). Social-media managers help charities spin a web of support. The Chronicle of Philanthropy, 7-9.

Guo, C., & Saxton, G. D. (2010). Voice-in, voice-out: Constituent participation and nonprofit advocacy. *Nonprofit Policy Forum, 1*(1), Article 5. doi:10.2202/2154-3348.1000

Guo, C., & Saxton, G. D. (2012). Tweeting social change: How social media are changing nonprofit advocacy. *Nonprofit and Voluntary Sector Quarterly*.

Hackler, D., & Saxton, G. D. (2007). The Strategic Use of Information Technology by Nonprofit Organizations: Increasing Capacity and Untapped Potential. *Public Administration Review*, *67*(3), 474–487. doi:10.1111/j.1540-6210.2007.00730.x

Kanter, B., & Fine, A. (2010). *The Networked Nonprofit: Connecting with Social Media to Drive Change*. New York, NY: John Wiley & Son.

Lovejoy, K., & Saxton, G. D. (2012). Information, community, and action: How nonprofit organizations use social media. *Journal of Computer-Mediated Communication*, *17*(3), 337–353. doi:10.1111/j.1083-6101.2012.01576.x

Lovejoy, K., Waters, R. D., & Saxton, G. D. (2012). Engaging stakeholders through Twitter: How nonprofit organizations are getting more out of 140 characters or less. *Public Relations Review*, *38*(2), 313–318. doi:10.1016/j.pubrev.2012.01.005

Saxton, G. D., Guo, C., & Brown, W. A. (2007). New dimensions of nonprofit responsiveness: The application and promise of Internet-based technologies. *Public Performance & Management Review.*, *3*(2), 144–173. doi:10.2753/PMR1530-9576310201

Saxton, G. D., & Wang, L. (2013). The social network effect: The determinants of giving through social media. *Nonprofit and Voluntary Sector Quarterly*, 1–19.

Suárez, D. F. (2009). Nonprofit Advocacy and Civic Engagement on the Internet: Administration and Society. Sage Publications.

Chapter 10
Models of Participation in Social Networks

Giulio Angiani
Università di Parma, Italy

Monica Mordonini
Università di Parma, Italy

Paolo Fornacciari
Università di Parma, Italy

Michele Tomaiuolo
Università di Parma, Italy

Eleonora Iotti
Università di Parma, Italy

ABSTRACT

The most important technological trend of the last years has been the rise of social networking systems to social phenomena involving hundreds of millions of people, attracting users from several social groups. Social networking systems blur the distinction between the private and working spheres, and users use such systems both at home and in the workplace, both professionally and with recreational goals. Social networking systems can be equally used to organize a work meeting, a dinner with colleagues or a birthday party with friends. For example, the chat systems that are embedded in social networking platforms are often the most practical way to contact a colleague to ask an urgent question, especially in technologically oriented companies. Moreover, several traditional information systems have been modified in order to include social aspects. Currently, social networking platforms are mostly used without corporate blessing, maintaining their status as feral systems.

DOI: 10.4018/978-1-5225-1963-8.ch010

INTRODUCTION

The most important technological trend of the last years has been the rise of social networking systems to social phenomena involving hundreds of millions of people all around the world, attracting users from several social groups, regardless of age, gender, education, or nationality.

Social networking systems blur the distinction between the private and working spheres, and users are known to use such systems both at home and in the workplace, both professionally and with recreational goals. Social networking systems can be equally used to organize a work meeting, a dinner with the colleagues, or a birthday party with friends. For example, the chat systems that are embedded in social networking platforms are often the most practical way to contact a colleague to ask an urgent question, especially in technologically oriented companies. Moreover, several traditional information systems have been modified in order to include social aspects. Several organizations allow external social networking platforms to be used (e.g., Facebook was available for Microsoft and Apple employees before the general public launch). Some organizations have created an internal social networking platform (DiMicco & Millen, 2007), or allow other social platforms for specific purposes (Millen et al., 2006).

Currently, social networking platforms are mostly used without corporate blessing, maintaining their status as feral systems. According to DiMicco (2008), most users that use social networking platforms for work purposes are primarily interested in accumulating social capital, either for career advancement or to gather support for their own projects inside the company. In order to understand how a social network could be used to increase interactions, information sharing and benefits in teams and organizations, it is useful to refer to analytical models, based on both network topology and users' own interests.

Social networks are typically studied using Social Network Analysis, a discipline that focuses on the structural and topological features of the network. Also, participation in such networks has long been studied as a social phenomenon according to different theories. Understanding the status of a social network, or the usage pattern of an online social networking platform, requires to study the system according to both static and dynamic models. Moreover, the theories of participation in social networks allow users not only to study, but also to guide the dynamics of a given social network.

The chapter is organized in the following way. First, we will describe the different kinds of virtual communities, social media technologies, and applications which are available. Then, we will focus on models and theories of participation in social media, discussing also various models of information spreading and the issue of anti-social behaviours. We will then highlight the challenges faced by organizations and firms in adopting social media, either in internal or public ways. Finally, we will provide some concluding remarks.

TECHNOLOGIES FOR SOCIAL ONLINE COLLABORATION

In general, Computer-Mediated Communication (CMC) is defined as any human communication that occurs through the use of two or more electronic devices (McQuail, 2005). Through CMC, users are able to create various kinds of virtual communities, i.e., networks of users whose connections mainly exist online. In the following paragraphs we discuss the features of the most typical kinds of virtual communities: Virtual Organizations, Virtual Teams, and Online Networks of Practice.

Types of Virtual Communities

Although there are several differences that clearly set the concepts apart, the things that set the different kinds of virtual communities apart are the lack of central authority, their temporary and impromptu nature, and the importance of reputation and trust as opposed to bureaucracy and law.

According to the definition given by Mowshowitz (1994), a Virtual Organization is "a temporary network of autonomous organizations that cooperate based on complementary competencies and connect their information systems to those of their partners via networks aiming at developing, making, and distributing products in cooperation." The term was then popularized by the Grid Computing community, referring to Virtual Organizations as "flexible, secure, coordinated resource sharing among dynamic collections of individuals, institutions, and resources" (Foster et al., 2001). The premise of Virtual Organizations is the technical availability of tools for effective collaboration among people located in different places, but their definition also emphasizes the possibility to share a large number of resources, including documents, data, knowledge and tools among interested people (Poggi & Tomaiuolo, 2010; Bergenti et al., 2005). Their importance is sustained by continuing trends in production and social forms, including the growing number of knowledge workers, the emergence of integrated industrial district and other aspects developing at an international level, like dynamic supply chains, just-in-time production, subcontracting, delocalization, externalization, global logistics and mass migrations which collectively are usually named "*globalization.*"

A Virtual Team, according to Powell et al. (2004), is a "group of geographically, organizationally and/or time dispersed workers brought together by information and telecommunication technologies to accomplish one or more organizational tasks." Virtual Teams can represent organizational structures within the context of Virtual Organizations, but they can also come into existence in other situations, where independent people collaborate on a project, for example an open source software.

An online Network of Practice (or interest) is a group of people who share a profession or a craft, whose main interactions occur through communication networks and tools, including forums and other discussion boards. The creation of the group typically occurs either:

1. In a spontaneous and natural way, because of a common interest of its members, or
2. It can be tailored exclusively to actual practitioners, forged specifically with the goal of sharing and increasing their professional skills and knowledge.

Requirements and Features of Online Social Networks

In OSNs there are at least three distinct functional elements: profile management, social graph management, and content production and discussion. In fact, by definition, a social network cannot lack social graph management and self-presentation, no matter how minimal. On the other hand, virtually no modern OSN lacks the content generation features.

According to these three main functional areas, it is also possible to draw three classifications of the OSNs. The first classification is systems where the profile and social graph management is prevalent. The second classification is systems where the content has a prominent role with respect to social networking activities and there are frequent interactions with people not closely related. The third consideration is systems where the two aspects have roughly the same importance.

The archetypal examples of the first category of systems are business-related and professional OSNs, like LinkedIn. People pay a great deal of attention to detail in creating their profile. In this type of system, there are usually various relationships among users, representing the variety of relationships that members may have in real life. Most users do not visit the site daily and do not add content to the system often (Skeels & Grudin, 2008).

The second type includes blogging, micro-blogging and media sharing websites, like Twitter. The "*follow*" relationships, which are typical for a system of this kind, are usually not symmetric. The focus is in information transmission; often the system does not support a proper profile and sometimes even the contacts may be hidden. Often weak semantic techniques such as Twitter hash-tags are used, in order to read content by subject instead than by author. Through collaborative tagging, the actors of the system may develop a sort of emergent semantics (Mika, 2007), possibly in the form of so-called "*folksonomies.*" Considering that tags usage is a heavy tailed power-law like distribution, i.e., most people actually uses very few tags, collaborative tagging usually produces a good classification of data (Halpin et al., 2007).

The third category includes the personal OSNs, like Facebook. In this type of system, users have a profile, partly public and partly confidential. Frequently, there is only one kind of relation, "*friendship,*" which is symmetric and requires approval by both users. These sites have extremely frequent updates: a noticeable percentage of users perform activities on the system at least on a daily basis.

One of the goals motivating the participation in online communities is the benefit of teamwork over solo work. Various studies (Van de Ven et al., 1976; Malone & Crowstone, 1994) describe the advantages and costs of coordinating team activities. In fact, while an increase in coordination can lead to greater effectiveness, typically it also produces a faster growth of coordination costs. As a consequence, a lot of effort is being devoted in creating tools and technologies that make group work more effective by containing the costs of their coordination. Virtual Teams assembly is another problem that online social platforms can help to solve. In fact, the success of a team depends largely on its assembly process, for identifying the best possible members.

Social collaboration platforms should also help to model and manage multidimensional networks. In fact, apart from direct relationships among people, such platforms should also include other resources. For example, in the area of academic research, a network model could include both people and the events they attend (Wasserman & Faust, 1994), thus creating a bimodal network. Su and Contractor (2011) propose a more complex multi-dimensional network model, including people, documents, datasets, tools, keywords/concepts, etc.

Additionally, in some online communities, participation may also strongly depend on adopted mechanisms and policies for preserving privacy, including confidentiality of messages and identity. For personal identity privacy, stable pseudonyms could be assigned at registration (Andrews, 2002). Moreover, in online communities and Virtual Teams, acquaintance may happen online, without previous connection in real life. In those cases, a member's reputation is directly related to his pseudonym, and ratability of his online activities may be more important than his real world identity for creating trust (Poggi et al., 2003). Complete anonymity may also have a value in some activities of Virtual Teams, apart from encouraging participation in general.

For example, an anonymous brainstorm activity may help opening a conversation about trust and ground rules for online meetings (Young, 2009).

For reaching wider and more effective adoption in open and dynamic online communities, including Virtual Organizations, Virtual Teams, and online Networks of Practice, we argue that social networking platforms should embrace an open approach (Franchi et al., 2016a; Poggi & Tomaiuolo, 2013). In fact, many isolated sites could not satisfy the need for an inter-organizational collaborative environment. On the other hand, organizations are not keen to rely on a single centralized site, which may pose risks to privacy and may control published data. Moreover, openness is important for participation, too. In fact, a closed environment can hardly reach the minimal dimension and variety required for activating the typical dynamics at the basis of the different theories taken into consideration by analysts, for explaining participation in OSNs.

INTEGRATION OF SOCIAL FEATURES INTO EXISTING APPLICATIONS

The trend toward introducing social media systems in the work environment has seen a massive increase in importance in recent years. At their first appearance, without indications from the management and without integration with internal information systems, social media took the form of feral systems. However, organizations and firms are finally coming to accept this situation as a matter of fact, trying to gain benefits from the same features that drove the introduction of social platforms in the first place. Thus, information systems are moving from the communication level to the coordination and collaboration levels, increasingly acknowledging and leveraging the various dimensions of social relations among people, both internally and across organization boundaries.

A first strategy, that some organizations and brands are adopting, is to use social media for improving their Customer Relationship Management (CRM). In fact, social media can be a means for firms and organizations to listen to customers and to cope with the difficulties in collecting data through interviews (Murphy et al., 2011). Social media allow the use of online sources of information, sometimes for free. So firms and organizations are moving to reduce costs and time needed by traditional survey researches. Moreover, in the last years several social media monitoring tools and platforms have been developed to listen to the social media users, analyze and measure their content in relation to a brand or enterprise business and so it is reducing the time necessary for extracting the useful information through the huge data provided by social media (Stavrakantonakis et al., 2012). However, this quite popular trend towards so-called "*Social CRM*" has not always been satisfactory. An IBM (2011) study shows that there is a large gap between the expectations of brand managers and social media users. In fact, only the 23% of users are keen to engage with brands on social media, and only 5% of users declare active participation. The majority, instead, limit their communications and shares with parents and relatives. Among the potentially interested people, many expect tangible benefits, including discounts, services, additional information and reviews about products. The study is in accordance with the difficulties that brands face to engage with users and to launch viral campaigns. Nevertheless, businesses continue to be greatly interested in using social media for rapid distribution of offers and content, reaching new people through trusted introducers, but also for improving customer care and research.

A second type of effort is directed to augment internal tools, in particular Knowledge Management (KM) systems, with explicit and rich data about relationships among involved people. The long term goal of KM, in fact, is to let insights and experiences existing in implicit way into an organization emerge and become easily accessible for wider internal adoption. Such knowledge can be either possessed by individuals or embedded into common practices. To provide effective access to valuable internal knowledge and expertise, it is essential to recognize and value the particular knowledge possessed by different persons, and then to have means to contact the relevant persons in a timely manner, thus making information-seeking an easier and more successful experience. In many regards, such a scenario can be fully developed only on the basis of the evolution of existing ICT tools and the creation of new ones, by making some typical features of social networking applications available in tools for daily activities.

This trend regards existing Information Systems and also, for some aspects, platforms for Enterprise Resource Planning (ERP). In fact, some aspects of traditional ERP systems are integrating features of social networking platforms, fostering collaboration among people on the basis of direct interpersonal links and simple knowledge sharing tools. The centralized and inward approach of early systems is being challenged also in the core area of production management software. The drift towards network of integrated enterprises is testified by an increasingly dynamic production environment, arranged in the form of complex Virtual Organizations and Virtual Enterprises. In this context, the tasks of supply chain management, project and activity management, data services, and access control management require the participation of actors of different organizations and possibly different places and cultures.

Models of Participation

The result of the interactions among the users in a social networking system is an Online Social Network, i.e., a special case of the more general concept of social network. A social network is defined as a set or sets of actors and the relations defined on them (Wasserman & Faust, 1994). Social networks are typically studied using social network analysis, a discipline that focuses on the structural and topological features of the network. More recently, additional dimensions have been added to the traditional social network analytic approach (Monge & Contractor 2003; Borgatti & Foster 2003; Parkhe et al. 2006; Hoang & Antoncic 2003).

Social Network Analysis

Social network analysis (SNA) is the process for studying social networks and understanding the behaviours of their members. Graph theory provides the basic foundations for representing and studying a social network. In fact, each member of the social network can be mapped onto a node of the graph and each relationship between two members onto an edge that connects two nodes.

In real life, it is very common to find examples of social networks: groups of friends, a company's employees, contributors with different aims, etc. In fact, SNA is currently used in many research fields including anthropology, biology, economics, geography, information science, organizational studies, political science, and social psychology.

The main goals of SNA are to:

- Investigate behaviours of some network users,
- Identify users' membership and position into sub-communities,
- Find possible relationships among some users,
- Discover changes in network structure over time.

Different aspects are useful for investigating the behaviours of a participant in a social network. The most relevant are his position in the social network (i.e., which other members it is connected to) and his contributions to discussions or collaborations (knowing which groups he belongs to could be an important information). Another important aspect is the kind of activity performed by a user in his social network (Klein, Ahlf & Sharma, 2015). Mainly, a user can be identified as *"active"* (when he produces contents, sends videos and photos, comments posts of other users, reports original texts and documents) or "*passive*" (when he is only a consumer of other users' contents, limiting himself to liking or unliking those contents).

A second aspect we want to focus on is the relationship between two members of the network (Golbeck & Hendler, 2006). Discovering the type of relationship between two members, their reciprocal trust and their distance in the network, is a basic information used by SNA to speculate about information diffusion and users contamination.

Another significant application of SNA is to find subgroups composed by different users, i.e., to perform community detection. For example, Fortunato (2010) presents a case study about the Belgian population, which can be split and clustered using phone communication data. Many users can be considered a community if existing connections between them are many more than the number of users (this situation is similar to a dense graph). Detecting the presence of a community allows analysts to recognize the paths followed by information for reaching the network users. According to a user's position, it is possible to identify three main metrics: Degree Centrality, Betweenness Centrality, and Closeness Centrality. Degree Centrality, strictly connected to the concept of graph-node degree, tells us the number of direct connections a node has. The higher the degree, the stronger the capability to spread information to other users is. Instead, Betweenness Centrality is a gauging of how much a user could be able to diffuse information from a community to another, especially if he belongs to many communities. A very interesting approach aims at identifying influential users on the basis of their activity level, comparing it with the activity and reactions of their followers/friends (Klein, Ahlf & Sharma, 2015). Finally, Closeness Centrality is a measurement connected to the concept of graph-path length. It provides information about how far a user is from all the users of his community: the shorter this value is, the greater the possibility to reach all the participants of the network is, when he posts a content.

The last major aspect SNA concentrates in is to discover the changes of a social network structure during time (Barabási et al., 2002). Studying the dynamics of a network allows analysts to detect persistent relationships, if they exist, and to discover the lead users. Lead users play an important role in the network, since they have the best marks, according to the main centrality metrics mentioned before, and remain stable in the network for a long period. Studying network changes can also be useful in predicting users' real connections (Wang et al., 2011).

Social Capital

An important theoretical foundation for the analysis of participation in social networks is constituted by social capital. Social capital represents a person's benefit due to his relations with other persons, including family, colleagues, friends and generic contacts. The concept originated in studies about communities, to underline the importance of collective actions and the associated enduring relations of trust and cooperation, for the functioning of neighborhoods in large cities (Jacobs, 1961).

Social capital has been studied as a factor providing additional opportunities to some players in a competitive scenario, and, from this point of view, it has been studied in the context of firms (Backer, 1990), nations (Fukuyama, 1995) and geographic regions (Putnam, 1995). In this sense, social capital is defined as a third kind of capital that is brought in the competitive arena, along with financial capital, which includes machinery and raw materials, and human capital, which includes knowledge and skills. Moreover, the role of social capital in the development of human capital has been studied by Loury and Coleman (Loury, 1987; Coleman, 1988).

Social capital is typically studied:

1. By drawing a graph of connected people and their own resources, creating a connection between each player's resources and those of his closest contacts, or
2. By analyzing social structures in their own right, and supposing that the network structure alone can be used to estimate some player's competitive advantage, at the social stance (Franchi et al., 2016b).

The size of the ego-centered social network is an important factor to estimate the social capital of one individual; however, the size alone does not provide enough information. According to Burt (1992) social capital is related with the number of non-redundant contacts and not directly with the simple number of contacts.

In fact, although information spreads rapidly among homogeneous, richly interconnected groups, Granovetter (1973) argues that new ideas and opportunities are introduced in the groups by contacts with people from outside the group. In order to explain this phenomenon, Granovetter distinguished among three types of ties:

1. Strong ties,
2. Weak ties, and
3. Absent ties.

A quantitative distinction between strong and weak ties has been subject of debate, but intuitively weak ties are simple acquaintances, while strong ties are reserved for close friends and family. The "*absent ties*" indicate missing relations in the network. Burt capitalizes on Granovetter's insight, and emphasizes the importance of absent ties, that create the "*structural holes*" in the network texture. According to Burt, structural holes allow the individuals that create a weak link among two otherwise separated communities to greatly increase their social capital.

Nahapiet & Goshal (1998) discuss the role of social capital in building intellectual capital inside organizations. The authors distinguish the structural, relational, and cognitive aspects of social networks. The structural properties describe the patterns of connection among actors and regard the social system as a whole. The relational properties describe the type of ties people have developed during their interactions, including relationships like friendship, trust, and respect. The cognitive properties refer to basic knowledge, representations, languages and other systems of meaning, shared among actors. Moreover, they focus on the development of intellectual capital, which is essentially an aspect of human capital but may also be owned by a social collectivity. In fact, they classify knowledge as implicit or explicit and as individual or social. In the case of social knowledge, they argue that social capital facilitates the creation of intellectual capital primarily by creating conditions for exchange and combination of knowledge. Finally, they discuss the features of an organization that are more effective for the development of intellectual capital, including duration of contacts, type and frequency of interactions, interdependence of actors, and closure of the community.

Contractor and Monge (2003) proposed a multifaceted approach with a Multi-theoretical multi-level (MTML) model for explaining the various motivations for the existence of social connections in a network. Their analysis considers the following theories:

- **Self-Interest:** According to the theories of self-interest, people create ties with other people and participate in team activities in order to maximize the satisfaction of their own goals. The most known theories of self-interest are based on the notion of social capital (Burt, 1992). Another foundation of these theories lies on transaction cost economics (Williamson, 1991).
- **Mutual Interest and Collective Action:** These theories study the coordinated action of individuals in a team. They explain collective actions as a mean for reaching outcomes which would be unattainable by individual action (Fulk et al., 2004). Thus, individuals collaborate in a community because they share mutual interests.
- **Homophily and Proximity:** The principle at the basis of these theories is that connections are mostly structured according to similarity (McPherson et al., 2001). Moreover, connections between dissimilar individuals break at a higher rate.
- **Exchange and Dependency:** Another founding motivation for the emergence of groups can be the exchange of available and required resources (Cook,

1982). Thus, these theories explain the creation of communities by analyzing the network structure together with the distribution and flow of resources in the network. Examples of exchange networks vary from data analysts to bands of musicians.

- **Co-Evolution:** The underlying principle of these theories is that evolution based on environmental selection can be applied to whole organizations, and not only to individuals. Thus, they study how organizations compete and cooperate to access limited resources, and how communities of individuals create ties both internally and towards other communities (Campbell, 1985; Baum, 1999).

- **Contagion:** For explaining the spread of innovations, contagion theories study how people are brought in contact through the social structure (Burt, 1987). Social contagion is described as a sort of interpersonal synapse through which ideas are spread. Conversely, some sort of social inoculations may prevent ideas from spreading to parts of the network.

- **Balance and Transitivity:** Since macroscopic patterns originate from local structures of social networks, balance theories (Holland & Leinhardt, 1975) start from the study of triads in a digraph, or a socio-matrix. The typical distributions of triads configurations in real social networks show that individuals' choices have a consistent tendency to be transitive.

- **Cognition:** Finally, another aspect of social network analysis regards the importance of knowledge and semantics in the development of teams and the impact of increasing specialization over collaboration. In this sense, the decision to form a collective depends on what possible members know (Hollingshead et al. 2002). These studies are grounded on the concept of transactive memory.

The study of structure of Online Social Networks, expressed as patterns of links among nodes, can exploit models and ideas from classical sociology and anthropology, with particular attention to contextual and relational approaches. In fact, all the results obtained in decades of studies of human networks are also at the basis of the analysis of Online Social Networks. However, these results cannot be simply applied to the different context of online relations. Instead they have to be evaluated and adapted to the new networks, which may have significantly different structure and dynamics. Moreover, online social networking platforms may greatly vary both technically and in their aims. They may be used by people for organizing quite diverse activities, in different virtual communities.

Information Spreading

In social network analysis, the study of information spreading processes is a critical topic. As a matter of fact, understanding the dynamics of information (or rumor) spread in social networks is very important for many different purposes, such as marketing campaigns, political influence, news diffusion and so on.

The way a piece of information reaches people and how much time it takes to do so are examples of analysis of information spreading processes. They depend mainly on network characteristics like topology, dynamism, and sparsity the meaning of the information content, and the influence of the source of information.

Several models have been developed in order to study such a phenomenon, but there is not a unique standard option, due to the heterogeneity of social networks (Moreno, Nekovee & Pacheco, 2004) that range from real-world ones to online social networks, such as micro-blogging services or forums.

Despite those diversities, social networks share common features that are taken as basis for the analysis. First of all, a network is often viewed as a graph G = (V, E), where V is a discrete finite set of nodes (or vertices) that represents the people or users involved, and E is a binary relation on V, that represents relationships among users. The neighborhood of a node is the set of other nodes directly connected to him.

Depending on networks, the topological characteristics of the graph change, and several models have been investigated to match the correct shape of a network. Examples of such models are complete graphs (Pittel, 1987), hypercubes (Feige et al., 1990), random graphs (Erdős & Rényi, 1959) and evolving random graphs (Clementi et al., 2015), preferential attachment graphs (Barabási & Albert, 1999; Doerr, Fouz & Friedrich, 2012), power-law degree graphs (Fountoulakis, Panagiotou & Sauerwald, 2012) and so on.

Among these models, there is not a "better" one. Choosing one of them depends on the problem to be addressed. For example, online social networks often present a scale-free structure, which can be successfully modeled by power-law degree graphs. If the focus is the time evolution of such a network, other models can be considered. As a matter of fact, evolving random graphs operates well in analyzing the problem of rumor spreading.

In literature, rumor spreading on a graph (thus, a social network) has been studied by means of two types of distributed mechanisms (Kuhn, Lynch & Oshman, 2010; Kuhn & Oshman, 2011): the push protocol and the flooding protocol. Both protocols are synchronous, i.e., time steps, or rounds, are used to describe the behavior of a node, and the piece of information or rumor originates by a single source node.

In flooding protocol, starting from the source at the first time step, each node forwards the information to all nodes in its neighborhood. In push protocol, on the other hand, at every time step, each informed node in the social network chooses uniformly at random another node, and share with it the piece of information. Behavior of such protocols are widely investigated for several types of graphs (Karp et al., 2000), and their performance, time of completion (Baumann, Crescenzi & Fraigniaud, 2011; Clementi et al., 2010) or other measures, such as conductance (Giakkoupis, 2011), are well-known.

The actual challenge is to understand when and how such protocols, or their variants, are suitable in order to describe information spreading in a certain social network, with its own topological model.

Answers to such problems differ according to social network characteristics and platforms, taking account of communication patterns. Examples for online social networks could include the Twitter retweet mechanism (Kwak et al., 2010; Ye & Wu, 2013), or the way Facebook users share posts (Fan & Yeung, 2013; Kee et al., 2016).

The study of information diffusion often gave rise to other inherent questions, such as how a topic becomes popular and what are the methods to make it viral (Zaman et al., 2010).

Those matters are analyzed by means of statistical models. Such models aim at predicting the future impact of a new information released within the social network.

Currently, "little is known about factors that could affect the dissemination of a single piece of information" (Wang et al., 2011), and several predictive models have been proposed. Each model have to face three main issues:

1. The impact of the topology of the underlying social network – with all the related formalizations,
2. The influence of the individual behaviour of users and, finally,
3. The communication patterns of the community (online or not).

A common approach is to assign a score to the characteristic features of the network (Shah & Zaman, 2011; Zhou et al., 2008; Zaman, Fox & Bradlow, 2014). In some networks, the underlying graph model is very important because diffusion is subordinated to connection among users, for example if the piece of information is visible only to a user's neighborhood. In other networks, messages or posts are public, and this fact overcome topological limits, bypassing relationship to address wide audience. Moreover, the propagation speed depends on the context in which the piece of information is introduced.

All those considerations are useful in gaining the correct score of a feature, and then the scores are put together to obtain an estimation of the diffusion probability of a single topic.

Such estimations are obtained, for example, by means of statistical methods such as the method of moments or the Maximum Likelihood Estimation (MLE), in which features represent the population of parameters to estimate.

MOTIVATIONS FOR PARTICIPATION

In order to understand the reasons that motivate the users in engaging in online social activities in general, and, more specifically, in sharing their valued knowledge in online communities, it is necessary to analyze

1. The nature and the structure of their relationships in the context of a specific community, and
2. Their implication over both online and offline reputation. Wasko & Faraj (2005), for example, analyze the motivations for participation in a specific online Network of Practice.

In particular, the analyzed network is a public online forum of legal professionals, who participate under their real identities. The study takes the following features into account as possible enablers of participation.

- **Individual Motivations:** One key aspect of social contribution is an individual's expectation that some new value will be created as result of his participation in the network. The individual should expect to receive some benefits from his contribution, even in the absence of direct acquaintance with other members of the community and without mechanisms enforcing or encouraging reciprocity. Increasing the reputation is one of the most important forms of return of investment, especially if the online reputation is believed to have a positive impact on the professional reputation.
- **Relational Capital:** Another enabling factor for contributions to an online community is represented by the personal relationships among individuals, as members of that community. Relational capital is directly related to the level of an individual's identification with the community, trust with other members (Tomaiuolo, 2013), perception of obligation to participate and reciprocate, acceptance of common norms. In particular, commitment can be associated with a community, apart from individuals.
- **Cognitive Capital:** Any meaningful interaction between two members of a community requires some basic shared understanding. All those common se-

mantic resources, including languages, interpretations, narratives, contexts, and norms, are usually described as cognitive capital. In fact, an individual can participate in community activities only if he possesses the required knowledge and, more generally, the required cognitive capital.

- **Structural Capital:** Communities characterized by dense internal connections are dialectically correlated with collective actions. In fact, individuals who are strongly embedded in a social network have many direct ties with other members and a habit of cooperation. On the other hand, an individual's position in the network influences his willingness to contribute, thus increasing both the number and quality of interactions.

Those factors have different weight in different social contexts. In the case study analyzed by Wasko & Faraj (2005), reputation plays a crucial role, since it also affects professional reputation. Other factors, though, also have significant correlation with the number and usefulness of contributions in the online community. The final results compare both the level and helpfulness of contributions against the following factors: reputation, willingness to help, centrality in the network structure, self-rated expertise, tenure in field, commitment, and reciprocity.

With regard to individual motivations, results for the case at hand show a stronger influence of reputation over intrinsic motivations, like willingness to help. Social capital, assessed by determining each individual's degree of centrality to the network, is confirmed to play the most significant role in knowledge exchange. Also cognitive capital, assessed by self-rated expertise and tenure in the field, shows a strong influence over participation, but this is mostly limited to the individual's experience in the field, while self-rated expertise is not quite as significant. Finally, in the analyzed Network of Practice, relational capital, assessed by commitment and reciprocity, is not strongly correlated with knowledge contribution, suggesting that these kinds of ties are more difficult to develop in an online network.

Both individuals and organizations also appreciate social media as they foster innovation, by improving collective thinking. In fact, creativity and innovation have long been notable subjects of organizational studies and social network analysis. According to Fedorowicz et al (2008) creative ideas rarely come from individuals. More often, they come from teams and groups, including those formed through social media. Dwyer (2011) argues that apart from the number of collaborators it is also important to measure the quality of collaboration. In fact, various collaborator segments can be identified with significant differences in the value of contributed ideas and the timing of participation. Thus, new metrics should be used, taking those differences into account and being based on information content. Hayne & Smith

(2005) note that groupware performance depends on the fit between the structure and task of the group. However, they argue that an important role may also be played by the cognitive structure, which also maps to the group structure. In fact, collaborative tasks may push human cognitive capabilities to their limits, in terms of perception, attention and memory. Thus, the authors argue for the integration of different areas of study, such as: psychology, especially with regard to abilities and limitations; theories of social interactions, with regard to group communication and motivation; studies of groupware structures and human interactions mediated by artifacts.

Anti-Social Behaviors and Trolling

In Computer-Mediated Communication (CMC), user behavior is very different from in face-to-face communication and every type of communication medium creates its own communication rules. Depending on the kind of CMC, users are allowed to variously adjust the degree of identity they reveal. The level of anonymity usually guaranteed in online discussions allows users to engage in behaviours they would otherwise be averse to carrying out in face-to-face discussion. This lack of identity has contributed to the codification of new communication behaviours, like trolling (Morrisey, 2010).

Trolls are often seen as corrupters within an online community. They often share a group's common interests and try to pass as a legitimate participants of the group (Donath, 1999). After that, they try to lead the conversation toward pointless discussion (Herring et al., 2002). Morrisey (2010) suggests that "trolling is an utterer producing an intentionally false or incorrect utterance with high-order intention to elicit from recipient a particular response, generally negative or violent."

A troll can damage a group in many ways. He can interrupt discussions, give bad advice, or undermine the mutual confidence of the user community. Trolls usually post messages into different sections (Cross-Posting). By doing this, they are able to annoy more groups simultaneously. Nowadays many companies are using tools such as blogs, forums, and social media (including self-developed ones) for their own interests. Trolls are therefore a threat to private social platforms as well as public ones.

The most widely used solution against trolls is to ignore provocations. Some systems provide filters (kill file, blacklist) that allow the exclusion of trolls from public discussions.

In recent years, many projects have been developed for the automatic detection of trolls in online communities. Some works (Seah et al., 2015) use a supervised learning algorithm, which allows certain people to classify the polarity of posts and identify trolls as users with a high number of negative messages. The classifiers are trained using examples of positive and negative sentences.

The polarity classifier is trained on a data set of movie reviews written in standard English. The Support Vector Machine algorithm is used to do binary classification of trolls. Since the data set contains messages from different topics (different forums), some domain adaptation techniques are used to get better results.

Furthermore, the frequency of messages, and possibly also the frequency of generated answers, is another factor for determining the presence of a troll in the network: the higher the frequency, the higher the probability that he or she is a troll (Buckels, Trapnell & Paulhus, 2014).

One study proposed a method to compute a ranking of the users in a social network in terms of their reliability (Ortega et al., 2012). The goal is to prevent malicious users to gain a good reputation in the network. To achieve this purpose, they create a graph taking the users of the network as the nodes. The edges represent the opinions of some users about others, and the weights of the edges correspond to the intensity of the relationship between the nodes.

In (Galán-García et al., 2015), the authors suppose that "it is possible to link a trolling account to the corresponding real profile of the user behind the fake account, analysing different features present in the profile, connections data and tweets characteristics, including text, using machine learning algorithms." In fact, machine learning techniques can be used to associate users' posts with various emotions, in addition to generic positive or negative sentiments (Fornacciari, Mordonini & Tomaiuolo, 2015).

More recently, researchers from Stanford and Cornell have developed an algorithm that can estimate the need to ban a member of an online community after observing only five to ten online posts (Cheng et al., 2015). In particular, the authors present a data-driven approach to detect antisocial behavior in online discussion. The data sets are collected from users that have been banned from a community.

RISKS AND CHALLENGES FOR FIRMS AND ORGANIZATIONS

The initial adoption of online collaboration tools and social networking platforms in the work environment has occurred largely on an individual basis. Faced with an increasingly decentralized, expanded, and interconnected environment, workers and members of organizations began adopting social networking platforms as better tools for connecting and collaborating with colleagues and partners (Franchi et al., 2016a). Thus, social media made their first appearance in firms and organizations mostly without indications from the management and without integration with internal information systems. In this sense, they took the form of feral systems. In fact, they were not "part of the corporation's accepted information technology infrastructure," and they were "designed to augment" that infrastructure, along with the definition of Feral Information Systems provided by Houghton & Kerr (2006).

In a study published by AT&T (2008), ten main challenges are listed for the adoption of social media by businesses. In fact, these challenges can be grouped in terms of organizational costs, risks of capital loss, and technical challenges.

About organizational costs, the first issue is that social networking has indirect benefits, which often are not fully appreciated. It is probably the main area of resistance, due to the perceived costs of networking time, not seen as cost efficient activity, and the necessity to allow employees to manage their working time with more freedom. However, traditional ROI methods make it difficult to incorporate all the benefits of social media, both direct and indirect. Thus new performance indicators will be needed. Another issue is the definition of an effective plan to reach the critical mass for the social network to be functional. In fact, common figures of users creating content and collaborating through social media are pretty low, typically from 1% to 20%. Resistance to adoption can come from both regular employee and cadres, possibly including managers and executives. Such a plan would also face the problem of timeliness. In fact, developments in the Web 2.0 environment occur very fast. Successful applications may reach millions of users in a couple of years, sometimes creating a new market.

Other challenges are related to the risk of loss of capital, faced by organizations in the adoption of social media. The capital at risk can include intellectual property, as well as human and social capital. In fact, organization members may easily and inadvertently leak sensible and protected content on social media, and such content may face rapid diffusion by "word of mouth" mechanisms. An even greater risk, however, may come from the increased mobility of organization members and employees. This risk is increased by the exposure of members' profiles to the outside world, including other organizations and competitors.

Finally, the adoption of Online Social Networks implies technical costs for creating and maintaining a more complex and open infrastructure. Some important challenges regard security, which is harder to enforce as intranets need to open to the external world for enabling social collaboration (Franchi et al., 2015). The risks include the malicious behavior of users, as well as the proliferation of viruses and malware. Also on the technical front, social media applications require increased levels of bandwidth, storage, and computational capacity to support interactions through videos and other forms of rich content. Moreover, the increased and differentiated use of social media will pose challenges for the interoperability of different applications, especially with regard to security and authentication schemes.

While the study of AT&T is formulated in reference to the business context, it is interesting to notice that similar considerations are also referred to government agencies and other types of organizations. For example, Bev et al. (2008) describe the case of government agencies. Among other issues, the study underlines the problems of

1. Employees wasting time on social networks,
2. Risk of malware and spyware coming from high traffic sites, and
3. Bandwidth requirements.

About the aspect of the organizational costs, the authors of the document argue that the problem is not specific to Web 2.0 technologies. In fact, a similar argument was used with respect to mobile phones, emails, etc. For this reason, it is better treated as a management problem instead of a technology problem. About security, efforts should be dedicated to at least mitigate the risks, if they cannot be canceled. Finally, with regard to bandwidth and other technological issues, enough resources should be deployed, to allow at least some selected employees to use rich-content media to communicate with the public, in the most effective way.

To leverage the advantages of social networking, organizations and firms should support their transition from the individual adoption as feral systems to the formal incorporation into existing information systems. To achieve this goal, knowledge management professionals should act as social networking architects, in conjunction with other managers and IT professionals. In fact, social network analysis can highlight the patterns of connection among individuals and the main knowledge flows in a whole organization. Thus, it can be used by managers as a basis for reshaping the organization and advancing towards the business goals. Anklam (2004) describes three main types of intervention, to conduct after a social network analysis:

1. Structural/organizational, i.e. change the organograms to improve the knowledge transfer;
2. Knowledge-network development, i.e. overcome resistance to action on the basis of evidence, instead of intuition;
3. Individual/leadership, i.e. resolve problems with the particular role of individuals, for example acting as factual gatekeepers and resulting in a knowledge bottleneck.

More generally, social network analysis can be useful to cope with common business problems including: launching distributed teams, retention of people with vital knowledge for the organization, and improving access to knowledge and increasing innovation.

Along the same lines, Roy (2012) discusses the profile of leaders in Virtual Teams. In fact, apart from usual technical and leadership capacities, to work effectively in a virtual environment, they also need abilities to build relationships among participants and to defuse frustrations. In fact, on the one hand, they need particular communication skills, as well as good knowledge for operating video conferencing software and other CSCW tools. On the other hand, they must be able to establish trust, embrace diversity, motivating team members, and fostering the team spirit.

CONCLUSION

In this chapter we investigated some crucial issues in the field of social network analysis, with particular reference to the theories of participation in social networks.

First of all, we presented the reasons and the benefits that people have in belonging to a social network, with particular reference to the theories of social capital. Then, we analyzed the problem of information spreading, which is crucial for understanding and improving the diffusion of knowledge and innovation inside and among online communities.

One problem that limits the potentialities of online social networks is their misuse by some participants who, for various reasons, adopt antisocial behaviours. The identification of so-called "*trolls*" is still an open research topic and, in part, it can be facilitated by an "*ad hoc*" knowledge on the network. Thus, it is important to join the different competences of computer engineers, data scientists, and knowledge management professionals.

The study of individual motivations in order to belong to an online social network can benefit from classical social networking models, that have been developed in the general context of human sociology. In assessing the performance of a social media, those models are of great importance. Also, it is crucial to find the appropriate parameters for measuring the success factors of online social networks and virtual communities.

A promising research area regards the study of the semantics of links in an online social network. In fact, this kind of knowledge could augment the topological analysis of a social graph, in order to refine the models of participation and their support in determining the corrective actions to improve the success of a certain social media initiative.

REFERENCES

Anklam, P. (2004). *KM and the Social Network*. Knowledge Management Magazine.

AT&T (2008). *The Business Impacts of Social Networking*. Author.

Baker, W. E. (1990). Market networks and corporate behavior. *American Journal of Sociology, 96*(3), 589–625. doi:10.1086/229573

Barabási, A. L., & Albert, R. (1999). Emergence of scaling in random networks. *Science, 286*(5439), 509–512. doi:10.1126/science.286.5439.509 PMID:10521342

Barabási, A.L., Jeong, H., Néda, Z., Ravasz, E., Schubert, A., & Vicsek, T. (2002). Evolution of the social network of scientific collaborations. *Physica A: Statistical Mechanics and Its Applications, 311*(3), 590-614.

Baum, J. A. (1999). Whole-part coevolutionary competition in organizations. *Variations in Organization Science*, 113-135.

Baumann, H., Crescenzi, P., & Fraigniaud, P. (2011). Parsimonious flooding in dynamic graphs. *Distributed Computing, 24*(1), 31–44. doi:10.1007/s00446-011-0133-9

Bergenti, F., Poggi, A., Tomaiuolo, M., & Turci, P. (2005). An Ontology Support for Semantic Aware Agents. In *Proc. Seventh International Bi-Conference Workshop on Agent-Oriented Information Systems* (AOIS-2005@ AAMAS).

Bev, G., Campbell, S., Levy, J., & Bounds, J. (2008). *Social media and the federal government: Perceived and real barriers and potential solutions*. Federal Web Managers Council.

Borgatti, S. P., & Foster, P. C. (2003). The network paradigm in organizational research: A review and typology. *Journal of Management, 29*(6), 991–1013. doi:10.1016/S0149-2063(03)00087-4

Buckels, E. E., Trapnell, P. D., & Paulhus, D. L. (2014). Trolls just want to have fun. *Personality and Individual Differences, 67*, 97–102. doi:10.1016/j.paid.2014.01.016

Burt, R. S. (1987). Social Contagion and Innovation: Cohesion versus Structural Equivalence. *American Journal of Sociology, 92*(6), 1287–1335. doi:10.1086/228667

Burt, R. S. (1995). *Structural holes: The social structure of competition*. Harvard University Press.

Campbell, J. H. (1985). An organizational interpretation of evolution. *Evolution at a Crossroads*, 133.

Cheng, J., Danescu-Niculescu-Mizil, C., & Leskovec, J. (2015). *Antisocial Behavior in Online Discussion Communities*. Academic Press.

Clementi, A., Crescenzi, P., Doerr, C., Fraigniaud, P., Pasquale, F., & Silvestri, R. (2015). Rumor spreading in random evolving graphs. *Random Structures and Algorithms*.

Clementi, A. E., Macci, C., Monti, A., Pasquale, F., & Silvestri, R. (2010). Flooding time of edge-markovian evolving graphs. *SIAM Journal on Discrete Mathematics*, *24*(4), 1694–1712. doi:10.1137/090756053

Coleman, J. S. (1988). Social capital in the creation of human capital. *American Journal of Sociology*, *94*, 95–120. doi:10.1086/228943

DiMicco, J. (2007). Identity management: multiple presentations of self in facebook.*6th International Conference on Supporting Group Work (GROUP'07)* (pp. 1–4). doi:10.1145/1316624.1316682

DiMicco, J., Millen, D., & Geyer, W. (2008). Motivations for social networking at work.*Conference on Computer Supported Cooperative Work (CSCW'08)* (pp. 711–720).

Doerr, B., Fouz, M., & Friedrich, T. (2012). Why rumors spread so quickly in social networks. *Communications of the ACM*, *55*(6), 70–75. doi:10.1145/2184319.2184338

Donath, J. S. (1999). Identity and deception in the virtual community. *Communities in Cyberspace, 1996*, 29-59.

Erdős, P., & Rényi, A. (1959). On Random Graphs. *Publ. Math.*, *6*, 290–297.

Fan, W., & Yeung, K. H. (2013). Virus Propagation Modeling in Facebook. In *The Influence of Technology on Social Network Analysis and Mining* (pp. 185–199). Vienna: Springer. doi:10.1007/978-3-7091-1346-2_8

Feige, U., Peleg, D., Raghavan, P., & Upfal, E. (1990). Randomized broadcast in networks. *Random Structures and Algorithms*, *1*(4), 447–460. doi:10.1002/rsa.3240010406

Fornacciari, P., Mordonini, M., & Tomaiuolo, M. (2015). A case-study for sentiment analysis on twitter.*CEUR Workshop Proceedings*.

Fornacciari, P., Mordonini, M., & Tomaiuolo, M. (2015). Social network and sentiment analysis on Twitter: Towards a combined approach.*CEUR Workshop Proceedings*.

Fortunato, S. (2010). Community detection in graphs. *Physics Reports*, *486*(3), 75–174. doi:10.1016/j.physrep.2009.11.002

Foster, I., Kesselman, C., & Tuecke, S. (2001). The anatomy of the grid: Enabling scalable virtual organizations. *International Journal of High Performance Computing Applications, 15*(3), 200–222. doi:10.1177/109434200101500302

Fountoulakis, N., Panagiotou, K., & Sauerwald, T. (2012, January). Ultra-fast rumor spreading in social networks. In *Proceedings of the twenty-third annual ACM-SIAM symposium on Discrete Algorithms* (pp. 1642-1660). SIAM. doi:10.1137/1.9781611973099.130

Franchi, E., Poggi, A., & Tomaiuolo, M. (2015). Information and password attacks on social networks: An argument for cryptography. *Journal of Information Technology Research, 8*(1), 25–42. doi:10.4018/JITR.2015010103

Franchi, E., Poggi, A., & Tomaiuolo, M. (2016a). Blogracy: A Peer-to-Peer Social Network. *International Journal of Distributed Systems and Technologies, 7*(2), 37–56. doi:10.4018/IJDST.2016040103

Franchi, E., Poggi, A., & Tomaiuolo, M. (2016b). Social media for online collaboration in firms and organizations. *International Journal of Information System Modeling and Design, 7*(1), 18–31. doi:10.4018/IJISMD.2016010102

Fukuyama, F. (1995). *Trust: The social virtues and the creation of prosperity*. New York, NY: Free Press.

Fulk, J., Heino, R., Flanagin, A. J., Monge, P. R., & Bar, F. (2004). A test of the individual action model for organizational information commons. *Organization Science, 15*(5), 569–585. doi:10.1287/orsc.1040.0081

Galán-García, P., De La Puerta, J. G., Gómez, C. L., Santos, I., & Bringas, P. G. (2015). Supervised machine learning for the detection of troll profiles in twitter social network: Application to a real case of cyberbullying. *Logic Journal of the IGPL*, jzv048. doi:10.1093/jigpal/jzv048

Giakkoupis, G. (2011). Tight bounds for rumor spreading in graphs of a given conductance.*Symposium on Theoretical Aspects of Computer Science (STACS2011)*.

Golbeck, J., & Hendler, J. (2006). Inferring binary trust relationships in web-based social networks. *ACM Transactions on Internet Technology, 6*(4), 497–529. doi:10.1145/1183463.1183470

Goldschlag, D., Reed, M., & Syverson, P. (1999). Onion routing. *Communications of the ACM, 42*(2), 39–41. doi:10.1145/293411.293443

Granovetter, M. S. (1973). The strength of weak ties. *American Journal of Sociology, 78*(6), 1360–1380. doi:10.1086/225469

Herring, S., Job-Sluder, K., Scheckler, R., & Barab, S. (2002). Searching for safety online: Managing trolling in a feminist forum. *The Information Society*, *18*(5), 371–384. doi:10.1080/01972240290108186

Hoang, H., & Antoncic, B. (2003). Network-based research in entrepreneurship: A critical review. *Journal of Business Venturing*, *18*(2), 165–187. doi:10.1016/S0883-9026(02)00081-2

Holland, P., & Leinhardt, S. (1974). *The Statistical Analysis of Local Structure in Social Networks*. National Bureau of Economic Research Working Paper Series 44.

Hollingshead, A. B., Fulk, J., & Monge, P. (2002). Fostering intranet knowledge sharing: An integration of transactive memory and public goods approaches. *Distributed Work*, 335-355.

Houghton, L., & Kerr, D. V. (2006). A study into the creation of feral information systems as a response to an ERP implementation within the supply chain of a large government-owned corporation. *International Journal of Internet and Enterprise Management*, *4*(2), 135–147. doi:10.1504/IJIEM.2006.010239

IBM Institute for Business Value. (2011). *From social media to Social CRM*. Retrieved 2012-10-20 from http://public.dhe.ibm.com/common/ssi/ecm/en/gbe03391usen/GBE03391USEN.PDF

Jacobs, J. (1961). *The death and life of great American cities*. Vintage.

Jones, B. F., Wuchty, S., & Uzzi, B. (2008). Multi-university research teams: Shifting impact, geography, and stratification in science. *Science*, *322*(5905), 1259–1262. doi:10.1126/science.1158357 PMID:18845711

Karp, R., Schindelhauer, C., Shenker, S., & Vocking, B. (2000). Randomized rumor spreading. In *Proceedings of the 41st Annual Symposium on Foundations of Computer Science 2000* (pp. 565-574). IEEE. doi:10.1109/SFCS.2000.892324

Kee, K. F., Sparks, L., Struppa, D. C., Mannucci, M. A., & Damiano, A. (2016). Information diffusion, Facebook clusters, and the simplicial model of social aggregation: A computational simulation of simplicial diffusers for community health interventions. *Health Communication*, *31*(4), 385–399. doi:10.1080/10410236.2014.960061 PMID:26362453

Klein, A., Ahlf, H., & Sharma, V. (2015). Social activity and structural centrality in online social networks. *Telematics and Informatics*, *32*(2), 321–332. doi:10.1016/j.tele.2014.09.008

Kuhn, F., Lynch, N., & Oshman, R. (2010). Distributed computation in dynamic networks. In *Proceedings of the forty-second ACM symposium on Theory of computing* (pp. 513-522). ACM. doi:10.1145/1806689.1806760

Kuhn, F., & Oshman, R. (2011). Dynamic networks: Models and algorithms. *ACM SIGACT News*, *42*(1), 82–96. doi:10.1145/1959045.1959064

Kwak, H., Lee, C., Park, H., & Moon, S. (2010). What is Twitter, a social network or a news media? In *Proceedings of the 19th international conference on World wide web* (pp. 591-600). ACM. doi:10.1145/1772690.1772751

Loury, G. C. (1987). Why should we care about group inequality? *Social Philosophy & Policy*, *5*(1), 249–271. doi:10.1017/S0265052500001345

Malone, T. W., & Crowstone, K. (1994). The Interdisciplinary Study of Coordination. *ACM Computing Surveys*, *26*(1), 87–119. doi:10.1145/174666.174668

McPherson, M., Smith-Lovin, L., & Cook, J. M. (2001). Birds of a Feather: Homophily in Social Networks. *Annual Review of Sociology*, *27*(1), 415–444. doi:10.1146/annurev.soc.27.1.415

McQuail, D. (2005). Processes and models of media effects. In McQuail's mass communication theory. Sage.

Millen, D. R., Feinberg, J., Kerr, B., Rogers, O., & Cambridge, S. (2006). *Dogear: Social Bookmarking in the Enterprise*. Academic Press.

Monge, P. R., & Contractor, N. (2003). *Theories of communication networks*. Oxford University Press.

Moreno, Y., Nekovee, M., & Pacheco, A. F. (2004). Dynamics of rumor spreading in complex networks. *Physical Review E: Statistical, Nonlinear, and Soft Matter Physics*, *69*(6), 066130. doi:10.1103/PhysRevE.69.066130 PMID:15244690

Morrissey, L. (2010). Trolling is an art: Towards a schematic classification of intention in internet trolling. *Griffith Working Papers in Pragmatics and Intercultural Communications, 3*(2).

Mowshowitz, A. (1994). Virtual organization: A vision of management in the information age. *The Information Society*, *10*(4), 267–288. doi:10.1080/01972243.1994.9960172

Murphy, J., Kim, A., Hagood, H., Richards, A., Augustine, C., Kroutil, L., & Sage, A. (2011). Twitter Feeds and Google Search Query Surveillance: Can They Supplement Survey Data Collection? *Shifting the Boundaries of Research*, 228.

Nahapiet, J., & Ghoshal, S. (1998). Social capital, intellectual capital, and the organizational advantage. *Academy of Management Review*, *23*(2), 242–266.

Ortega, F. J., Troyano, J. A., Cruz, F. L., Vallejo, C. G., & Enríquez, F. (2012). Propagation of trust and distrust for the detection of trolls in a social network. *Computer Networks*, *56*(12), 2884–2895. doi:10.1016/j.comnet.2012.05.002

Parkhe, A., Wasserman, S., & Ralston, D. A. (2006). New frontiers in network theory development. *Academy of Management Review*, *31*(3), 560–568. doi:10.5465/AMR.2006.21318917

Pittel, B. (1987). On spreading a rumor. *SIAM Journal on Applied Mathematics*, *47*(1), 213–223. doi:10.1137/0147013

Poggi, A., & Tomaiuolo, M. (2010). Integrating peer-to-peer and multi-agent technologies for the realization of content sharing applications. *Studies in Computational Intelligence*, *324*, 93–107.

Poggi, A., & Tomaiuolo, M. (2013). A DHT-based multi-agent system for semantic information sharing. In *New Challenges in Distributed Information Filtering and Retrieval* (pp. 197–213). Springer Berlin Heidelberg. doi:10.1007/978-3-642-31546-6_12

Poggi, A., Tomaiuolo, M., & Vitaglione, G. (2003). Security and trust in agent-oriented middleware. In *OTM Confederated International Conferences On the Move to Meaningful Internet Systems* (pp. 989-1003). Springer Berlin Heidelberg. doi:10.1007/978-3-540-39962-9_95

Powell, A., Piccoli, G., & Ives, B. (2004). Virtual Teams: A Review of Current Literature and Directions for Future Research. *The Data Base for Advances in Information Systems*, *35*(1), 7. doi:10.1145/968464.968467

Putnam, R. D. (1995). Bowling alone: Americas declining social capital. *Journal of Democracy*, *6*(1), 65–78. doi:10.1353/jod.1995.0002

Roy, S. R. (2012). Digital Mastery: The Skills Needed for Effective Virtual Leadership. *International Journal of e-Collaboration*, *8*(3), 56–66. doi:10.4018/jec.2012070104

Seah, C. W., Chieu, H. L., Chai, K. M. A., Teow, L. N., & Yeong, L. W. (2015, July). Troll detection by domain-adapting sentiment analysis. In *18th International Conference on Information Fusion (Fusion) 2015* (pp. 792-799). IEEE.

Shah, D., & Zaman, T. (2011). Rumors in a network: Whos the culprit? *IEEE Transactions on Information Theory*, *57*(8), 5163–5181. doi:10.1109/TIT.2011.2158885

Stavrakantonakis, I., Gagiu, A. E., Kasper, H., Toma, I., & Thalhammer, A. (2012). An approach for evaluation of social media monitoring tools. *Common Value Management, 52*.

Su, C., & Contractor, N. (2011). A multidimensional network approach to studying team members information seeking from human and digital knowledge sources in consulting firms. *Journal of the American Society for Information Science and Technology, 62*(7), 1257–1275. doi:10.1002/asi.21526

Tomaiuolo, M. (2013). Trust Management for Web Services. *International Journal of Information Security and Privacy, 7*(3), 53–67. doi:10.4018/jisp.2013070104

Tomaiuolo, M. (2013). Trust management and delegation for the administration of web services. In *Organizational* (pp. 18–37). Legal, and Technological Dimensions of Information System Administration.

Van de Ven, A., Delbecq, A., & Koenig, R. (1976). Determinants of coordination modes within organizations. *American Sociological Review, 41*(2), 322–338. doi:10.2307/2094477

Wang, D., Pedreschi, D., Song, C., Giannotti, F., & Barabasi, A. L. (2011, August). Human mobility, social ties, and link prediction. In *Proceedings of the 17th ACM SIGKDD international conference on Knowledge discovery and data mining* (pp. 1100-1108). ACM. doi:10.1145/2020408.2020581

Wang, D., Wen, Z., Tong, H., Lin, C. Y., Song, C., & Barabási, A. L. (2011, March). Information spreading in context. In *Proceedings of the 20th international conference on World wide web* (pp. 735-744). ACM.

Wasko, M. M., & Faraj, S. (2005). Why should I share? examining social capital and knowledge contribution in electronic networks of practice. *Management Information Systems Quarterly, 29*(1), 35–57.

Wasserman, S., & Faust, K. (1994). *Social network analysis: Methods and applications* (Vol. 8). Cambridge University Press. doi:10.1017/CBO9780511815478

Williamson, O. E. (1991). Comparative Economic Organization: The Analysis of Discrete Structural Alternatives. *Administrative Science Quarterly, 36*(2), 219–244. doi:10.2307/2393356

Wuchty, S., Jones, B. F., & Uzzi, B. (2007). The increasing dominance of teams in production of knowledge. *Science, 316*(5827), 1036–1039. doi:10.1126/science.1136099 PMID:17431139

Ye, S., & Wu, F. (2013). Measuring message propagation and social influence on Twitter.com. *International Journal of Communication Networks and Distributed Systems*, *11*(1), 59–76. doi:10.1504/IJCNDS.2013.054835

Zaman, T., Fox, E. B., & Bradlow, E. T. (2014). A Bayesian approach for predicting the popularity of tweets. *The Annals of Applied Statistics*, *8*(3), 1583–1611. doi:10.1214/14-AOAS741

Zaman, T. R., Herbrich, R., Van Gael, J., & Stern, D. (2010, December). Predicting information spreading in twitter. In *Workshop on computational social science and the wisdom of crowds, nips* (*Vol. 104*, No. 45, pp. 17599-601). Citeseer.

Zhou, Y., Guan, X., Zhang, Z., & Zhang, B. (2008, June). Predicting the tendency of topic discussion on the online social networks using a dynamic probability model. In *Proceedings of the hypertext 2008 workshop on Collaboration and collective intelligence* (pp. 7-11). ACM. doi:10.1145/1379157.1379160

Chapter 11
Invest, Engage, and Win:
Online Campaigns and Their Outcomes in an Israeli Election

Moran Yarchi
The Interdisciplinary Center (IDC), Israel

Tal Samuel-Azran
The Interdisciplinary Center (IDC), Israel

Gadi Wolfsfeld
The Interdisciplinary Center (IDC), Israel

Elad Segev
Tel-Aviv University, Israel

ABSTRACT

Though the use of social media for political campaigning has been widely studied, its correlation with electoral success has not received much attention. The current study uses the 2013 Israeli elections to examine the impact of social media on campaigns as a process. Findings indicate that parties and candidates that invest in social media are more likely to achieve social media success, which in turn increases their chances of achieving electoral success. Some may dispute the level of influence of social media; however, study findings suggest that being active in the digital arena has become a significant element in achieving ballot box success.

DOI: 10.4018/978-1-5225-1963-8.ch011

INTRODUCTION

One of the most challenging political communication questions concerns social media in election campaigns. These days, social media serve as a public stage for political deliberation (Bode et al., 2014; Dvir-Gvirsman et al., 2014; Kushin & Kitchener, 2009; Zhang et al., 2010). As the new media become an increasingly important part of every campaign (Dimitrova et al., 2014; Trent & Friedenberg, 2008; Trippi, 2013), researchers and practitioners have been attempting to understand whether social media popularity can be linked to electoral success. This study deals directly with that issue by looking at the role of Facebook in the 2013 Israeli elections.

In the U.S., the 2008 presidential campaign was considered a social media turning point. Indeed, in 2008, CNN went so far as to ask whether the presidential election would be won on Facebook (Rawlinson, 2007). In 2012, the Obama digital campaign made several significant changes, and the general impression was that these contributed to the President's re-election (Trippi, 2013).

Previous studies have examined this phenomenon from various perspectives. Some that examined political preferences and election results (Ceron et al., 2013; Lui et al., 2011) found that social media activity can be used to forecast results in Italy and France (Ceron et al., 2013). Others looked at how citizens use social media during election campaigns (Baumgartner & Morris, 2010; Fernandes et al., 2010; Kushin & Yamamoto, 2010; Robertson el al., 2010; Small, 2008), and how candidates were portrayed (Woolley et al., 2010). Some studies dealt with the impact of social media on political participation (Bakker & de Vreese, 2011; Baumgartner & Morris 2010; Conroy et al., 2012; Dimitrova et al., 2014; Vitak et al., 2011; Wolfsfeld et al., 2013; Zhang et al., 2010) and social capital (Pasek et al., 2009; Valenzuela et al., 2009; Gil de Zúñiga et al., 2012), while others focused on candidates' use of social media (Bronstein, 2013; Church, 2010; Gueorguieva, 2008; Metzgar & Maruggi, 2009; Perlmutter, 2008; Robertson et al., 2010; Wen, 2014).

The current study examines the impact of social media on election campaigns as a process, beginning with the amount of resources a political party invests in digital media, the extent to which this investment leads to greater social media success, and the extent to which this second variable can be translated into electoral success. To better understand this process, the authors took into consideration additional factors such as the parties' initial Knesset1 size and their relative success in the traditional news media. The 2013 Israeli elections were considered by many to be the first Facebook elections in Israel, since social media hosted an extensive part of the campaigns and political discussions. Using Israel as a case study provides a more international perspective (compared to most studies in the field, which were conducted in the US). The characteristics of the Israeli political system enable us to compare these variables in a multi-party parliamentary system.

INVESTING IN DIGITAL MEDIA

Early studies focused on mass media investments and their role in changing voters' attitudes. Most scholars agree that traditional media coverage of issues and events influences public opinion (de Vreese et al., 2011; Entman, 2003; McQuail, 1994), especially when dealing with political issues, such as election campaigns (Hopmann et al., 2010; van Aelst et al., 2008). For example, Norris et al. (1999) found that the media can have direct effects on political opinions. Thus, media shapes its recipients' conceptions of political reality, while setting the frames of reference that they use to interpret public events (McQuail, 1994; de Vreese et al., 2011). Previous studies have indicated a link between traditional media coverage and audience attitudes (Beck et al., 2002; de Vreese et al., 2011; Druckman, 2005; Entman, 1993; Gamson, 1992; Mazzoleni & Schulz, 1999; Mendelsohn, 1996), taking into consideration that other factors, such as personal experience and interactions with peers, also affect audience views (Neuman et al., 1992). Previous studies also found that financial investment in media campaigning provides resourceful candidates with an advantage over their rivals (Davis, 2000; Ganz, 1994, 2000).

Whereas the above studies relate mostly to traditional media, the emergence of Web campaigns sparked an important new line of research. The question was whether the lower costs of internet use provided a way for candidates and political parties to compete on a more equal basis. Proponents of the equalization hypothesis argued that creating a website requires many fewer resources than using public relations and advertising agencies (Corrado & Firestone, 1996; Gibson & Ward, 1998; Rash, 1997). Conversely, critics argued that the Web reflects the traditional power play, because candidates with better resources have better online media. Effective web campaigns are expensive, and operating professional websites requires significant resources (Margolis & Resnick, 2000).

The majority of early studies supported the normalization hypothesis and identified that the larger parties had more advanced and well-designed websites, and were able to generate a significantly greater volume of traffic (Bowers-Brown & Gunter, 2002; Gibson & Ward 1998; Gibson & Ward, 2000; Norris, 2001; Ward & Gibson, 2003). The growth of social networking services renewed the debate and led to further studies.

Indeed, the Web 2.0 era provides wider evidence for the equalization hypothesis. The 2008 US Democratic primaries, as well as Obama's victory, were widely influenced by skillful use of social media, again in favor of the candidate originally perceived as the underdog (Harfoush, 2009; Hindman, 2009; Trippi, 2013). Similar trends were found in Scandinavia (Carlson & Strandberg, 2008; Kalnes, 2009), Australia (Gibson & McAllister, 2009), and Germany (Zittel, 2009). In contrast, Schweitzer's 2011 study of German online campaigns indicated normalization, because larger parties used social media to their advantage much more efficiently. Studies in the UK and US also regularly point in the direction of normalization (Gibson, 2010; Gulati & Williams, 2013; Williams & Gulati, 2013).

Does Success with Social Media Lead to Electoral Success?

Media attention during the election campaign is seen as vital to the election outcome (Harrop, 1987; Hopmann et al., 2010; van Aelst et al., 2008), and politicians are convinced that media attention is crucial for their electoral success (van Aelst et al., 2008). Media attention was found to contribute to the electoral success of parties and candidates (Brosius & Kepplinger, 1992; Gerth & Siegert, 2011; Maddens et al., 2006; Sheafer & Weimann, 2005; van Aelst et al., 2008).

The impact of social media on election outcomes, however, has not received enough scholarly attention. A related topic that has been studied is the impact of social media on political participation and civic engagement. Social media's political use was found to correlate with civic engagement, and enhance both digital and traditional political participation (Bode et al., 2014; Gil de Zúñiga et al., 2012; Wolfsfeld et al., 2013; Xenos et al., 2014; Zhang et al., 2010). If so, it is reasonable to expect social media campaigning to affect political processes.

To date, there are only a few studies that have dealt with the impact of online campaigns on election outcomes. One of the earliest (D'Alessio, 1997) found that investing in online campaigns is linked to electoral success. Findings did not clearly indicate whether Web campaigns directly affect the election outcomes; rather, they suggested that such campaigns reflect the parties' size and power, as well as their level of campaign preparation, thus supporting the normalization hypothesis. Given the increasing use of the internet in political contexts, more studies supported this trend. Gibson and McAllister (2006; 2011) studied the impact of digital campaigning on voting in the Australian elections in a Web 1.0 environment during the 2004 elections, and in a Web 2.0 environment during the 2007 elections, generally finding that online campaigns constitute an important component of a winning election strategy, but those effects are moderated by the party and the tools used (Gibson & McAllister, 2011). Their findings indicated that Web-based techniques are nontraditional, providing a clear advantage in election outcomes (Gibson & McAllister, 2006). Similarly, while examining the 2006 US midterm congressional elections, Wagner and Gainous (2009) found that digital campaigning and Web presence were significant predictors of the total votes candidates garnered, even when controlling for funding, incumbency, and experience. Further, Sudulich and Wall (2010) found that Web-based campaigns are more effective in areas with higher internet penetration. Apart from website presence, Rackaway (2007) emphasized the influence of blogs and "grassroots mobilizing sites" to the success of campaigns.

Investment in Web 2.0 platforms made the study of online campaign outcomes even more complex and challenging, mainly because users are able to directly engage and channel campaigns in several directions, making it harder for the candidates to control the process. Thus, Gueorguieva (2008) found that YouTube and Myspace indeed offer greater potential for new candidates to spread their messages. However, once the message is reproduced and changed by users, candidates lose control over it. Zittel (2009), reporting on the 2005 German federal elections, further found that young candidates and those running in districts with a high share of young voters were more likely to engage in and benefit from social media campaigning. Hence, the use of interactive online platforms may particularly leverage the outcomes of parties that employ them. It seems, for example, that parties that can appeal to the younger audience may benefit more from employing Web 2.0 tools in their election campaigns.

Engagement:[2] The Mediating Factor

The engagement of online audiences is therefore an important and perhaps crucial factor for evaluating the election outcomes. Park and Perry (2008) showed that online campaigns clearly influence the level of engagement and the social interaction between users, who further spread information to their friends. In recent years, social networking platforms, particularly Facebook, have been embraced by many political candidates as a platform for engaging and mobilizing their supporters. Hong and Nadler (2012) explored the relationship between presidential candidates' use of social media channels by measuring the number of mentions they received on Twitter. Their findings showed that high levels of presidential candidate Twitter activity had only minimal effects on their mentions by users in this channel. This provides another indication that investment in social media has a certain independence from both candidates' actions and election outcomes. To conclude, most studies on election campaigns conducted on the internet examine the relationship either between online investment and election success, or between online investment and audience engagement. As far as can be discerned, no previous studies have systematically explored the relationship among the three stages: investment in digital media, social media success, and electoral success.

The theoretical argument is straightforward: all other things being equal, political parties that make a significant investment in social media during an election campaign are more likely to have citizens react positively to the party and/or candidate posts on Facebook. Social media success should, in turn, lead to electoral success. Investing in digital media is the independent variable, social media success is the intervening variable, and the dependent variable is electoral success.

The underlying logic is that social media represents a powerful tool for encouraging potential voters emotionally and ideologically. The traditional electoral campaign, which is vastly different from what happens in the digital era, is based on two major communication channels: the mainstream news media and political advertisements, that is, two inherently passive types of communication that can nevertheless attract success at the ballot box. Social media, however, enables potential supporters to become actively engaged in the campaign, which the authors believe offers major advantages. In addition, potential supporters receiving the political messages from their "friends" increases the likelihood that such communications will be read and watched. The term "potential" is critical here. The assumption is that political parties that are able to successfully exploit the social media are in a better position to reach voters who consider that party or candidate as a viable voting option. A massive investment in social media by an inherently unpopular party will not save it. In addition, in a multi-party system, most voters identify with a certain ideological camp, and few will consider voting for a party that is opposed to their core political beliefs. Thus, the authors expect strong correlations between the three variables, but do not see investment in the social media as something that always brings electoral success.

The study's hypothesis claims that the impact of social media on election campaigns is a process; the amount of resources a political party invests in digital media leads to greater levels of social media success, which in turn can lead to electoral success. Success on social media is expected to serve as a mediator variable between the parties' and candidates' investment on digital media and their electoral success.

METHOD

This study examines the 19th Israeli parliament (the Knesset) elections, held on January 22, 2013. Israel has a multi-party proportionate representation system, which has always led to coalition governments. In the 2013 elections, 32 parties ran for the Knesset (many did not have a realistic chance of being elected, due to the two-percent threshold that is required to secure any representation). The 19th Knesset's 120 seats are distributed between 12 parties. The citizens in Israel vote for their preferred party, but due to the tendency in western democratic countries to emphasize and personalize candidates (Balmas et al., 2014)—and a few changes that were made in the Israeli voting system3— – candidates (and especially party leaders) play a significant role in the election campaign. As such, the authors decided to also examine the impact of Facebook pages for both parties and certain candidates. Social media played a central role in the 2013 Israeli election campaigns, and politicians' use of new media tools is correspondingly vast. Almost all political parties had a digital campaign (including Facebook pages), and their financial investment was 50 percent of the total budget (Mann & Lev-On, 2014). The authors selected the parties and candidates for this study based on their chances to pass the two-percent threshold, as reflected in the polls before the elections. The final list included 14 parties and nine candidates.4

In keeping with the study's goals, several interviews with the parties' campaign managers and new media managers were conducted. The parties and candidates' online activity was Web-mined via monitoring their Facebook activity and mentions in prominent news websites (see below). The indicator for candidates' political success was the election result.

Investment in Digital Media

The information about the three investment variables was collected through 27 interviews with campaign staff members.5 During those post-election interviews, the campaign managers provided us with information about their parties' financial, personnel, and time investments in digital media.

To assess the parties' commitment to digital media, the authors examined three indicators:

1. Financial investment (the percentage of the total media budget invested in digital media);
2. The number of the campaign's digital media staff members; and
3. The length of the digital media campaign (measured in weeks).

These three aspects, which were presented as part of the factors of political campaigns professionalism in previous studies (Gibson & Römmele, 2001; 2009; Tenscher et al., 2012), together provided a broad, albeit imperfect, assessment of parties' investment in digital media.

Investment in Digital Media Scale

To effectively estimate the parties' investment in digital media, the authors constructed the Investment in Digital Media scale. The scale was calculated using the three indicators mentioned: the parties' financial investment in new media, the number of the campaign's digital media staff members, and the length of the digital media's campaign. The scale's range was determined by merging those three indicators' standardized scores, and confirmed using a factor analysis (with loadings of no less than 0.807 for any of the items).

Online Activity and Success

The authors chose to focus on Facebook because it is by far the most popular social network site in Israel, with 4.3 million users (more than 50 percent of the population), 95 percent of whom are over the age of 18 and considered potential voters, according to official Facebook figures (Kabir & Urbach, 2013).6 For each party and candidate, the authors collected activity data during 52 days before the elections (between December 1, 2012 and January 21, 2013).7 Specifically, the authors looked at the daily party and candidate mentions in mainstream online newspapers, and the number of likes given to their official Facebook pages. Because most online activity in Israel is conducted in Hebrew, the authors measured only Hebrew content. The authors recorded Facebook activity on the relevant official pages of the parties and the candidates, using the following measurements:

Online News

This variable consisted of the daily average number of news mentions of each party and candidate. The authors used the full names of the candidates and the official names of their parties as appeared on the official Israeli government website (The Israeli elections website, n.d.). The data on news mentions were retrieved using software called Makam (Makam, n.d.) that systematically mined thousands of Web pages using pre-selected keywords. For the news data, the authors looked at the number of items mentioning each political party or candidate in all mainstream sites in Israel including Ynet, Walla, NRG, Haaretz, The Marker, Globes, Nana10, and News1. For the purpose of this study, even when a party or a candidate was mentioned more than once in the same news item, it was counted only as one mention. Given the massive amount of content, no attempt was made to assess whether the news stories were considered "positive" or "negative." Thus, the measure is meant to convey media standing rather than legitimacy.

Facebook Data

After identifying the official Facebook pages of the parties and their candidates, the authors used three measurements to examine their success:

1. *Facebook's "talking about this" (TAT) scale*, which refers to the number of people who responded to a post in a page mainly by sharing, liking, or commenting on it during the last seven days. The authors calculated the average TAT for each party or candidate between December 1, 2012 and January 21, 2013.

2. *Facebook Likes added to the page during the campaign.* For each party or candidate, the authors calculated the number of likes added during the campaign by subtracting those in the beginning of December from the number on the day of the elections. This measurement gives us a general overview of the party or candidate's pages.
3. *Facebook Likes (daily average)* compensates for this general overview by providing the information on a daily basis.[8]

Overall Facebook Success Scale

In order to get a better estimation of the parties' and candidates' success on Facebook, the *Overall Facebook Success scale* was calculated using the three indicators noted: Facebook's TAT scale, the number of Facebook Likes added to the page during the campaign, and the daily average number of Facebook Likes. The scale was gauged by merging those three indicators' standardized scores, and confirmed using a factor analysis (with loadings of no less than 0.900 for any individual item).

Political Success

The election results were used to measure the parties and candidates' political success. Two indicators were used:

1. The *number of Knesset seats* won by the respective parties in the elections, and
2. The *change in the party's number of seat from the last elections.* This last represents the rise or decline of the parties' political power during the elections.

The examination of the absolute number of seats won provides us with a completely objective measure of electoral success, since winning seats is the ultimate goal of every political party. However, the disadvantage of this measurement is its problematic assumption that every party starts from zero, ignoring the major advantages that existing parties have in terms of resources and voter loyalty. An examination of the change in each party's number of seats compared to the last elections solves this problem. While there are many factors that affect the ability of parties to improve their Knesset representation, it is important to see whether social media is among the factors that contribute to that success.

In addition to the political success in the 2013 election, the *number of seats of each party in the previous Knesset* (according to the 2009 elections) was taken into account and served as a controlling variable in the study's analysis. An examination of the number of existing seats in the beginning of the campaign is important, because party size affects both its resources (because the state's election funding relies on party size) and its political success in the current elections (because, as mentioned above, the party's Knesset size has an effect on its ability to attract voters). Table 1 presents the distribution of the variables used in the study.

RESULTS AND DISCUSSION

This section will examine the study's hypotheses, beginning by examining the correlation between the parties' and candidates' investment and social media success, and conclude by examining the full model, beginning with the parties' and candidates' investment in digital media, through their success on it, and on to their political success in the elections.

It is important to note that in contrast to most studies, the statistical significance of the results is less of a concern. The reason is that the authors were basically examining all the political parties with a reasonable chance of entering the Knesset. The major reason to examine statistical significance is to attempt to generalize from the sample to a more general population. In general, the authors found that the correlations were strong (Table 2), although due to the small number of cases (23) not always statistically significant.

Table 1. Summary of variables

Variables Distribution (Means and Standard Deviations)			
	N	Mean	SD
Facebook's Talking about this scale	23	20,545.30	22,460.61
Facebook's Likes added to page during the campaign	23	14,048.65	19,315.04
Facebook Likes (daily average)	23	464.28	597.43
Overall Facebook Success	23	0	0.72
Online News Exposure	23	50.31	45.10
Financial investment in digital media	18	19.08	14.644
Number of digital media staff members	18	6.67	3.56
Digital media's campaign length	18	25.22	25.55
Digital Investment	18	0.07	0.71
Seats in last elections	23	9.26	11.03
Number of seats in the Knesset	23	10.22	10.30
Change in the number of seats since the last elections	23	0.96	11.77

Table 2. Controlling for party size

	Digital Investment, Social Media Success, and Online News Exposure				
	Overall Facebook Success	Facebook's Talking about This Scale	Facebook's Likes Added to Page during the Campaign	Facebook Likes (Daily Average)	Online News Exposure
Digital Investment - controlling for party size. (zero-order correlation)	.494* (.473*)	.424* (.364)	.623* (.641**)	.227 (.232)	.503* (.256)

Note: Entries are Pearson's R scores.
*$p \leq .05$. **$p \leq .01$. ***$p \leq .001$, N=23

In accordance with the hypothesis and as shown in Table 2, a relatively strong correlation was found between the parties' and candidates' investment in social media and their subsequent success. The findings indicate that an increase in the investment in digital media leads to more success in all three Facebook variables: the Overall Facebook Success scale ($r = 0.494$); and online news coverage,[9] while controlling for the number of seats in the previous elections, a variable that also tells us the amount of state funding the party received for the election campaign (the zero sum correlation between the investment and the success on the different digital media variables is presented in Table 2).[10]

This relationship between investment in digital media and success on Facebook certainly makes sense, but is far from obvious, and there are surely political parties that make a major investment in social media, but either their messages or their candidates fail to resonate. These results suggest, however, that most parties do receive a return on their social media investments. Parties and candidates that invest more heavily in digital media will generally be more successful in social media, regardless of their party size.

As presented in model 1 of Tables 3 and 4, parties' and candidates' investments in digital media can predict their political success in the elections for both indicators. The more heavily a party or candidate invests in digital media, the greater their political success. Model 2 (of Tables 3 and 4) adds success in digital media (the Overall Facebook Success scale) as a predictor. Findings indicate that it explains the effect of parties' and candidates' investment in digital media on both indicators of their political success (Hayes, 2013). Investment in digital media leads to parties and candidates' popularity there, which leads to election success. Model 3 (of Tables 3 and 4) adds the number of seats in the previous elections as a control

Table 3. Predicting overall electoral success (number of Knesset seats) using investment and social media success and existing Knesset size (regression model)

	Model 1	Model 2	Model 3	SE
Digital Investment	0.439*	0.224	0.390	3.112
Overall Facebook Success		0.454*	0.378*	5.461
Seats in last elections			0.432**	0.195
N	18	18	18	
Total *(adjusted)*	0.142	0.267	0.415	

Note: Entries are standardized beta coefficients and standard errors.
*$p \leq .1$. **$p \leq .05$. ***$p \leq .01$.

Table 4. Predicting relative electoral success (change in the number of seats since the last elections), using investment and social media success, and existing Knesset size (regression model)

	Model 1	Model 2	Model 3	SE
Digital Investment	0.626***	0.220	0.322	3.133
Overall Facebook Success		0.522**	0.312*	5.461
Seats in last elections			-0.524***	0.195
N	18	18	18	
Total *(adjusted)*	0.354	0.430	0.603	

Note: Entries are standardized beta coefficients and standard errors.
*$p \leq .1$. **$p \leq .05$. ***$p \leq .01$.

variable, and exhibits similar findings. The model in Table 3 explains more than 41 percent of the variance of the number of seats, and the model in Table 3 explains more than 60 percent of the same.

Surprisingly, the number of seats in the previous elections serves as a negative predictor for the change (Table 4). One possible explanation is that this result had to do with the particularities of this election and not any theoretical issue that can be generalized; during the 2013 elections in Israel, two small parties received a large amount of votes (*Yesh Atid,* a new party, went from zero seats to 19, and *Habayit Hayehudi* went from three seats to 12). At the same time, the largest party in the previous elections, Kadima, lost 26 seats (from 28 seats to only two).

Similar to the concept of advertising and public relations (Reis & Reis, 2002), the findings suggest that while dealing with election campaigns in the Web 2.0

era, investment in digital media leads to political power. In addition, the evidence provides some support to the normalization hypothesis (Bowers-Brown & Gunter, 2002; Gibson & Ward, 2000; Norris, 2001). Table 5 gives more detail on social media success when controlling for party size.

CONCLUSION

The findings provide strong support for the hypothesis. In the Israeli election campaign of 2013, digital media investment was clearly worth every shekel spent (Israel's currency). These findings should assist both scholars and practitioners in the field of political communication.

One reason to treat these findings with a bit of caution is that the authors decided to focus on parties and leaders who had a realistic chance of passing the two-percent threshold and getting into the Knesset. This decision makes theoretical sense because the authors do not believe that an investment in Facebook will save a party with little initial support. As argued, the assumption is that investment in social media allows parties and leaders to attract *potential* voters. There are certainly unpopular parties that did invest in social media and never made it into the Knesset. This reality is

Table 5. Digital investment (the different components), social media success, and online news exposure, controlling for party size

	Overall Facebook Success	Facebook's Talking about This Scale	Facebook's Likes Added to Page during the Campaign	Facebook Likes (Daily Average)	Online News Exposure
Financial investment in digital media - controlling for party size. (zero-order correlation)	.652* (.752**)	.659* (.730**)	.700* (.796**)	.355 (.505)	.525 (.278)
Number of digital media staff members - controlling for party size. (zero-order correlation)	.488 (.515*)	.397 (.455)	.581* (.529*)	.258 (.291)	.398 (.492)
Digital media's campaign length - controlling for party size. (zero-order correlation)	.060 (.057)	.061 (.004)	.169 (.231)	-.113 (-.082)	.062 (-.164)

$*p \leq .05. **p \leq .01. ***p \leq .001, N=23$

important to keep in mind, especially for those who might exaggerate the potential of social media to compensate for other, more inherent problems facing political parties and leaders.

Nevertheless, this assumption may be more problematic in some types of elections than others. In the US, for example, the primary system provides opportunities for completely unknown candidates to become popular. In this context, the use of social media may prove critical in generating some initial excitement about a candidate. It would be indeed worthwhile to look at *all* candidates and parties running in different types of elections. One would also assume that social media are more effective in some countries than in others. If so, future studies should examine similar research questions in other countries and other political systems. In addition, it would be interesting to review the topic over time; in different election campaigns in the same country, it will allow us to get a better understanding of the impact over time.

Another limitation has to do with the relatively small number of cases used in the study. The authors measured 14 parties and 9 candidates that had a realistic chance to get elected, constituting a small data set. Since the study deals with the whole range of Israeli political parties, and the findings indicate substantial correlations between the variables, the findings and conclusion are meaningful notwithstanding the small number of cases tested.

Despite these caveats, the findings do tell us that being active in the digital arena has become a significant element in achieving ballot box success.

REFERENCES

Bakker, T. P., & de Vreese, C. H. (2011). Good news for the future? Young people, internet use, and political participation. *Communication Research*, *38*(4), 451–470. doi:10.1177/0093650210381738

Balmas, M., Rahat, G., Sheafer, T., & Shenhav, S. R. (2014). Two routes to personalized politics: Centralized and decentralized personalization. *Party Politics*, *20*(1), 37–51. doi:10.1177/1354068811436037

Baumgartner, J. C., & Morris, J. S. (2010). MyFaceTube Politics: Social Networking web sites and political engagement of young adults. *Social Science Computer Review*, *28*(1), 24–44. doi:10.1177/0894439309334325

Beck, P., Dalton, R., Greene, S., & Huckfeldt, R. (2002). The social calculus of voting: Interpersonal, media, and organizational influences on presidential choices. *The American Political Science Review*, *96*(1), 57–74. doi:10.1017/S0003055402004239

Bode, L., Vraga, E. K., Borah, P., & Shah, D. V. (2014). A new space for political behavior: Political social networking and its democratic consequences. *Journal of Computer-Mediated Communication*, *19*(3), 414–429. doi:10.1111/jcc4.12048

Bowers-Brown, J., & Gunter, B. (2002). Political parties use of the web during the 2001 general election. *Aslib Proceedings*, *54*(3), 166–176. doi:10.1108/00012530210441719

Bronstein, J. (2013). Like me! Analyzing the 2012 presidential candidates Facebook pages. *Online Information Review*, *37*(2), 173–192. doi:10.1108/OIR-01-2013-0002

Brosius, H. B., & Kepplinger, H. M. (1992). Beyond agenda-setting: The influence of partisanship and television reporting on the electorates voting intentions. *The Journalism Quarterly*, *69*(4), 893–901. doi:10.1177/107769909206900409

Carlson, T., & Strandberg, K. (2008). Riding the web 2.0 wave: Candidates on YouTube in the 2007 Finnish national elections. *Journal of Information Technology & Politics*, *5*(2), 159–174. doi:10.1080/19331680802291475

Ceron, A., Curini, L., Iacus, S. M., & Porro, G. (2013). Every tweet counts? How sentiment analysis of social media can improve our knowledge of citizens political preferences with an application to Italy and France. *New Media & Society*, *16*(2), 340–358. doi:10.1177/1461444813480466

Church, S. H. (2010). YouTube politics: YouChoose and leadership rhetoric during the 2008 election. *Journal of Information Technology & Politics*, *7*(2).

Conroy, M., Feezell, J. T., & Guerrero, M. (2012). Facebook and political engagement: A study of online political group membership and offline political engagement. *Computers in Human Behavior*, *28*(5), 1535–1546. doi:10.1016/j.chb.2012.03.012

Corrado, A., & Firestone, C. (1996). *Elections in cyberspace: Toward a new era in American politics*. Washington, DC: Aspen Institute.

DAlessio, D. W. (1997). Use of the web in the 1996 US election. *Electoral Studies*, *16*(4), 489–501. doi:10.1016/S0261-3794(97)00044-9

Davis, A. (2000). Public relations, news production and changing patterns of source access in the British national media. *Media Culture & Society*, *22*(1), 39–59. doi:10.1177/016344300022001003

de Vreese, C. H., Boomgaarden, H. G., & Semetko, H. A. (2011). (In)direct framing effects: The effects of news media framing on public. *Communication Research*, *38*(2), 179–205. doi:10.1177/0093650210384934

Dimitrova, D. V., Shehata, A., Strömbäck, J., & Nord, L. W. (2014). The effects of digital media on political knowledge and participation in election campaigns evidence from panel data. *Communication Research*, *41*(1), 95–118. doi:10.1177/0093650211426004

Druckman, J. N. (2005). Media matter: How newspapers and television news cover campaigns and influence voters. *Political Communication*, *22*(4), 463–481. doi:10.1080/10584600500311394

Dvir-Gvirsman, S., Tzfati, Y., & Menchen-Trevino, E. (2014). The extent and nature of ideological selective exposure online: Combining survey responses with actual web log data from the 2013 Israeli elections. *New Media & Society*.

Entman, R. M. (1993). Framing: Towards clarification of a fractured paradigm. *Journal of Communication*, *43*(4), 51–58. doi:10.1111/j.1460-2466.1993.tb01304.x

Entman, R. M. (2003). *Projections of power: Framing news, public opinion, and US Foreign policy*. Chicago: The University of Chicago Press. doi:10.7208/chicago/9780226210735.001.0001

Fernandes, J., Giurcanu, M., Bowers, K. W., & Neely, J. C. (2010). The writing on the wall: A content analysis of college students Facebook groups for the 2008 presidential election. *Mass Communication & Society*, *13*(5), 653–675. doi:10.1080/15205436.2010.516865

Gamson, W. A. (1992). *Talking politics*. New York, NY: Cambridge University Press.

Ganz, M. (1994). Voters in the crosshairs: How markets and technology are destroying politics. *The American Prospect, 16*, 100-109. Retrieved from http://prospect.org/article/voters-crosshairs

Ganz, M. (2000). Resources and resourcefulness: Leadership, strategy and organization in the unionization of California agriculture. *American Journal of Sociology, 105*(4), 1003–1062. doi:10.1086/210398

Gerth, M. A., & Siegert, G. (2011). Patterns of consistence and constriction: How news media frame the coverage of direct democratic campaigns. *The American Behavioral Scientist, 56*(3), 279–299. doi:10.1177/0002764211426326

Gibson, R. K. (2010). *Open source campaigning? UK party organisations and the use of the new media in the 2010 general election.* Academic Press.

Gibson, R. K., & McAllister, I. (2006). Does cyber-campaigning win votes? Online communication in the 2004 Australian election. *Journal of Elections, Public Opinion, and Parties, 16*(3), 243–263. doi:10.1080/13689880600950527

Gibson, R. K., & McAllister, I. (2009, September). *Revitalising participatory politics?: The internet, social capital and political action.* Paper presented at the APSA Annual Meeting, Toronto, Canada.

Gibson, R. K., & McAllister, I. (2011). Do online election campaigns win votes? The 2007 Australian YouTube election. *Political Communication, 28*(2), 227–244. doi:10.1080/10584609.2011.568042

Gibson, R. K., & Römmele, A. (2001). A party centered theory of professionalized campaigning. *The Harvard International Journal of Press/Politics, 6*(4), 31–44. doi:10.1177/108118001129172323

Gibson, R. K., & Römmele, A. (2009). Measuring the professionalization of political campaigning. *Party Politics, 15*(3), 265–293. doi:10.1177/1354068809102245

Gibson, R. K., & Ward, S. (1998). U.K. political parties and the internet: Politics as usual in the new media? *The Harvard International Journal of Press/Politics, 3*(3), 14–38. doi:10.1177/1081180X98003003003

Gibson, R. K., & Ward, S. (2000). An outsiders medium? The European elections and UK party competition on the Internet. *British Elections & Parties Yearbook, 10*(1), 173–191. doi:10.1080/13689880008413043

Gil de Zúñiga, H., Jung, N., & Valenzuela, S. (2012). Social media use for news and individuals social capital, civic engagement and political participation. *Journal of Computer-Mediated Communication*, *17*(3), 319–336. doi:10.1111/j.1083-6101.2012.01574.x

Goldenberg, R. (2013). *The tweets have died: Why did Twitter service fail in Israel.* Globes.

Gueorguieva, V. (2008). Voters, Myspace, and YouTube: The impact of alternative communication channels on the 2006 election cycle and beyond. *Social Science Computer Review*, *26*(3), 288–300. doi:10.1177/0894439307305636

Gulati, G. J., & Williams, C. B. (2013). Social media and campaign 2012: Developments and trends for Facebook adoption. *Social Science Computer Review*, *31*(5), 577–588. doi:10.1177/0894439313489258

Harfoush, R. (2009). *Yes we did! An inside look at how social media built the Obama brand.* Berkeley, CA: New Riders.

Harrop, M. (1987). Voters. In J. Seaton & B. Pimlott (Eds.), The media in British politics (pp. 45-63). Aldershot, UK: Dartmouth.

Hayes, A. F. (2013). *Introduction to mediation, moderation, and conditional process analysis: A regression-based approach.* New York, NY: Guilford Press.

Hindman, D. B. (2009). Mass media flow and differential distribution of politically disputed beliefs: The belief gap hypothesis. *Journalism & Mass Communication Quarterly*, *86*(4), 790–808. doi:10.1177/107769900908600405

Hong, S., & Nadler, D. (2012). Which candidates do the public discuss online in an election campaign?: The use of social media by 2012 presidential candidates and its impact on candidate salience. *Government Information Quarterly*, *29*(4), 455–461. doi:10.1016/j.giq.2012.06.004

Hopmann, D. N., Vliegenthart, R., de Vreese, C., & Erik Albæk, E. (2010). Effects of election news coverage: How visibility and tone influence party choice. *Political Communication*, *27*(4), 389–405. doi:10.1080/10584609.2010.516798

Kabir, M., & Urbach, A. (2013, May 21). Facebook exposes: How many Israelis are surfing the social network? *Calcalist.* (in Hebrew)

Kalnes, Ø. (2009). Norwegian parties and web 2.0. *Journal of Information Technology & Politics*, *6*(3/4), 251–266. doi:10.1080/19331680903041845

Kushin, M., & Kitchener, K. (2009). Getting political on social network sites: Exploring online political discourse on Facebook. *First Monday*, 14.

Kushin, M. J., & Yamamoto, M. (2010). Did social media really matter? College students use of online media and political decision making in the 2008 election. *Mass Communication & Society*, *13*(5), 608–630. doi:10.1080/15205436.2010.516863

Lui, C., Metaxas, P. T., & Mustafaraj, E. (2011, March). On the predictability of the US elections through search volume activity. In *Proceedings of the IADIS International Conference on e-Society*.

Maddens, B., Wauters, B., Noppe, J., & Fiers, S. (2006). Effects of campaign spending in an open list pr-system: The 2003 legislative elections in Flanders/Belgium. *West European Politics*, *29*(1), 161–168. doi:10.1080/01402380500389398

Makam. (n.d.). Retrieved from http://www.makam.co.il

Mann, R., & Lev-On, A. (2014). *Annual report: The Israeli media in 2013 agendas, uses and trends*. Ariel, Israel: The Institute for the Study of New Media, Politics and Society.

Margolis, M., & Resnick, D. (2000). Politics as usual: The "Cyberspace Revolution". Thousand Oaks, CA: Sage Publications.

Mazzoleni, G., & Schulz, W. (1999). Mediatization of politics: A challenge for democracy? *Political Communication*, *16*(3), 247–261. doi:10.1080/105846099198613

McQuail, D. (1994). *Mass communication theory*. London: Sage.

Mendelsohn, M. (1996). The media and interpersonal communications: The priming of issues, leaders, and party identification. *The Journal of Politics*, *58*(1), 112–125. doi:10.2307/2960351

Metzgar, E., & Maruggi, A. (2009). Social media and the 2008 US Presidential election. *Journal of New Communications Research*, *4*(1), 141–165.

Neuman, W. R., Just, M. R., & Crigler, A. N. (1992). Common knowledge: News and the construction of political meaning. Chicago, IL: University of Chicago Press.

Norris, P. (2001). *Digital divide*. Cambridge, UK: Cambridge University Press. doi:10.1017/CBO9781139164887

Norris, P., Curtice, J., Sanders, D., Scammell, M., & Semetko, H. A. (1999). *On message: Communicating the campaign*. London: Sage.

Park, H. M., & Perry, J. L. (2008). Do campaign web sites really matter in electoral civic engagement? Empirical evidence from the 2004 post-election internet tracking survey. *Social Science Computer Review*, 26(2), 190–212. doi:10.1177/0894439307309026

Pasek, J., More, E., & Romer, D. (2009). Realizing the social internet? Online social networking meets offline civic engagement. *Journal of Information Technology & Politics*, 6(3-4), 197–215. doi:10.1080/19331680902996403

Perlmutter, D. D. (2008). *Blogwars: The new political battleground*. New York, NY: Oxford University Press.

Rackaway, C. (2007). Trickle-down technology? The use of computing and network technology in state legislative campaigns. *Social Science Computer Review*, 25(4), 466–483. doi:10.1177/0894439307305625

Rash, W. (1997). *Politics on the nets: Wiring the political process*. New York, NY: W.H. Freeman.

Rawlinson, L. (2007). Will the 2008 USA election be won on Facebook? *CNN*. Retrieved from http://www.cnn.com/2007/TECH/05/01/election.facebook/

Ries, A., & Ries, L. (2002). *The fall of advertising and the rise of pr*. New York, NY: Harper Collins.

Robertson, S. P., Vatrapu, R. K., & Medina, R. (2010). Off the wall political discourse: Facebook use in the 2008 US presidential election. *Information Polity*, 15(1), 11–31.

Schweitzer, E. J. (2011). Normalization 2.0: A longitudinal analysis of German online campaigns in the national elections 2002–9. *European Journal of Communication*, 26(4), 310–327. doi:10.1177/0267323111423378

Sheafer, T., & Weimann, G. (2005). Agenda building, agenda setting, priming, individual voting intentions, and the aggregate results: An analysis of four Israeli elections. *Journal of Communication*, 55(2), 347–365. doi:10.1111/j.1460-2466.2005. tb02676.x

Small, T. (2008). The Facebook effect? Online campaigning in the 2008 Canadian and US elections. *Policy Options*, 85, 84–87.

Sudulich, M., & Wall, M. (2010). Cyber campaigning in the 2007 Irish general election. *Journal of Information Technology & Politics*, 7(4), 340–355. doi:10.1080/19331680903473485

Tenscher, J., Mykkänen, J., & Moring, T. (2012). Modes of professional campaigning: A four-country- comparison in the European parliamentary elections 2009. *The International Journal of Press/Politics, 17*(2), 145–168. doi:10.1177/1940161211433839

The Israeli Elections Website. (n.d.). Retrieved from http://www.bechirot.gov.il/elections19/eng/list/ListIndex_eng.aspx

Trent, J. S., & Friedenberg, R. V. (2008). *Political campaign communication: Principles and practices*. Plymouth, UK: Rowman & Littlefield.

Trippi, J. (2013). Technology has given politics back its soul. *Technology Review, 116*(1), 34–36.

Valenzuela, S., Park, N., & Kee, K. F. (2009). Is there social capital in a social network site? Facebook use and college students life satisfaction, trust, and participation. *Journal of Computer-Mediated Communication, 14*(4), 875–901. doi:10.1111/j.1083-6101.2009.01474.x

van Aelst, P., Maddens, B., Noppe, J., & Fiers, S. (2008). Politicians in the news: Media or party logic? Media attention and electoral success in the Belgian election campaign of 2003. *European Journal of Communication, 2*(2), 193–210. doi:10.1177/0267323108089222

Vitak, J., Zube, P., Smock, A., Carr, C. T., Ellison, N., & Lampe, C. (2011). Its complicated: Facebook users political participation in the 2008 election. *Cyberpsychology, Behavior, and Social Networking, 14*(3), 107–114. doi:10.1089/cyber.2009.0226 PMID:20649449

Wagner, K. M., & Gainous, J. (2009). Electronic grassroots: Does online campaigning work? *Journal of Legislative Studies, 15*(4), 502–520. doi:10.1080/13572330903302539

Ward, S., & Gibson, R. K. (2003). On-line and on message? Candidate websites in the 2001 general election. *British Journal of Politics and International Relations, 5*(2), 108–256. doi:10.1111/1467-856X.00103

Wen, W. C. (2014). Facebook political communication in Taiwan: 1.0/2.0 messages and election/post-election messages. *Chinese Journal of Communication, 7*(1), 19–39. doi:10.1080/17544750.2013.816754

Williams, C. B., & Gulati, G. J. (2013). Social networks in political campaigns: Facebook and the congressional elections of 2006 and 2008. *New Media & Society, 15*(1), 52–71. doi:10.1177/1461444812457332

Wolfsfeld, G., Yarchi, M., & Samuel-Azran, T. (2013, July). *Media repertoires and political participation: evidence from the Israeli electorate*. Paper presented at the ISPP annual meeting, Herzliya, Israel.

Woolley, J. K., Limperos, A. M., & Oliver, M. B. (2010). The 2008 presidential election, 2.0: A content analysis of user-generated political Facebook groups. *Mass Communication & Society*, *13*(5), 631–652. doi:10.1080/15205436.2010.516864

Xenos, M., Vromen, A., & Loader, B. D. (2014). The great equalizer? Patterns of social media use and youth political engagement in three advanced democracies. *Information Communication and Society*, *17*(2), 151–167. doi:10.1080/136911 8X.2013.871318

Zhang, W., Johnson, T. J., Seltzer, T., & Bichard, S. L. (2010). The revolution will be networked: The influence of social networking sites on political attitudes and behavior. *Social Science Computer Review*, *28*(1), 75–92. doi:10.1177/0894439309335162

Zittel, T. (2009). Lost in technology? Political parties and the online campaigns of constituency candidates in Germanys mixed member electoral system. *Journal of Information Technology & Politics*, *6*(3/4), 298–311. doi:10.1080/19331680903048832

KEY TERMS AND DEFINITIONS

"Facebook Elections": This term refers to the notion that contemporary elections are won through successful Facebook campaigns due to the rise of social networks as the key campaigning arena.

Engagement on Social Media: A salient indicator of social media's success is the ability to promote audiences' emotional involvement in its messages. Audience engagement can be measured using various methods, including the number of "Likes" and "Shares" a post receives and the "talking about this" scale.

Investment in Digital Media: Political actors invest resources to promote their messages through digital media based on their appreciation of its role in today's reality. The factors that can help us better understand such investments include the amount of money, the digital campaign's duration, and the number of people working on it.

Political Deliberation: The process of thoughtfully weighing options, usually prior to political decision-making. Deliberation emphasizes the use of logic and reason as opposed to power struggles via the active involvement of citizens in the political process.

Political Success in Election Campaigns: Political success is measured by the election outcomes. In parliamentary elections, political success is measured in the number of seats a party receives.

The Equalization-Normalization Debate in Social Media: A debate regarding the ability of social networks to promote equality between incumbents and challengers, due to the ease with which social media campaigns are launched in comparison to the mainstream media campaigns. Equalization refers to social media's ability to promote equal standing whereas normalization refers to maintenance of the former inequality.

The Israeli Political System: Israel has a multi-party proportionate representation system, which has always led to the formation of coalition governments. The Israeli Parliament ("the Knesset") has 120 seats, and the citizens in Israel vote for their preferred party.

ENDNOTES

[1]   The Israeli parliament.

[2]   The term "engagement" in social media refers to all activity on a party or a candidate's page (as shown in the number of "Likes", the Facebook "Talking about this" scale, etc.). The level of online engagement reflects political success on social media.

[3]   In the 1996, 1999, and 2001 election campaigns, the electoral system was changed to a "direct election of the Prime Minister" system. Citizens were given two ballots and were asked to vote for a particular candidate for Prime Minister and a political party for the Knesset. In the 2003 elections, Israel returned to the original system with some changes, but some believe this further accelerated the more personalized type of voting.

[4]   The candidates examined in the study are: Netanyahu, Lapid, Yachimovich, Bennett, Yishi, Liberman, Galon, Livni, and Mofaz. The parties are: HaLikud, Yesh Atid, Haavoda (Labor), Habait Hayehudi, Shas, Meretz, HaTnua, Kadima, Am Shalem, Kalkala, Ale Yarok, Otzma LeIsrael, DaAm, and Eretz Hadasha. Only four parties that were elected for the Knesset in the 2013 elections were not examined in the study. All of them represent sectorial groups in the Israeli society, and do not turn to the average, Hebrew-speaking Israeli for his vote. Three of the parties are Arab political parties that together have 11 of the 120 seats in the 19th Knesset, and their campaigns (both in the traditional and digital media) are in Arabic. The fourth is Yahadut Hatora (with seven seats in the 19th Knesset)—an Ultra-Orthodox party that does not campaign online (or

in the mainstream traditional media), since it turns to Ultra-Orthodox voters that do not tend to use digital media for religious reasons.

5   Interviews were conducted with campaign staff members of 12 of the 14 parties, and all candidates studied. For most parties, at least two interviews (one of which was with the campaign manager or digital campaign manager) were conducted.

6   Unlike many other countries, Twitter is not popular in Israel: only 150,000 Israelis have Twitter accounts (Goldenberg, 2013).

7   Not all Facebook pages of candidates and parties were available for analysis at the same time. Some Facebook pages were mined starting from December 5, 2012, and others from December 24, 2012 due to data availability. The Facebook measurements are based on the daily average of activity.

8   The number of likes can be reduced if users "unlike" a page.

9   Although our hypotheses do not deal with online news coverage, nor whether such coverage is positive, the correlation can help us better understand the influence of digital investment on the parties and candidates overall level of publicity.

10   An examination of the correlations between each component of the investment in digital media by itself and digital media success is presented in Table 5.

Compilation of References

Aaker, J., & Smith, A. (2010). The dragonfly effect: Quick, effective, and powerful ways to use social media to drive social change. San Francisco, CA: Jossey-Bass.

Aaker, J., & Smith, A. (2010). The Dragonfly Effect: Quick, Effective, and Powerful Ways to Use Social Media to Drive Social Change. San Francisco, CA: Jossey-Bass.

Aichner, T., & Jacob, F. (2015). Measuring the degree of corporate social media use. *International Journal of Market Research, 57*(2), 257–275.

Akhras, A., & Akhras, C. (2013). Interactive, Asynchronous, Face-to-Face: Does It Really Make a Difference? *Procedia: Social and Behavioral Sciences, 83,* 337–341. doi:10.1016/j.sbspro.2013.06.066

Albors, J., Ramos, J. C., & Hervas, J. L. (2008). New learning network paradigms: Communities of objectives, crowdsourcing, wikis and open source. *International Journal of Information Management, 28*(3), 194–202. doi:10.1016/j.ijinfomgt.2007.09.006

Andaleeb, S. S. (1996). An experimental investigation of satisfaction and commitment in marketing channels: The role of trust and dependence. *Journal of Retailing, 72*(1), 77–93. doi:10.1016/S0022-4359(96)90006-8

Anderson, P. (2007). *What is Web 2.0? Ideas, technologies and implications for education.* Bristol: JISC.

Anklam, P. (2004). *KM and the Social Network.* Knowledge Management Magazine.

Arceneaux, N., & Schmitz, W. A. (2010). Seems stupid until you try it: Press coverage of twitter, 2006–9. *New Media & Society, 12*(8), 1262–1279. doi:10.1177/1461444809360773

Arguello, J., Elsas, J. L., Callan, J., & Carbonell, J. G. (2008). *Document representation and query expansion models for blog recommendation.Second International Conference on Weblogs and Social Media,* Washington, DC.

Arnold, J., & Ewing, R. (2012). Issues management methods for reputational management. In *The handbook of strategic public relations and integrated marketing communications New York* (pp. 335–352). McGraw Hill.

Arnstein, S. R. (1969). A Ladder of Citizen Participation. *Journal of the American Institute of Planners*, *35*(4), 216–224. doi:10.1080/01944366908977225

AT&T (2008). *The Business Impacts of Social Networking*. Author.

Atkinson, R. D., & McKay, A. S. (2007). *Digital prosperity: Understanding the economic benefits of the information technology revolution*. The Information Technology and Innovation Foundation.

Auh, S., Bell, S. J., McLeod, C. S., & Shih, E. (2007). Co-production and customer loyalty in financial services. *Journal of Retailing*, *83*(3), 359–370. doi:10.1016/j.jretai.2007.03.001

Bachmann, R., Knights, D., & Sydow, J. (2001). Special Issue: Trust and control in organizational relations. *Organization Studies*, *22*(2). doi:10.1177/0170840601222007

Baker, W. E. (1990). Market networks and corporate behavior. *American Journal of Sociology*, *96*(3), 589–625. doi:10.1086/229573

Bakker, T. P., & de Vreese, C. H. (2011). Good news for the future? Young people, internet use, and political participation. *Communication Research*, *38*(4), 451–470. doi:10.1177/0093650210381738

Balmas, M., Rahat, G., Sheafer, T., & Shenhav, S. R. (2014). Two routes to personalized politics: Centralized and decentralized personalization. *Party Politics*, *20*(1), 37–51. doi:10.1177/1354068811436037

Bandura, A., & Walters, R. H. (1977). *Social learning theory*. Academic Press.

Bandura, A. (1977). *Social learning theory*. Englewood Cliffs, NJ: Prentice Hall.

Bandura, A. (1986). *Social foundations of thought and action: a social cognitive theory*. Englewood Cliffs, NJ: Prentice-Hall.

Bandura, A. (2002). Social cognitive theory in cultural context. *Applied Psychology*, *51*(2), 269–290. doi:10.1111/1464-0597.00092

Bane, C. M., Cornish, M., Erspamer, N., & Kampman, L. (2010). Self-disclosure through weblogs and perceptions of online and real-life friendships among female bloggers. *Cyberpsychology, Behavior, and Social Networking*, *13*(2), 131–139. doi:10.1089/cyber.2009.0174 PMID:20528268

Barabási, A.L., Jeong, H., Néda, Z., Ravasz, E., Schubert, A., & Vicsek, T. (2002). Evolution of the social network of scientific collaborations. *Physica A: Statistical Mechanics and Its Applications, 311*(3), 590-614.

Barabási, A. L., & Albert, R. (1999). Emergence of scaling in random networks. *Science, 286*(5439), 509–512. doi:10.1126/science.286.5439.509 PMID:10521342

Barassi, V., & Treré, E. (2012). Does Web 3.0 come after Web 2.0? Deconstructing theoretical assumptions through practice. *New Media & Society, 0*(0), 1–17.

Barnes, N. G. (n.d.). Social Media Usage Now Ubiquitous Among US Top Charities, Ahead of All Other Sectors. Center for Marketing Research. *University of Massachusetts.*

Barnes, N. G., & Lescault, A. M. (n.d.). Executives Concerned about ROI, Name Facebook Most Effective, Blogs Continue Decline: The 2015 Inc. 500 and Social Media. Center for Marketing Research. *University of Massachusetts.*

Barry, F. (2012). *2012 Nonprofit social networking benchmark report.* Academic Press.

Baum, J. A. (1999). Whole-part coevolutionary competition in organizations. *Variations in Organization Science*, 113-135.

Baumann, H., Crescenzi, P., & Fraigniaud, P. (2011). Parsimonious flooding in dynamic graphs. *Distributed Computing, 24*(1), 31–44. doi:10.1007/s00446-011-0133-9

Baumgartner, J. C., & Morris, J. S. (2010). MyFaceTube Politics: Social Networking web sites and political engagement of young adults. *Social Science Computer Review, 28*(1), 24–44. doi:10.1177/0894439309334325

Bearman, Guynup, & Milevski. (1985). Information and Productivity. *Journal of the American Society for Information Science, 36*(6), 369.

Beck, P., Dalton, R., Greene, S., & Huckfeldt, R. (2002). The social calculus of voting: Interpersonal, media, and organizational influences on presidential choices. *The American Political Science Review, 96*(1), 57–74. doi:10.1017/S0003055402004239

Bergenti, F., Poggi, A., Tomaiuolo, M., & Turci, P. (2005). An Ontology Support for Semantic Aware Agents. In *Proc. Seventh International Bi-Conference Workshop on Agent-Oriented Information Systems* (AOIS-2005@ AAMAS).

Berthon, P. R., Pitt, L. F., Plangger, K., & Shapiro, D. (2012). Marketing meets Web 2.0, social media, and creative consumers: Implications for international marketing strategy. *Business Horizons, 55*(3), 261–271. doi:10.1016/j.bushor.2012.01.007

Bettencourt, L. A., Ostrom, A. L., Brown, S. W., & Roundtree, R. I. (2002). Client Co-Production in Knowledge-Intensive Business Services. *California Management Review*, *44*(4), 100–128. doi:10.2307/41166145

Bev, G., Campbell, S., Levy, J., & Bounds, J. (2008). *Social media and the federal government: Perceived and real barriers and potential solutions*. Federal Web Managers Council.

Bode, L., Vraga, E. K., Borah, P., & Shah, D. V. (2014). A new space for political behavior: Political social networking and its democratic consequences. *Journal of Computer-Mediated Communication*, *19*(3), 414–429. doi:10.1111/jcc4.12048

Booz, Allen, & Hamilton. (1982). *New products management for the 1980s*. New York: Booz, Allen & Hamilton.

Borgatti, S. P., & Foster, P. C. (2003). The network paradigm in organizational research: A review and typology. *Journal of Management*, *29*(6), 991–1013. doi:10.1016/S0149-2063(03)00087-4

Bowers-Brown, J., & Gunter, B. (2002). Political parties use of the web during the 2001 general election. *Aslib Proceedings*, *54*(3), 166–176. doi:10.1108/00012530210441719

Boyd, D. (2010). Social network sites as networked publics: Affordances, dynamics, and implications. In *Networked self: Identity, community, and culture on social network sites* (pp. 39–58). New York, NY: Routledge.

Brabham, D. C. (2008). Crowdsourcing as a Model for Problem Solving an Introduction and 87 Cases. *The International Journal of Research into New Media Technologies*.

Bressolles, G. (2012). *L'e-marketing*. Dunod.

Brigida, D., & Colman, J. D. (2010). How successful are your social media efforts? In *Internet Management for Nonprofits: Strategies, Tools, & Trade Secrets. (181 – 202)*. Hoboken, NJ: John Wiley & Sons.

Briones, R. L., Kuch, B., Liu, F., & Jin, Y. (2011). Keeping up with the digital age: How the American Red Cross uses social media to build relationships. *Public Relations Review*, *37*(1), 37–43. doi:10.1016/j.pubrev.2010.12.006

Bronstein, J. (2013). Like me! Analyzing the 2012 presidential candidates Facebook pages. *Online Information Review*, *37*(2), 173–192. doi:10.1108/OIR-01-2013-0002

Broom, C., & Sha, B. (2013). Effective public relations (11th ed.). Boston, MA: Pearson Education, Inc.

Brosius, H. B., & Kepplinger, H. M. (1992). Beyond agenda-setting: The influence of partisanship and television reporting on the electorates voting intentions. *The Journalism Quarterly*, *69*(4), 893–901. doi:10.1177/107769909206900409

Brown, M. A. (2011). *Social networking and individual performance: Examining predictors of participation*. Old Dominion University.

Brown, M. Sr. (2011). *Social networking and individual performance: Examining predictors of participation Ph.D.* Old Dominion University.

Brownstein, J. S., Freifeld, C. C., & Madoff, L. C. (2009). Influenza A (H1N1) virus, 2009 – online monitoring. *The New England Journal of Medicine*, *360*(21), 21–56. doi:10.1056/NEJMp0904012 PMID:19423868

Bruns, A. (2008). *Blogs, Wikipedia, second life and beyond: From production to produsage*. New York, NY: Peter Lang.

Buckels, E. E., Trapnell, P. D., & Paulhus, D. L. (2014). Trolls just want to have fun. *Personality and Individual Differences*, *67*, 97–102. doi:10.1016/j.paid.2014.01.016

Bullock, C. (2007). Framing domestic violence fatalities: Coverage by Utah newspapers. *Womens Studies in Communication*, *30*(1), 34–63. doi:10.1080/07491409.2007.10162504

Burt, R. S. (1987). Social Contagion and Innovation: Cohesion versus Structural Equivalence. *American Journal of Sociology*, *92*(6), 1287–1335. doi:10.1086/228667

Burt, R. S. (1995). *Structural holes: The social structure of competition*. Harvard University Press.

Campbell, J. H. (1985). An organizational interpretation of evolution. *Evolution at a Crossroads*, 133.

Campbell, S. W., & Kwak, N. (2011). Mobile Communication and Civil Society: Linking Patterns and Places of Use to Engagement with Others in Public. *Human Communication Research*, *37*(2), 207–222. doi:10.1111/j.1468-2958.2010.01399.x

Carlson, T., & Strandberg, K. (2008). Riding the web 2.0 wave: Candidates on YouTube in the 2007 Finnish national elections. *Journal of Information Technology & Politics*, *5*(2), 159–174. doi:10.1080/19331680802291475

Cavazza, F. (2008). *Panorama des médias sociaux*. FredCavazza.net.

Ceron, A., Curini, L., Iacus, S. M., & Porro, G. (2013). Every tweet counts? How sentiment analysis of social media can improve our knowledge of citizens political preferences with an application to Italy and France. *New Media & Society, 16*(2), 340–358. doi:10.1177/1461444813480466

Cerulo, K. A. (1990). To Err Is Social: Network Prominence and Its Effects on Self-Estimation. *Sociological Forum, 5*(4), 619–634. doi:10.1007/BF01115394

Chang, Y. O., & Zhu, D. H. (2012). The role of perceived social capital and flow experience in building users continuance intention to social networking sites in China. *Computers in Human Behavior, 28*(3), 995–1001. doi:10.1016/j.chb.2012.01.001

Cheng, J., Danescu-Niculescu-Mizil, C., & Leskovec, J. (2015). *Antisocial Behavior in Online Discussion Communities*. Academic Press.

Cheng, J., Sun, A., Hu, D., & Zeng, D. (2010). An information diffusion-based recommendation framework for micro-blogging. *Journal of the Association for Information Systems, 12*, 463–486.

Chen, H. (2006). Flow on the net: Detecting web users positive affects and their flow states. *Computers in Human Behavior, 22*(2), 221–223. doi:10.1016/j.chb.2004.07.001

Chen, H., Wigand, R., & Nilan, M. S. (1999). Optimal Experience of Web Activities. *Computers in Human Behavior, 15*(5), 585–608. doi:10.1016/S0747-5632(99)00038-2

Cheung, M. F. Y., & To, W. M. (2011). Customer involvement and perceptions: The moderating role of customer co-production. *Journal of Retailing and Consumer Services, 18*(4), 271–277. doi:10.1016/j.jretconser.2010.12.011

Chinese Internet Network Information Center. (2007). *Statistical report of Chinese Internet development 2007*. Author.

Chinese Internet Network Information Center. (2015). *The 36th statistical report on Internet development in China*. Author.

Church, S. H. (2010). YouTube politics: YouChoose and leadership rhetoric during the 2008 election. *Journal of Information Technology & Politics, 7*(2).

Clayton, R. B., Leshner, G., & Almond, A. (2015). The extended iSelf: The impact of iPhone separation on cognition, emotion, and physiology. *Journal of Computer-Mediated Communication, 20*(2), 119–135. doi:10.1111/jcc4.12109

Clementi, A. E., Macci, C., Monti, A., Pasquale, F., & Silvestri, R. (2010). Flooding time of edge-markovian evolving graphs. *SIAM Journal on Discrete Mathematics*, *24*(4), 1694–1712. doi:10.1137/090756053

Clementi, A., Crescenzi, P., Doerr, C., Fraigniaud, P., Pasquale, F., & Silvestri, R. (2015). Rumor spreading in random evolving graphs. *Random Structures and Algorithms*.

Cohen, S. (2013, March 7). Sandy marked a shift for social media use in disasters. *Emergency Management*. Retrieved from http://www.emergencymgmt.com/disaster/Sandy-Social-Media-Use-in-Disasters.html

Coleman, J. S. (1988). Social capital in the creation of human capital. *American Journal of Sociology*, *94*, 95–120. doi:10.1086/228943

Conroy, M., Feezell, J. T., & Guerrero, M. (2012). Facebook and political engagement: A study of online political group membership and offline political engagement. *Computers in Human Behavior*, *28*(5), 1535–1546. doi:10.1016/j.chb.2012.03.012

Constantinides, E. (2014). Foundations of Social Media Marketing. *Procedia: Social and Behavioral Sciences*, *148*, 40–57. doi:10.1016/j.sbspro.2014.07.016

Coombs, W. (2007). Protecting Organization Reputations During a Crisis: The Development and Application of Situational Crisis Communication Theory. *Corporate Reputation Review*, *10*(3), 163–176. doi:10.1057/palgrave.crr.1550049

Cooper, A., & Sportolari, L. (1997). Romance in cyberspace: Understanding online attraction. *Journal of Sex Education and Therapy*, *22*(1), 7–14.

Cooper, R. K. (1997). Applying Emotional Intelligence in the Workplace. *Training & Development*, *51*(12), 31–38.

Corrado, A., & Firestone, C. (1996). *Elections in cyberspace: Toward a new era in American politics*. Washington, DC: Aspen Institute.

Coutant, A., & Stenger, Th. (2009). Les configurations sociotechniques sur le Web et leurs usages: le cas des réseaux sociaux numériques. 7ème Colloque du chapitre français de l'ISKO 27-34.

Cova, B., & Cova, V. (2009). Les figures du nouveau consommateur: Une genèse de la gouvernementalité du consommateur. *Recherche et Applications en Marketing*, *24*(3), 3. doi:10.1177/076737010902400305

Crandall, W., Parnell, J., & Spillan, J. (2014). Crisis management. Los Angeles, CA: Sage Publications, Inc.

Csikszentmihalyi, M. (1975). Beyond boredom and anxiety. San Francisco, CA: Jossey-Bass.

Csikszentmihalyi, M. (1990). *Flow*. New York, NY: Harper and Row.

Csikszentmihalyi, M. (1997). *Finding flow*. New York, NY: Basic.

Csikszentmihalyi, M. (2004). *Vivre la psychologie du Bonheur*. Paris: Edition Robert Laffont.

Csikszentmihalyi, M., & LeFevre, J. (1989). Optimal experience in work and leisure. *Journal of Personality and Social Psychology*, *56*(5), 815–822. doi:10.1037/0022-3514.56.5.815 PMID:2724069

Curtis, L., Edwards, C., Fraser, K. L., Gudelsky, S., Holmquist, J., Thornston, K., & Sweetser, K. (2010). Adoption of social media for public relations by nonprofit organizations. *Public Relations Review*, *36*(1), 90–92. doi:10.1016/j.pubrev.2009.10.003

Daft, R. L., & Lengel, R. H. (1986). Organizational information requirements, media richness, and structural design. *Management Science*, *32*(5), 554–571. doi:10.1287/mnsc.32.5.554

DAlessio, D. W. (1997). Use of the web in the 1996 US election. *Electoral Studies*, *16*(4), 489–501. doi:10.1016/S0261-3794(97)00044-9

Dance, F. E. (1970). The concept of communication. *Journal of Communication*, *20*(2), 201–210. doi:10.1111/j.1460-2466.1970.tb00877.x

Davis, C. (2013). *An Analysis of Financially Successful Special Fundraising Events* (Master's Thesis). University of Akron.

Davis, J. (2012, April 24). *The 5 Easy Steps To Measure Your Social Media Campaigns*. Retrieved from https://blog.kissmetrics.com/social-media-measurement/

Davis, A. (2000). Public relations, news production and changing patterns of source access in the British national media. *Media Culture & Society*, *22*(1), 39–59. doi:10.1177/016344300022001003

Davis, F. D. (1989). Perceived Usefulness, Perceived Ease of Use, and User Acceptance of Information Technology. *Management Information Systems Quarterly*, *13*(3), 319–340. doi:10.2307/249008

Davis, T. R. V., & Luthans, F. (1980). A Social Learning Approach to Organizational Behavior. *Academy of Management Review*, *5*(2), 281–290.

Dawes, S., Cresswell, A., & Pardopublic, T. (2009). From need to know to need to share: Tangled problems, information boundaries, and the building of public sector knowledge networks. *Public Administration Review*, *69*(3), 63–84. doi:10.1111/j.1540-6210.2009.01987_2.x

de Vreese, C. H., Boomgaarden, H. G., & Semetko, H. A. (2011). (In)direct framing effects: The effects of news media framing on public. *Communication Research*, *38*(2), 179–205. doi:10.1177/0093650210384934

Deighton, J., & Kornfeld, L. (2009). Interactivitys Unanticipated Consequences for Markets and Marketing. *Journal of Interactive Marketing*, *23*(1), 1, 2–12. doi:10.1016/j.intmar.2008.10.001

Delk, J. (1995). *MOUT: A domestic case study*. Los Angeles, CA: Rand Corporation. Retrieved from https://www.rand.org/content/dam/rand/pubs/conf_proceedings/CF148/CF148.appd.pdf

Dennis, A. R., & Valacich, J. S. (1994). Group, Sub-Group, and Nominal Group Idea Generation: New Rules for a New Media? *Journal of Management*, *20*(4), 723–736. doi:10.1177/014920639402000402

Depover, C., Karsenti, T., & Komis, V. (2007). *Enseigner avec les technologies, Favoriser les apprentissages, développer des compétences*. Presses de l'Université du Québec.

DiMicco, J. (2007). Identity management: multiple presentations of self in facebook.*6th International Conference on Supporting Group Work (GROUP'07)* (pp. 1–4). doi:10.1145/1316624.1316682

DiMicco, J., Millen, D., & Geyer, W. (2008). Motivations for social networking at work.*Conference on Computer Supported Cooperative Work (CSCW'08)* (pp. 711–720).

Dimitrova, D. V., & Connolly-Ahern, C. (2007). A tale of two wars: Framing analysis of online news sites in Coalition countries and the Arab world during the Iraq War. *The Howard Journal of Communications*, *18*(2), 153–168. doi:10.1080/10646170701309973

Dimitrova, D. V., Shehata, A., Strömbäck, J., & Nord, L. W. (2014). The effects of digital media on political knowledge and participation in election campaigns evidence from panel data. *Communication Research, 41*(1), 95–118. doi:10.1177/0093650211426004

Ding, D. X., Hu, P. J., Verma, R., & Wardell, D. (2010). The Impact of Service System Design and Flow Experience on Customer Satisfaction in Online Financial Services. *Journal of Service Research, 13*, 1.

Doerr, B., Fouz, M., & Friedrich, T. (2012). Why rumors spread so quickly in social networks. *Communications of the ACM, 55*(6), 70–75. doi:10.1145/2184319.2184338

Donath, J. S. (1999). Identity and deception in the virtual community. *Communities in Cyberspace, 1996*, 29-59.

Drago, E. (2015). The Effect of Technology on Face-to-Face Communication. *Elon Journal of Undergraduate Research in Communications, 6*(1).

Druckman, J. N. (2005). Media matter: How newspapers and television news cover campaigns and influence voters. *Political Communication, 22*(4), 463–481. doi:10.1080/10584600500311394

Dvir-Gvirsman, S., Tzfati, Y., & Menchen-Trevino, E. (2014). The extent and nature of ideological selective exposure online: Combining survey responses with actual web log data from the 2013 Israeli elections. *New Media & Society*.

Edelman, R. (2012). PR and the media cloverleaf. In *The handbook of strategic public relations and integrated marketing communications* (pp. 258–261). McGraw Hill.

Efimova, L. (2009). *Passion at work: Blogging practices of knowledge workers.* Enschede, The Netherlands: Novay.

Ehrlich, K., & Shami, N. S. (2010, May). *Microblogging inside and outside the workplace.4th International AAAI Conference on Weblogs and Social Media (IC-WSM)*, Washington, DC.

Elías, M. V., & Alkadry, M. G. (2011). Constructive conflict, participation, and shared governance. *Administration & Society*.

Englehart, H. (2012). *Crisis communications: brand new channels, same old static. The handbook of strategic public relations and integrated marketing communications* (pp. 401–413). McGraw Hill.

Entman, R. M. (1993). Framing: Toward a clarification of a fractured paradigm. *Journal of Communication, 43*(4), 51–58. doi:10.1111/j.1460-2466.1993.tb01304.x

Entman, R. M. (2003). *Projections of power: Framing news, public opinion, and US Foreign policy*. Chicago: The University of Chicago Press. doi:10.7208/chicago/9780226210735.001.0001

Erdoğmuş, İ., & Çiçek, M. (2012). The impact of social media marketing on brand loyalty. *Procedia: Social and Behavioral Sciences, 58*, 1353–1360. doi:10.1016/j.sbspro.2012.09.1119

Erdős, P., & Rényi, A. (1959). On Random Graphs. *Publ. Math., 6*, 290–297.

Erkan, I., & Evans, C. H. (2016). The influence of eWOM in social media on consumers purchase intentions: An extended approach to information adoption. *Computers in Human Behavior, 61*, 47–55. doi:10.1016/j.chb.2016.03.003

Eyrich, N., Padman, M. L., & Sweetser, K. D. (2008). PR practitioners use of social media tools and communication technology. *Public Relations Review, 34*(4), 412–414. doi:10.1016/j.pubrev.2008.09.010

Falkheimer, J., & Heide, M. (2010). Crisis communicators in change: From plans to improvisations. In Handbook of crisis communication (pp. 511-526). Academic Press.

Fan, W., & Yeung, K. H. (2013). Virus Propagation Modeling in Facebook. In *The Influence of Technology on Social Network Analysis and Mining* (pp. 185–199). Vienna: Springer. doi:10.1007/978-3-7091-1346-2_8

Farrell, H., & Drezner, D. (2008). The power and politics of blogs. *Public Choice, 134*(1-2), 15–30. doi:10.1007/s11127-007-9198-1

Fearn-Banks, K. (2007). *Crisis communications: a casebook approach* (3rd ed.). Mahwah, NJ: Lawrence Erlbaum Associates, Inc.

Feige, U., Peleg, D., Raghavan, P., & Upfal, E. (1990). Randomized broadcast in networks. *Random Structures and Algorithms, 1*(4), 447–460. doi:10.1002/rsa.3240010406

Fernandes, J., Giurcanu, M., Bowers, K. W., & Neely, J. C. (2010). The writing on the wall: A content analysis of college students Facebook groups for the 2008 presidential election. *Mass Communication & Society, 13*(5), 653–675. doi:10.1080/15205436.2010.516865

Fernandez, S., & Rainey, H. (2006). Managing successful organizational change in the public sector. *Public Administration Review, 66*(2), 168–176. doi:10.1111/j.1540-6210.2006.00570.x

Firat, A. F., & Venkatesh, A. (1993). Postmodernity: The Age of Marketing. *International Journal of Research in Marketing, 10*(3), 227–249. doi:10.1016/0167-8116(93)90009-N

Fisk, R. P., Brown, S. W., & Bitner, M. J. (1993). Tracking the evolution of the services marketing literature. *Journal of Retailing, 69*(1), 61–103. doi:10.1016/S0022-4359(05)80004-1

Flandez, R. (2010). Social-media managers help charities spin a web of support. The Chronicle of Philanthropy, 7-9.

Fornacciari, P., Mordonini, M., & Tomaiuolo, M. (2015). A case-study for sentiment analysis on twitter. *CEUR Workshop Proceedings*.

Fornacciari, P., Mordonini, M., & Tomaiuolo, M. (2015). Social network and sentiment analysis on Twitter: Towards a combined approach. *CEUR Workshop Proceedings*.

Fornerino, M., Helme-Guizon, A., & Gotteland, D. (2008). Expériences cinématographiques en état dimmersion: Effets sur la satisfaction. *Recherche et Applications en Marketing, 23*(3), 93–111. doi:10.1177/205157070802300306

Fortunato, S. (2010). Community detection in graphs. *Physics Reports, 486*(3), 75–174. doi:10.1016/j.physrep.2009.11.002

Foster, I., Kesselman, C., & Tuecke, S. (2001). The anatomy of the grid: Enabling scalable virtual organizations. *International Journal of High Performance Computing Applications, 15*(3), 200–222. doi:10.1177/109434200101500302

Fountoulakis, N., Panagiotou, K., & Sauerwald, T. (2012, January). Ultra-fast rumor spreading in social networks. In *Proceedings of the twenty-third annual ACM-SIAM symposium on Discrete Algorithms* (pp. 1642-1660). SIAM. doi:10.1137/1.9781611973099.130

Franchi, E., Poggi, A., & Tomaiuolo, M. (2015). Information and password attacks on social networks: An argument for cryptography. *Journal of Information Technology Research, 8*(1), 25–42. doi:10.4018/JITR.2015010103

Franchi, E., Poggi, A., & Tomaiuolo, M. (2016a). Blogracy: A Peer-to-Peer Social Network. *International Journal of Distributed Systems and Technologies, 7*(2), 37–56. doi:10.4018/IJDST.2016040103

Franchi, E., Poggi, A., & Tomaiuolo, M. (2016b). Social media for online collaboration in firms and organizations. *International Journal of Information System Modeling and Design*, 7(1), 18–31. doi:10.4018/IJISMD.2016010102

Fukuyama, F. (1995). *Trust: The social virtues and the creation of prosperity*. New York, NY: Free Press.

Fulk, J., Heino, R., Flanagin, A. J., Monge, P. R., & Bar, F. (2004). A test of the individual action model for organizational information commons. *Organization Science*, 15(5), 569–585. doi:10.1287/orsc.1040.0081

Galán-GarcÍa, P., De La Puerta, J. G., Gómez, C. L., Santos, I., & Bringas, P. G. (2015). Supervised machine learning for the detection of troll profiles in twitter social network: Application to a real case of cyberbullying. *Logic Journal of the IGPL*, jzv048. doi:10.1093/jigpal/jzv048

Gambetta, D. (1988). *Trust: Making and breaking cooperative relations*. New York, NY: B. Blackwell.

Gamble, J., Peteraf, M., & Thompson, A. (2017). Evaluating a company's external environment. In Essentials of Strategic Management: The quest for competitive advantage (5th ed.; pp. 40-50). New Yok: McGraw-Hill.

Gamson, W. A. (1992). *Talking politics*. New York, NY: Cambridge University Press.

Gandy, O. H. Jr, & Li, Z. (2005). Framing comparative risk: A preliminary analysis. *The Howard Journal of Communications*, 16(2), 71–86. doi:10.1080/10646170590948956

Ganz, M. (1994). Voters in the crosshairs: How markets and technology are destroying politics. *The American Prospect, 16*, 100-109. Retrieved from http://prospect.org/article/voters-crosshairs

Ganz, M. (2000). Resources and resourcefulness: Leadership, strategy and organization in the unionization of California agriculture. *American Journal of Sociology*, 105(4), 1003–1062. doi:10.1086/210398

Gao, H., Barbier, G., & Goolsby, R. (2011). *Harnessing the crowdsourcing power of social media for disaster relief. In IEEE Intelligent Systems* (pp. 10–14). IEEE Computer Society.

Gao, L., & Bai, X. (2014). Online consumer behaviour and its relationship to website atmospheric induced flow: Insights into online travel agencies in China. *Journal of Retailing and Consumer Services*, 21(4), 653–665. doi:10.1016/j.jretconser.2014.01.001

Gerth, M. A., & Siegert, G. (2011). Patterns of consistence and constriction: How news media frame the coverage of direct democratic campaigns. *The American Behavioral Scientist, 56*(3), 279–299. doi:10.1177/0002764211426326

Gheorghiță & Pădurețu. (2014). Social Networks And Interpersonal Communication. *System, 2*(3), 5.

Giakkoupis, G. (2011). Tight bounds for rumor spreading in graphs of a given conductance.*Symposium on Theoretical Aspects of Computer Science (STACS2011).*

Gibson, R. K. (2010). *Open source campaigning? UK party organisations and the use of the new media in the 2010 general election.* Academic Press.

Gibson, R. K., & McAllister, I. (2009, September). *Revitalising participatory politics?: The internet, social capital and political action.* Paper presented at the APSA Annual Meeting, Toronto, Canada.

Gibson, R. K., & McAllister, I. (2006). Does cyber-campaigning win votes? Online communication in the 2004 Australian election. *Journal of Elections, Public Opinion, and Parties, 16*(3), 243–263. doi:10.1080/13689880600950527

Gibson, R. K., & McAllister, I. (2011). Do online election campaigns win votes? The 2007 Australian YouTube election. *Political Communication, 28*(2), 227–244. doi:10.1080/10584609.2011.568042

Gibson, R. K., & Römmele, A. (2001). A party centered theory of professionalized campaigning. *The Harvard International Journal of Press/Politics, 6*(4), 31–44. doi:10.1177/108118001129172323

Gibson, R. K., & Römmele, A. (2009). Measuring the professionalization of political campaigning. *Party Politics, 15*(3), 265–293. doi:10.1177/1354068809102245

Gibson, R. K., & Ward, S. (1998). U.K. political parties and the internet: Politics as usual in the new media? *The Harvard International Journal of Press/Politics, 3*(3), 14–38. doi:10.1177/1081180X98003003003

Gibson, R. K., & Ward, S. (2000). An outsiders medium? The European elections and UK party competition on the Internet. *British Elections & Parties Yearbook, 10*(1), 173–191. doi:10.1080/13689880008413043

Giddens, A. (1984). The constitution of society. Cambridge, MA: Polity Press.

Gil de Zúñiga, H., Jung, N., & Valenzuela, S. (2012). Social media use for news and individuals social capital, civic engagement and political participation. *Journal of Computer-Mediated Communication, 17*(3), 319–336. doi:10.1111/j.1083-6101.2012.01574.x

Girard, A., & Fallery B. (2009). *Réseaux Sociaux Numériques: revue de littérature et perspectives de recherche*. Academic Press.

Goi, C. L. (2009). A Review of Marketing Mix: 4Ps or More? Internation. *Journal of Marketing Studies, 1*(1), 1–15.

Golbeck, J., & Hendler, J. (2006). Inferring binary trust relationships in web-based social networks. *ACM Transactions on Internet Technology, 6*(4), 497–529. doi:10.1145/1183463.1183470

Goldenberg, R. (2013). *The tweets have died: Why did Twitter service fail in Israel.* Globes.

Goldschlag, D., Reed, M., & Syverson, P. (1999). Onion routing. *Communications of the ACM, 42*(2), 39–41. doi:10.1145/293411.293443

Goldstein, S. (2015, November 4). A social media checklist for your crisis communications plan. *PR News Online.* Retrieved from http://www.prnewsonline.com/water-cooler/2015/11/04/how-to-integrate-social-media-into-your-crisis-plan/

González-Herreo, A., & Smith, S. (2008). Crisis communications management on the web: How internet-based technologies are changing the way public relations professionals handle business crises. *Journal of Contingencies and Crisis Management, 16*(3), 143–153. doi:10.1111/j.1468-5973.2008.00543.x

Google, Inc. (2016a). *Google analytics solutions website.* Retrieved from https://www.google.com/analytics/#?modal_active=none

Google, Inc. (2016b). *Google analytics features website.* Retrieved from: http://www.google.com/analytics/standard/features/

Gottfried, J., & Shearer, E. (2016). *News across social media platforms.* PEW Research Center.

Granovetter, M. S. (1973). The Strength of Weak Ties. *American Journal of Sociology, 78*(6), 1360–1380. doi:10.1086/225469

Granovetter, M. S. (1982). *The strength of weak ties: A network theory revisited. In Social structure and network analysis* (pp. 105–130). New York: John Wiley and Sons.

Greene, S. (2001). Astride the digital divide. *The Chronicle of Philanthropy, 13*(6), 18–19.

Grønbjerg, K. (1991). Managing grants and contracts: The case of four nonprofit social service organizations [Electronic version]. *Nonprofit and Voluntary Sector Quarterly, 20*(1), 5–24. doi:10.1177/089976409102000103

Grönroos, C. (2006). *What Can a Service Logic Offer Marketing Theory?* Academic Press.

GSMA. (2016). London, UK: GSMA Mobile Economy.

Gueorguieva, V. (2008). Voters, Myspace, and YouTube: The impact of alternative communication channels on the 2006 election cycle and beyond. *Social Science Computer Review, 26*(3), 288–300. doi:10.1177/0894439307305636

Gulati, G. J., & Williams, C. B. (2013). Social media and campaign 2012: Developments and trends for Facebook adoption. *Social Science Computer Review, 31*(5), 577–588. doi:10.1177/0894439313489258

Gunawardena, C. N. (1995). Social presence theory and implications for interaction and collaborative learning in computer conferences. *International Journal of Educational Telecommunications, 1*(2), 147–166.

Guo, C., & Saxton, G. D. (2010). Voice-in, voice-out: Constituent participation and nonprofit advocacy. *Nonprofit Policy Forum, 1*(1), Article 5. doi:10.2202/2154-3348.1000

Guo, C., & Saxton, G. D. (2013). Tweeting social change: How social media are changing nonprofit advocacy. *Nonprofit and Voluntary Sector Quarterly.*

Hackler, D., & Saxton, G. D. (2007). The Strategic Use of Information Technology by Nonprofit Organizations: Increasing Capacity and Untapped Potential. *Public Administration Review, 67*(3), 474–487. doi:10.1111/j.1540-6210.2007.00730.x

Hallahan, K., Holtzhausen, D., Van Ruler, B., Verčič, D., & Sriramesh, K. (2007). Defining strategic communication. *International Journal of Strategic Communication, 1*(1), 3–35. doi:10.1080/15531180701285244

Handley, A., & Chapman, C. C. (2011). *Content Rules: How to Create Killer Blogs, Webinars, (and More) that Engage Customers and Ignite Your Business.* Hoboken, NJ: John Wiley & Sons, Inc.

Harfoush, R. (2009). *Yes we did! An inside look at how social media built the Obama brand*. Berkeley, CA: New Riders.

Hargrave, S. (2004). *The blog busters*. The Guardians.

Harrop, M. (1987). Voters. In J. Seaton & B. Pimlott (Eds.), The media in British politics (pp. 45-63). Aldershot, UK: Dartmouth.

Hayes, A. F. (2013). *Introduction to mediation, moderation, and conditional process analysis: A regression-based approach*. New York, NY: Guilford Press.

Heller Baird, C., & Parasnis, G. (2011). From social media to social customer relationship management. *Strategy and Leadership*, *39*(5), 30–37. doi:10.1108/10878571111161507

Herring, S., Job-Sluder, K., Scheckler, R., & Barab, S. (2002). Searching for safety online: Managing trolling in a feminist forum. *The Information Society*, *18*(5), 371–384. doi:10.1080/01972240290108186

Hindman, D. B. (2009). Mass media flow and differential distribution of politically disputed beliefs: The belief gap hypothesis. *Journalism & Mass Communication Quarterly*, *86*(4), 790–808. doi:10.1177/107769900908600405

Hindman, M., Tsioutsiouliklis, K., & Johnson, J. (2003). *'Googlearchy': How are few heavily-linked sites dominate politics online*. Philadelphia, PA: American Political Science Association.

Hoang, H., & Antoncic, B. (2003). Network-based research in entrepreneurship: A critical review. *Journal of Business Venturing*, *18*(2), 165–187. doi:10.1016/S0883-9026(02)00081-2

Ho, C. T., Li, C. T., & Lin, S. D. (2011). *Modeling and visualizing information propagation in a micro-blogging platform*. Kaohsiung, Taiwan: Advances in Social Networks Analysis and Mining. doi:10.1109/ASONAM.2011.37

Hodkinson, P. (2006). Subcultural blogging? Online journals and group involvement among U.K. Goths. In *Uses of blogs* (pp. 187–198). New York, NY: Peter Lang.

Hoffman, D. L., & Novak, T. H. P. (2009). Flow Online: Lessons Learned and Future Prospects. *Journal of Interactive Marketing*, *23*(1), 23–34. doi:10.1016/j.intmar.2008.10.003

Hoffman, D. L., & Novak, T. P. (1996). Marketing in Hypermedia Computer-Mediated Environments: Conceptual Foundations. *Journal of Marketing*, *60*(3), 50–68. doi:10.2307/1251841

Holbrook, M. B., & Hirschman, E. C. (1982). The experiential aspects of consumption: Consumer fantasies, feeling, and fun. *The Journal of Consumer Research, 9*(2), 132–14.

Holland, P., & Leinhardt, S. (1974). *The Statistical Analysis of Local Structure in Social Networks*. National Bureau of Economic Research Working Paper Series 44.

Hollingshead, A. B., Fulk, J., & Monge, P. (2002). Fostering intranet knowledge sharing: An integration of transactive memory and public goods approaches. *Distributed Work*, 335-355.

Hong, S., & Nadler, D. (2012). Which candidates do the public discuss online in an election campaign?: The use of social media by 2012 presidential candidates and its impact on candidate salience. *Government Information Quarterly, 29*(4), 455–461. doi:10.1016/j.giq.2012.06.004

Hopmann, D. N., Vliegenthart, R., de Vreese, C., & Erik Albæk, E. (2010). Effects of election news coverage: How visibility and tone influence party choice. *Political Communication, 27*(4), 389–405. doi:10.1080/10584609.2010.516798

Hossain, L., & de Silva, A. (2009). Exploring user acceptance of technology using social networks. *The Journal of High Technology Management Research, 20*(1), 1–18. doi:10.1016/j.hitech.2009.02.005

Houghton, L., & Kerr, D. V. (2006). A study into the creation of feral information systems as a response to an ERP implementation within the supply chain of a large government-owned corporation. *International Journal of Internet and Enterprise Management, 4*(2), 135–147. doi:10.1504/IJIEM.2006.010239

Howard, A. (2011). 2011 Gov 2.0 year in review: A look at the Gov 2.0 themes, moments and achievements that made an impact in 2011. *O'Reilly Radar*. Retrieved from http://radar.oreilly.com/2011/12/2011-gov2-year-in-review.html

Huang, M.-H. (2003). Designing Website Attributes to Induce Experiential Encounters. *Computers in Human Behavior, 19*(4), 425–442. doi:10.1016/S0747-5632(02)00080-8

Huy, Q. N. (1999). Emotional Capability, Emotional Intelligence, and Radical Change. *Academy of Management Review, 24*(2), 325–345.

IBM Institute for Business Value. (2011). *From social media to Social CRM*. Retrieved 2012-10-20 from http://public.dhe.ibm.com/common/ssi/ecm/en/gbe03391usen/GBE03391USEN.PDF

Igbaria, M., & Tan, M. (1997). The consequences of information technology acceptance on subsequent individual performance. *Information & Management, 32*(3), 113–121. doi:10.1016/S0378-7206(97)00006-2

Igwe, C. F. (2008). *Beyond the digital divide into computer-mediated communications: A content analysis of the role of community weblogs in building Oldenburg's virtual third places in back America* (Unpublished doctoral dissertation). Pennsylvania State University.

Infante, D. A. (1975). Differential functions of desirable and undesirable consequences in predicting attitude and attitude change toward proposals. *Speech Monographs, 42*(2), 115–134. doi:10.1080/03637757509375886

International Association for the Measurement and Evaluation of Communications. (2014). *Program and Business Channel Social media* [artwork]. Retrieved from http://amecorg.com/wp-content/uploads/2014/06/Program-Business-and-Channel-Social-Media-Measurement-Framework.pdf

Ivancevich, J. M. Konopaske, R., & Matteson, M. T. (2008). Organizational Behavior and Management. New York: McGraw-Hill/Irwin.

Ivancevich, J. M., Konopaske, R., & Matteson, M. T. (2008). Organizational Behavior and Management. New York.

Iyengar, S. (1991). Is anyone responsible? How television frames political issues. Chicago, IL: University of Chicago Press. doi:10.7208/chicago/9780226388533.001.0001

Jacobs, J. (1961). *The death and life of great American cities*. Vintage.

Jansen, B. J., Zhang, M., Sobel, K., & Chowdury, A. (2009). Twitter power: Tweets as electronic word of mouth. *Journal of the American Society for Information Science and Technology, 60*(11), 2169–2188. doi:10.1002/asi.21149

Java, A., Song, X., Finin, T., & Tseng, B. (2007). *Why we twitter: Understanding microblogging usage and communities*. 9th WEBKDD and 1st SNA-KDD Workshop on Web mining and social analysis, San Jose, CA.

Jones, B. F., Wuchty, S., & Uzzi, B. (2008). Multi-university research teams: Shifting impact, geography, and stratification in science. *Science, 322*(5905), 1259–1262. doi:10.1126/science.1158357 PMID:18845711

Kabir, M., & Urbach, A. (2013, May 21). Facebook exposes: How many Israelis are surfing the social network? *Calcalist*. (in Hebrew)

Kalnes, Ø. (2009). Norwegian parties and web 2.0. *Journal of Information Technology & Politics*, *6*(3/4), 251–266. doi:10.1080/19331680903041845

Kanter, B. (2010). The ROI of Social Media: The "I" stands for insight and impact. In T. Hart, S. MacLaughlin, J. M. Greenfield, & P. H. Greier Jr., (Eds.), *Internet Management for Nonprofits: Strategies, Tools, & Trade Secrets*. Hoboken, NJ: John Wiley & Sons.

Kanter, B., & Fine, A. (2010). *The Networked Nonprofit: Connecting with Social Media to Drive Change*. New York, NY: John Wiley & Son.

Kanter, B., & Paine, K. D. (2012). *Measuring the networked nonprofit: Using data to change the world*. John Wiley & Sons.

Kaplan, A. M., & Haenlein, M. (2011). The early bird catches the news: Nine things you should know about micro-blogging. *Business Horizons*, *54*(2), 105–113. doi:10.1016/j.bushor.2010.09.004

Kaplan, A., & Haenlein, M. (2010). Users of the world, unite! The challenges and opportunities of Social Media. *Business Horizons*, *53*(1), 59–68. doi:10.1016/j.bushor.2009.09.003

Karp, R., Schindelhauer, C., Shenker, S., & Vocking, B. (2000). Randomized rumor spreading. In *Proceedings of the 41st Annual Symposium on Foundations of Computer Science 2000* (pp. 565-574). IEEE. doi:10.1109/SFCS.2000.892324

Kee, K. F., Sparks, L., Struppa, D. C., Mannucci, M. A., & Damiano, A. (2016). Information diffusion, Facebook clusters, and the simplicial model of social aggregation: A computational simulation of simplicial diffusers for community health interventions. *Health Communication*, *31*(4), 385–399. doi:10.1080/10410236.2014.960061 PMID:26362453

Kent, M. L., Carr, B. J., Husted, R. A., & Pop, R. A. (2011). Learning web analytics: A tool for strategic communication. *Public Relations Review*, *37*(5), 563–543. doi:10.1016/j.pubrev.2011.09.011

Kietzmann, J. H., Hermkens, K., McCarthy, I. P., & Silvestre, B. S. (2011). Social Media? Get Serious! Understanding the Functional Building Blocks of Social Media. *Business Horizons*, *54*(1), 241–251. doi:10.1016/j.bushor.2011.01.005

Kim, D. H. (1993). The link between individual learning and organizational learning. *Sloan Management Review*, *35*(Fall), 379–500.

King, C. (2010). Emergent communication strategies. *International Journal of Strategic Communication*, *4*(1), 19–38. doi:10.1080/15531180903415814

Klein, A., Ahlf, H., & Sharma, V. (2015). Social activity and structural centrality in online social networks. *Telematics and Informatics*, *32*(2), 321–332. doi:10.1016/j.tele.2014.09.008

Komchenko, S. (1997). *Civil-military relations in domestic support operations. The California national guard in Los Angeles 1992 riots and Northridge earthquake of 1994* (Master's thesis). Monterey, CA: Naval Postgraduate School.

Kotler, P., Kartajaya, H., & Setiawan, I. (2012). *Marketing 3.0: produits, clients, facteurs humains*. Edition De Boeck.

Kramer, R. M. (1996). *Trust in organizations: Frontiers of theory and research*. Thousand Oaks, CA: Sage Publications.

Krishen, A. S., Berezan, O., Agarwal, S., & Kachroo, P. (2016). The generation of virtual needs: Recipes for satisfaction in social media networking. *Journal of Business Research*, *69*(11), 5248–5254. doi:10.1016/j.jbusres.2016.04.120

Krishnamurthy, B., Gill, P., & Arlitt, M. (2008). *A few chirps about Twitter*. 1st workshop on online social networks (WOSN'08)., Seattle, WA.

Kuhn, F., Lynch, N., & Oshman, R. (2010). Distributed computation in dynamic networks. In *Proceedings of the forty-second ACM symposium on Theory of computing* (pp. 513-522). ACM. doi:10.1145/1806689.1806760

Kuhn, F., & Oshman, R. (2011). Dynamic networks: Models and algorithms. *ACM SIGACT News*, *42*(1), 82–96. doi:10.1145/1959045.1959064

Kumar, K. (2015, October 20). The beginner's checklist to planning your social and digital media strategy. *Social Media Week*. Retrieved from http://socialmediaweek.org/blog/2015/10/beginners-checklist-planning-social-digital-media-strategy/

Kushin, M. J., & Yamamoto, M. (2010). Did social media really matter? College students use of online media and political decision making in the 2008 election. *Mass Communication & Society*, *13*(5), 608–630. doi:10.1080/15205436.2010.516863

Kushin, M., & Kitchener, K. (2009). Getting political on social network sites: Exploring online political discourse on Facebook. *First Monday*, 14.

Kwak, H., Lee, C., Park, H., & Moon, S. (2010). What is Twitter, a social network or a news media? In *Proceedings of the 19th international conference on World wide web* (pp. 591-600). ACM. doi:10.1145/1772690.1772751

Lane, C., & Bachmann, R. (1998). *Trust within and between organizations: Conceptual issues and empirical applications.* New York: Oxford University Press.

Langley, Q. (2014). *Brandjack.* New York, NY: Palgrave Macmillan. doi:10.1057/9781137375360

Leighninger, M. (2011). Citizenship and governance in a wild, wired world: How should citizens and public managers use online tools to improve democracy? *National Civic Review, 100*(2), 20–29. doi:10.1002/ncr.20056

Levinson, J. C., Adkins, F., & Forbes, C. (2010). *Guerrilla Marketing for Nonprofits. 250 Tactics to Promote, Recruit, Motivate, and Raise More Money.* Entrepreneur Press.

Lévy, P. (1997). *L'intelligence collective: pour une anthropologie du cyberspace.* La Découverte.

Li, Q. (2013). Bile bear IPO halted as opponents cheer. *Global Times.*

Lievrouw, L. (2002). Determination and contingency in new media development: Diffusion of innovations and social shaping of technology perspectives. In *Handbook of new media* (pp. 183–199). London, UK: Sage. doi:10.4135/9781446206904.n14

Li, G., Hoi, S. C. H., Chang, K., & Jain, R. (2010). Micro-blogging sentiment detection by collaborative online learning. *IEEE International Conference on Data Mining* (pp. 893-898). doi:10.1109/ICDM.2010.139

Linden, R. (2010). *Leading across boundaries: Creating collaborative agencies in a networked world.* San Francisco, CA: Jossey-Bass.

Lorenzo-Romeroa, C. L., Constantinides, E., & Brüninkc, L. A. (2014). Co-Creation: Customer Integration in Social Media Based Product and Service Development. *Procedia: Social and Behavioral Sciences, 148*, 383–396. doi:10.1016/j.sbspro.2014.07.057

Loury, G. C. (1987). Why should we care about group inequality? *Social Philosophy & Policy, 5*(1), 249–271. doi:10.1017/S0265052500001345

Lovejoy, K., & Saxton, G. D. (2012). Information, community, and action: How nonprofit organizations use social media. *Journal of Computer-Mediated Communication, 17*(3), 337–353. doi:10.1111/j.1083-6101.2012.01576.x

Lovejoy, K., Waters, R. D., & Saxton, G. D. (2012). Engaging stakeholders through Twitter: How nonprofit organizations are getting more out of 140 characters or less. *Public Relations Review, 38*(2), 313–318. doi:10.1016/j.pubrev.2012.01.005

Lovelock, C. H., & Young, R. F. (1979). Look to Consumers to Increase Productivity. *Harvard Business Review, 57,* 168–178.

Luhmann, N. (1988). *Familiarity, confidence, trust: Problems and alternatives. In Trust: Making and breaking cooperative relations.* New York: Basil Blackwell.

Lui, C., Metaxas, P. T., & Mustafaraj, E. (2011, March). On the predictability of the US elections through search volume activity. In *Proceedings of the IADIS International Conference on e-Society.*

Lundby, K. (2009). *Mediatization: Concept, changes, consequences.* Peter Lang.

M+R. (2014). *2014 M+R Benchmarks.* Available from http://www.mrbenchmarks.com

MacLaughlin, S. (2010). Demystifying online metrics: Understanding the hits, clicks, and errors. In T. Hart, S. MacLaughlin, J. M. Greenfield, & P. H. Greier Jr., (Eds.), *Internet Management for Nonprofits: Strategies, Tools, & Trade Secrets.* Hoboken, NJ: John Wiley & Sons.

MacNamara, J., & Zerfass, A. (2012). Social media communication in organizations: The challenges of balancing openness, strategy, and management. *International Journal of Strategic Communication, 6*(4), 287–308. doi:10.1080/1553118X.2012.711402

Madden, M. (2005). *Hurricane Katrina: In the face of disaster and chaos, people use the internet to coordinate relief.* Pew Research Center. Retrieved on May 22, 2016 from http://www.pewinternet.org/2005/09/07/hurricane-katrina-in-the-face-of-disaster-and-chaos-people-use-the-internet-to-coordinate-relief/

Madden, M., & Jones, S. (2008). *Networked Workers.* Washington, DC: Pew Research Center.

Maddens, B., Wauters, B., Noppe, J., & Fiers, S. (2006). Effects of campaign spending in an open list pr-system: The 2003 legislative elections in Flanders/Belgium. *West European Politics, 29*(1), 161–168. doi:10.1080/01402380500389398

Mahoney, M. J., & Thoresen, C. E. (1974). *Self-control: power to the person.* Monterey, CA: Brooks/Cole Pub. Co.

Makam. (n.d.). Retrieved from http://www.makam.co.il

Malone, T. W., & Crowstone, K. (1994). The Interdisciplinary Study of Coordination. *ACM Computing Surveys*, *26*(1), 87–119. doi:10.1145/174666.174668

Mann, R., & Lev-On, A. (2014). *Annual report: The Israeli media in 2013 agendas, uses and trends*. Ariel, Israel: The Institute for the Study of New Media, Politics and Society.

Manz, C. C., & Sims, H. P. Jr. (1981). Vicarious Learning: The Influence of Modeling on Organizational Behavior. *Academy of Management Review*, *6*(1), 105–113.

Margolis, M., & Resnick, D. (2000). Politics as usual: The "Cyberspace Revolution". Thousand Oaks, CA: Sage Publications.

Marolt, P. W. (2008). *Blogging in China: Individual agency, the production of cyburban 'spaces of dissent' in Beijing, and societal transformation in China* (Unpublished doctoral dissertation). University of Southern California.

Mayo, E. (1949). *Hawthorne and the Western Electric Company: The Social Problems of an Industrial Civilisation*. New York: Routledge.

Mayol, S. (2011). *Le marketing 3.0*. Editions Duno.

Mazzoleni, G., & Schulz, W. (1999). Mediatization of politics: A challenge for democracy? *Political Communication*, *16*(3), 247–261. doi:10.1080/105846099198613

McCombs, M., & Ghanem, S. I. (2003). The convergence of agenda setting and framing. In *Framing public life: Perspectives on media and our understanding of the social world* (pp. 67–81). Mahwah, NJ: Lawrence Erlbaum.

McConnell-Henry, T., Chapman, Y., & Francis, K. (2009). Husserl and Heidegger: Exploring the disparity. *International Journal of Nursing Practice*, *15*(1), 7–15. doi:10.1111/j.1440-172X.2008.01724.x PMID:19187164

McEvily, B., Perrone, V., & Zaheer, A. (2003). Introduction to the special issue on trust in an organizational context. *Organization Science*, *14*(1), 1–4. doi:10.1287/orsc.14.1.1.12812

McPhee, P., & Bare, J. (2001). Introduction. In C. J. De Vita & C. Fleming (Eds.), *Building Capacity in Nonprofit Organizations* (pp. 1–4). Washington, DC: Urban Institute.

McPherson, M., Smith-Lovin, L., & Cook, J. M. (2001). Birds of a Feather: Homophily in Social Networks. *Annual Review of Sociology, 27*(1), 415–444. doi:10.1146/annurev.soc.27.1.415

McQuail, D. (2005). Processes and models of media effects. In McQuail's mass communication theory. Sage.

McQuail, D. (1994). *Mass communication theory*. London: Sage.

Mencarelli, R., & Pulh, M. (2009). La communication 2.0: Un dialogue sous conditions. *Décisions Marketing, 54*, 71–75.

Mendelsohn, M. (1996). The media and interpersonal communications: The priming of issues, leaders, and party identification. *The Journal of Politics, 58*(1), 112–125. doi:10.2307/2960351

Mendel, W. (1996). *Combat in cities: The LA riots and operation Rio*. Foreign Military Studies Office.

Menzel, D. (2010). Ethics moments in government: Cases and controversies. Boca Raton, FL: Taylor & Francis.

Mercier, P.A. (2008). Liens faibles sur courants faibles: Réseaux sociaux et technologies de communication. *Informations sociales, 147*, 20-31.

Metzgar, E., & Maruggi, A. (2009). Social media and the 2008 US Presidential election. *Journal of New Communications Research, 4*(1), 141–165.

Meuter, M. L., Bitner, M. J., Ostrom, A. L., & Brown, S. W. (2005). Choosing Among Alternative Service Delivery Modes: An Investigation of Customer Trial of Self-Service Technologies. *Journal of Marketing, 69*(2), 61–83. doi:10.1509/jmkg.69.2.61.60759

Millen & Fontaine. (2003). Improving individual and organizational performance through communities of practice. *Proceedings of the 2003 international ACM SIGGROUP conference on Supporting group work*. Sanibel Island, FL: ACM. doi:10.1145/958160.958192

Millen, D. R., Feinberg, J., Kerr, B., Rogers, O., & Cambridge, S. (2006). *Dogear: Social Bookmarking in the Enterprise*. Academic Press.

Misra, S., Cheng, L., Genevie, J., & Yuan, M. (2016). The iPhone Effect: The Quality of In-Person Social Interactions in the Presence of Mobile Devices. *Environment and Behavior, 48*(2), 275–298. doi:10.1177/0013916514539755

Monge, P. R., & Contractor, N. (2003). *Theories of communication networks*. Oxford University Press.

Moreno, Y., Nekovee, M., & Pacheco, A. F. (2004). Dynamics of rumor spreading in complex networks. *Physical Review E: Statistical, Nonlinear, and Soft Matter Physics*, *69*(6), 066130. doi:10.1103/PhysRevE.69.066130 PMID:15244690

Morrissey, L. (2010). Trolling is an art: Towards a schematic classification of intention in internet trolling. *Griffith Working Papers in Pragmatics and Intercultural Communications, 3*(2).

Mowshowitz, A. (1994). Virtual organization: A vision of management in the information age. *The Information Society*, *10*(4), 267–288. doi:10.1080/01972243.1994.9960172

Munnukka, J., & Järvi, P. (2013). *Perceived risks and risk management of social media in an organizational context*. Institute of Information Management, University of St. Gallen.

Murphy, J., Kim, A., Hagood, H., Richards, A., Augustine, C., Kroutil, L., & Sage, A. (2011). Twitter Feeds and Google Search Query Surveillance: Can They Supplement Survey Data Collection? *Shifting the Boundaries of Research*, 228.

Nahapiet, J., & Ghoshal, S. (1998). Social capital, intellectual capital, and the organizational advantage. *Academy of Management Review*, *23*(2), 242–266.

Nakamura, J., & Csikszentmihalyi, M. (2002). The concept of flow. In *Handbook of positive psychology* (pp. 89–105). New York, NY: Oxford University Press.

Nardi, B., Schiano, D., Gumbrecht, M., & Swartz, L. (2004). Why we blog. *Communications of the ACM*, *47*(12), 41–46. doi:10.1145/1035134.1035163

Neuman, W. R., Just, M. R., & Crigler, A. A. (1992). Common knowledge: News and the construction of political meaning. Chicago, IL: The University of Chicago Press.

Neuman, W. R., Just, M. R., & Crigler, A. N. (1992). Common knowledge: News and the construction of political meaning.Chicago, IL: University of Chicago Press.

Newell, S., & Swan, J. (2000). Trust and inter-organizational networking. *Human Relations*, *53*(10), 1287–1328.

Norris, P. (2001). *Digital divide*. Cambridge, UK: Cambridge University Press. doi:10.1017/CBO9781139164887

Norris, P., Curtice, J., Sanders, D., Scammell, M., & Semetko, H. A. (1999). *On message: Communicating the campaign.* London: Sage.

Novak, T. P., Hoffman, D. L., & Yung, Y.-F. (2000). Measuring the customer experience in online environments: A structural modeling approach. *Marketing Science, 19*(1), 22–42. doi:10.1287/mksc.19.1.22.15184

O'Reilly, T. (2005). *What is Web 2.0: Design patterns and business models for the next generation of software.* Academic Press.

Obar, J., Zube, P., & Lampe, C. (2011). *Advocacy 2.0: An analysis of how advocacy groups in the United States perceive and use social media as tools for facilitating civic engagement and collective action.* Social Science Research Network. Retrieved from: http://ssrn.com/abstract=1956352

O'Connor, B., Balasubramanyan, R., Routledge, B., & Smith, N. (2010). *From tweets to polls: Linking text sentiment to public opinion time series.4th International AAAI Conference on Weblogs and Social Media (ICWSM),* Washington, DC.

Ojoa, A., Esteveza, E., & Janowskia, T. (2010). Semantic interoperability architecture for governance 2.0. *Information Polity, 15,* 105–123.

Orlikowski, W., & Scott, S. (2009). Sociomateriality: Challenging the separation of technology, work and organization. *The Academy of Management Annals, 2*(1), 433–474. doi:10.1080/19416520802211644

Ortega, F. J., Troyano, J. A., Cruz, F. L., Vallejo, C. G., & Enríquez, F. (2012). Propagation of trust and distrust for the detection of trolls in a social network. *Computer Networks, 56*(12), 2884–2895. doi:10.1016/j.comnet.2012.05.002

Pablo, E., Desouza, K. C., Schäfer-Jugel, A., & Kurzawa, M. (2006). Business customer communities and knowledge sharing: Exploratory study of critical issue. *European Journal of Information Systems, 15*(5), 511–524. doi:10.1057/palgrave.ejis.3000643

Pace, S. (2004). A Grounded Theory of the Flow Experiences of Web User. *International Journal of Human-Computer Studies, 60*(3), 327–363. doi:10.1016/j.ijhcs.2003.08.005

Paine, K. (2011). *Measure what matters.* Hoboken, NJ: John Wiley & Sons, Inc.

Paino, M., & Rossett, A. (2008). Performance Support That Adds Value to Everyday Lives. *Performance Improvement, 47*(1), 37–44. doi:10.1002/pfi.177

Pallotta, D. (2008). Uncharitable. Medford, MA: Tufts University Press.

Pan, P. P. (2006). Bloggers who pursue change confront fear and mistrust. *Washington Post*, p. A01.

Park, H. M., & Perry, J. L. (2008). Do campaign web sites really matter in electoral civic engagement? Empirical evidence from the 2004 post-election internet tracking survey. *Social Science Computer Review*, 26(2), 190–212. doi:10.1177/0894439307309026

Parkhe, A., Wasserman, S., & Ralston, D. A. (2006). New frontiers in network theory development. *Academy of Management Review*, 31(3), 560–568. doi:10.5465/AMR.2006.21318917

Pasek, J., More, E., & Romer, D. (2009). Realizing the social internet? Online social networking meets offline civic engagement. *Journal of Information Technology & Politics*, 6(3-4), 197–215. doi:10.1080/19331680902996403

Pelet, J.E. (2011). *Le e-commerce renforcé par les réseaux sociaux numériques: résultats d'une application expérimentale de la méthode Delphi*. Academic Press.

Perlmutter, D. D. (2008). *Blogwars: The new political battleground*. New York, NY: Oxford University Press.

Perrow, C. (1967). A Framework for the Comparative Analysis of Organizations. *American Sociological Review*, 32(2), 194–208. doi:10.2307/2091811

Pilke, E. M. (2004). Flow Experiences in Information Technology Use. *International Journal of Human-Computer Studies*, 61(3), 347–357. doi:10.1016/j.ijhcs.2004.01.004

Piper, P., & Ramos, M. (2006, June). A Failure to Communicate Politics, Scams, and Information Flow During Hurricane Katrina. *Searcher Magazine, 14*(6). Retrieved on from http://www.infotoday.com/searcher/jun06/Piper_Ramos.shtml

Pittel, B. (1987). On spreading a rumor. *SIAM Journal on Applied Mathematics*, 47(1), 213–223. doi:10.1137/0147013

Placing, K., Ward, M.-H., Peat, M., & Teixeira, P. T. (2005). A blog on blogging in science education. 2004 National UniServe Science Conference, Sydney, Australia.

Poggi, A., Tomaiuolo, M., & Vitaglione, G. (2003). Security and trust in agent-oriented middleware. In *OTM Confederated International Conferences On the Move to Meaningful Internet Systems* (pp. 989-1003). Springer Berlin Heidelberg. doi:10.1007/978-3-540-39962-9_95

Poggi, A., & Tomaiuolo, M. (2010). Integrating peer-to-peer and multi-agent technologies for the realization of content sharing applications. *Studies in Computational Intelligence*, *324*, 93–107.

Poggi, A., & Tomaiuolo, M. (2013). A DHT-based multi-agent system for semantic information sharing. In *New Challenges in Distributed Information Filtering and Retrieval* (pp. 197–213). Springer Berlin Heidelberg. doi:10.1007/978-3-642-31546-6_12

Pope, J., Isely, A., & Asamoa-Tutu, F. (2009, April). Developing a marketing strategy for nonprofit organizations: An exploratory study. *Journal of Nonprofit & Public Sector Marketing*, *21*(2), 184–201. doi:10.1080/10495140802529532

Porras, J. J., Hargis, K., Patterson, K. J., Maxfield, D. G., Roberts, N., & Bies, R. J. (1982). Modeling-Based Organizational Development: A Longitudinal Assessment. *The Journal of Applied Behavioral Science*, *18*(4), 433–446. doi:10.1177/002188638201800405

Powell, A., Piccoli, G., & Ives, B. (2004). Virtual Teams: A Review of Current Literature and Directions for Future Research. *The Data Base for Advances in Information Systems*, *35*(1), 7. doi:10.1145/968464.968467

Poynter, R. & Lawrence, G. (2008). Insight 2.0: Nouveaux médias, nouvelles règles, nouvelle vision approfondie. *Revue Française du Marketing*, 25 – 38.

Prahalad, C. K. (2004). "The Cocreation of Value," in Invited Commentaries on "Evolving to a New Dominant Logic for Marketing". *Journal of Marketing*, 68.

Prahalad, C. K., & Ramaswamy, V. (2000). Co-opting Customer Competence. *Harvard Business Review*, *78*, 79–87.

Prahalad, C. K., & Ramaswamy, V. (2004a). Co-creation Experiences: The Next Practice in Value Creation. *Journal of Interactive Marketing*, *18*(3), 3, 5–14. doi:10.1002/dir.20015

Przybylski, A. K., & Weinstein, N. (2013). Can you connect with me now? How the presence of mobile communication technology influences face-to-face conversation quality. *Journal of Social and Personal Relationships*, *30*(3), 237–246. doi:10.1177/0265407512453827

Putnam, R. D. (1993). *Bowling Alone*. New York: Simon & Schuster Paperbacks.

Putnam, R. D. (1995). Bowling alone: Americas declining social capital. *Journal of Democracy*, *6*(1), 65–78. doi:10.1353/jod.1995.0002

Pynes, J. (2009). Human resources management for public and nonprofit organizations. San Francisco, CA: Jossey-Bass.

Raab, C., Berezan, O., Krishen, A., & Tanford, S. (2015). What's in a word? Building program loyalty through social media communication. *Cornell Hospitality Quarterly*.

Rackaway, C. (2007). Trickle-down technology? The use of computing and network technology in state legislative campaigns. *Social Science Computer Review*, *25*(4), 466–483. doi:10.1177/0894439307305625

Radian 6 Overview. (n.d.). Retrieved from http://www.webanalyticsworld.net/analytics-measurement-and-management-tools/radian-6-overview, May 9, 2016.

Rash, W. (1997). *Politics on the nets: Wiring the political process*. New York, NY: W.H. Freeman.

Rawlinson, L. (2007). Will the 2008 USA election be won on Facebook? *CNN*. Retrieved from http://www.cnn.com/2007/TECH/05/01/election.facebook/

Rayan, D. & Jones C. (2009). *Understanding Digital Marketing, Marketing strategies for engaging the digital generation*. Kogan.

Reagle, D. (2012). *10 Years of Mobile Industry History in 10 Minutes*. Academic Press.

Reese, S. D., & Dai, D. (2009). Citizen journalism in the global news arena: China's new media critics. In *Citizen journalism: Global perspectives* (pp. 221–232). New York, NY: Peter Lang.

Regnaud, D. (2003). Le trompe-l'oeil du client roi, pour une vraie relation de service dans les services grand public. *Lettre de CISTE*, *35*, 1–6.

Rice, R. E. (1992). Task Analyzability, Use of New Media, and Effectiveness: A Multi-Site Exploration of Media Richness. *Organization Science*, *3*(4), 475–500. doi:10.1287/orsc.3.4.475

Ries, A., & Ries, L. (2002). *The fall of advertising and the rise of pr*. New York, NY: Harper Collins.

Robertson, S. P., Vatrapu, R. K., & Medina, R. (2010). Off the wall political discourse: Facebook use in the 2008 US presidential election. *Information Polity*, *15*(1), 11–31.

Rogers, E. (2003). *Diffusion of innovations* (5th ed.). New York, NY: Free Press.

Rousseau, D. M., Sitkin, S. B., Burt, R. S., & Camerer, C. (1998). Not so different after all: A cross-discipline view of trust. Academy of Management. *Academy of Management Review, 23*(3), 393–404. doi:10.5465/AMR.1998.926617

Roy, S. R. (2012). Digital Mastery: The Skills Needed for Effective Virtual Leadership. *International Journal of e-Collaboration, 8*(3), 56–66. doi:10.4018/jec.2012070104

Safko, L. (2012). *The social media bible.* Hoboken, NJ: John Wiley & Sons, Inc.

Sako, M. (1992). *Prices, quality, and trust: inter-firm relations in Britain and Japan.* Cambridge, UK: Cambridge University Press. doi:10.1017/CBO9780511520723

Salamon, L. (2003). *The resilient sector.* Washington, DC: Brookings Institution Press.

Saxton, G. D., Guo, C., & Brown, W. A. (2007). New dimensions of nonprofit responsiveness: The application and promise of Internet-based technologies. *Public Performance & Management Review., 3*(2), 144–173. doi:10.2753/PMR1530-9576310201

Saxton, G. D., & Wang, L. (2013). The social network effect: The determinants of giving through social media. *Nonprofit and Voluntary Sector Quarterly,* 1–19.

Schaefer, G., & Hersey, L. N. (2015). Enhancing Organizational Capacity and Strategic Planning Through the Use of Social Media. In Cases on Strategic Social Media Utilization. Hershey, PA: IGI Global.

Scheid, F., Vaillant, R., & De Montaigu, G. (2012). *Le marketing digital: développer sa stratégie à l'ère numérique.* Ed Eyrolle.

Scheidt, L. A. (2006). Adolescent diary weblogs and the unseen audience. In *Digital generations: Children, young people, and new media* (pp. 1–25). London, UK: Erlbaum.

Schelling, T. (1960). The strategy of conflict. Cambridge, MA: Harvard University Press.

Schipul, E. (2009). Social Media Programs: Cultivate, Don't Control. *Public Relations Tactics, 16*(1).

Schmidt, J. H. (2011). *(Micro)blogs: Practices of privacy management. In Privacy online* (pp. 159–173). New York, NY: Springer. doi:10.1007/978-3-642-21521-6_12

Schmitt, B. H. (1999). *Experiential Marketing: How to get customers to sense, feel, think, act, and to relate to your company and brands.* New York, NY: Free Press.

Schöbel, M. (2009). Trust in high-reliability organizations. *Social Sciences Information. Information Sur les Sciences Sociales, 48*(2), 315–333. doi:10.1177/0539018409102416

Schultz, F., Utz, S., & Göritz, A. (2011). Is the medium the message? Perceptions of and reactions to crisis communication via twitter, blogs and traditional media. *Public Relations Review, 37*(1), 20–27. doi:10.1016/j.pubrev.2010.12.001

Schweitzer, E. J. (2011). Normalization 2.0: A longitudinal analysis of German online campaigns in the national elections 2002–9. *European Journal of Communication, 26*(4), 310–327. doi:10.1177/0267323111423378

Seah, C. W., Chieu, H. L., Chai, K. M. A., Teow, L. N., & Yeong, L. W. (2015, July). Troll detection by domain-adapting sentiment analysis. In *18th International Conference on Information Fusion (Fusion) 2015* (pp. 792-799). IEEE.

Shah, D., & Zaman, T. (2011). Rumors in a network: Whos the culprit? *IEEE Transactions on Information Theory, 57*(8), 5163–5181. doi:10.1109/TIT.2011.2158885

Sheafer, T., & Weimann, G. (2005). Agenda building, agenda setting, priming, individual voting intentions, and the aggregate results: An analysis of four Israeli elections. *Journal of Communication, 55*(2), 347–365. doi:10.1111/j.1460-2466.2005.tb02676.x

Sherman, A. (2011). How law enforcement agencies are using social media to better serve the public. *Mashable.* Retrieved from: http://mashable.com/2011/08/31/law-enforcement- social-media-use/

Shetzer, L. (1993). A social information processing model of employee participation. *Organization Science, 4*(2), 252–268. doi:10.1287/orsc.4.2.252

Shirky, C. (2008). *Here comes everybody: the power of organizing without organizations.* New York, N.Y.: Penguin Books.

Short, J., Williams, E., & Christie, B. (1976). *The social psychology of telecommunications.* Hoboken, NJ: John Wiley.

Small, T. (2008). The Facebook effect? Online campaigning in the 2008 Canadian and US elections. *Policy Options, 85*, 84–87.

SpannerWorks. (2007). *What is social media.* Retrieved from www.spannerworks.com/ebooks

Stavrakantonakis, I., Gagiu, A. E., Kasper, H., Toma, I., & Thalhammer, A. (2012). An approach for evaluation of social media monitoring tools. *Common Value Management, 52.*

Suárez, D. F. (2009). Nonprofit Advocacy and Civic Engagement on the Internet: Administration and Society. Sage Publications.

Su, C., & Contractor, N. (2011). A multidimensional network approach to studying team members information seeking from human and digital knowledge sources in consulting firms. *Journal of the American Society for Information Science and Technology, 62*(7), 1257–1275. doi:10.1002/asi.21526

Sudulich, M., & Wall, M. (2010). Cyber campaigning in the 2007 Irish general election. *Journal of Information Technology & Politics, 7*(4), 340–355. doi:10.1080/19331680903473485

Svendsen, G., & Sørensen, J. F. L. (2006). The socioeconomic power of social capital. *The International Journal of Sociology and Social Policy, 26*(9/10), 411–429. doi:10.1108/01443330610690550

Tapscott, D., & Williams, D. A. (2008). *Wikinomics – How Mass Collaboration Changes Everything*. Portfolio.

Tardanico, S. (2012, April 30). Is social media sabotaging real communication? *Forbes*. Retrieved from http://www. forbes. com/sites/susantardanico/2012/04/30/is-social-media-sabotaging-real-communication/Published

Taylor, I. (2008). *Why Social Media Should Be a Key Ingredient in Your Marketing Mix*. Academic Press.

Tenscher, J., Mykkänen, J., & Moring, T. (2012). Modes of professional campaigning: A four-country-comparison in the European parliamentary elections 2009. *The International Journal of Press/Politics, 17*(2), 145–168. doi:10.1177/1940161211433839

The Israeli Elections Website. (n.d.). Retrieved from http://www.bechirot.gov.il/elections19/eng/list/ListIndex_eng.aspx

Tiago, M. T., & Verissimo, J. M. (2014). Digital Marketing and Social Media: Why Bother? *Business Horizons, 57*(6), 703–708. doi:10.1016/j.bushor.2014.07.002

Tomaiuolo, M. (2013). Trust management and delegation for the administration of web services. In *Organizational* (pp. 18–37). Legal, and Technological Dimensions of Information System Administration.

Tomaiuolo, M. (2013). Trust Management for Web Services. *International Journal of Information Security and Privacy*, *7*(3), 53–67. doi:10.4018/jisp.2013070104

Torp, S. (2011). *The strategic turn: On the history and broadening of the strategy concept in communication.* Paper presented at the International Communication Association 2011 pre-conference, Strategic communication: A concept at the Center of Applied Communications, Boston, MA.

Tremayne, M. (2007). Harnessing the active audience: Synthesizing blog research and lessons for the future of media. In *Blogging, citizenship, and the future of media* (pp. 261–272). New York, NY: Routledge.

Trent, J. S., & Friedenberg, R. V. (2008). *Political campaign communication: Principles and practices*. Plymouth, UK: Rowman & Littlefield.

Trippi, J. (2013). Technology has given politics back its soul. *Technology Review*, *116*(1), 34–36.

Turcotte-choquette, A. & Parmentier, M-A. (2011). Le web 2.0: mieux le comprendre pour mieux l'utiliser. *Cahier de recherche*, *11*(2).

Turkle, S. (2012). *Alone together: Why we expect more from technology and less from each other*. Basic books.

Utz, S., Schultz, F., & Glocka, S. (2013). Crisis communication online: How medium, crisis type and emotions affected public reactions in the fukushima daiichi nuclear disaster. *Public Relations Review*, *39*(1), 40–46. doi:10.1016/j.pubrev.2012.09.010

Valenzuela, S., Park, N., & Kee, K. F. (2009). Is there social capital in a social network site? Facebook use and college students life satisfaction, trust, and participation. *Journal of Computer-Mediated Communication*, *14*(4), 875–901. doi:10.1111/j.1083-6101.2009.01474.x

van Aelst, P., Maddens, B., Noppe, J., & Fiers, S. (2008). Politicians in the news: Media or party logic? Media attention and electoral success in the Belgian election campaign of 2003. *European Journal of Communication*, *2*(2), 193–210. doi:10.1177/0267323108089222

Van de Ven, A., Delbecq, A., & Koenig, R. (1976). Determinants of coordination modes within organizations. *American Sociological Review*, *41*(2), 322–338. doi:10.2307/2094477 van Ruler, B. (2015). Agile public relations planning: The Reflective Communication Scrum. *Public Relations Review, 41*(2), 187–194. doi:10.1016/j.pubrev.2014.11.008

Vandercammen, M. (2012). *Marketing: l'essentiel pour comprendre, décider, agir.* Deboeck.

Vargo, S. L., & Lusch, R. F. (2004a). Evolving to a New Dominant Logic for Marketing. *Journal of Marketing, 68*(1), 1–17. doi:10.1509/jmkg.68.1.1.24036

Vitak, J., Zube, P., Smock, A., Carr, C. T., Ellison, N., & Lampe, C. (2011). Its complicated: Facebook users political participation in the 2008 election. *Cyberpsychology, Behavior, and Social Networking, 14*(3), 107–114. doi:10.1089/cyber.2009.0226 PMID:20649449

Von Hippel & Katz. (2002). Shifting innovation to users via toolkits. *Management Science, 48*(7), 821-833.

Wagner, K. M., & Gainous, J. (2009). Electronic grassroots: Does online campaigning work? *Journal of Legislative Studies, 15*(4), 502–520. doi:10.1080/13572330903302539

Walker, M. (2011). *Disaster response increasingly linked to social media.* FierceGovernmentIT.

Wang, D., Pedreschi, D., Song, C., Giannotti, F., & Barabasi, A. L. (2011, August). Human mobility, social ties, and link prediction. In *Proceedings of the 17th ACM SIGKDD international conference on Knowledge discovery and data mining* (pp. 1100-1108). ACM. doi:10.1145/2020408.2020581

Wang, D., Wen, Z., Tong, H., Lin, C. Y., Song, C., & Barabási, A. L. (2011, March). Information spreading in context. In *Proceedings of the 20th international conference on World wide web* (pp. 735-744). ACM.

Ward, S., & Gibson, R. K. (2003). On-line and on message? Candidate websites in the 2001 general election. *British Journal of Politics and International Relations, 5*(2), 108–256. doi:10.1111/1467-856X.00103

Wasko, M. M., & Faraj, S. (2005). Why should I share? examining social capital and knowledge contribution in electronic networks of practice. *Management Information Systems Quarterly, 29*(1), 35–57.

Wasserman, S., & Faust, K. (1994). *Social network analysis: Methods and applications* (Vol. 8). Cambridge University Press. doi:10.1017/CBO9780511815478

Waters, R. D. (2010). The Use of Social Media by Nonprofit Organizations: An Examination from the Diffusion of Innovations Perspective. In T. Dumova, & R. Fiordo (Eds.), *Handbook of Research on Social Interaction Technologies and Collaboration Software: Concepts and Trends* (pp. 473-485). Hershey, PA: Information Science Reference.

Waters, R. D., & Jamal, J. Y. (2011). Tweet, tweet, tweet: A content analysis of nonprofit organizations Twitter updates. *Public Relations Review*, *37*(3), 321–324. doi:10.1016/j.pubrev.2011.03.002

Wathieu, L., Brenner, L., Carmon, Z., Chattopadhay, A., Wetenbroch, K., Drolet, A., & Wu, G. et al. (2002). Consumer control and Empowerment: A Primer. *Marketing Letters*, *13*(3), 297–305. doi:10.1023/A:1020311914022

Watson, D. L., & Tharp, R. G. (1977). *Self-directed behavior: self-modification for personal adjustment*. Monterey, CA: Brooks/Cole Pub. Co.

Weber, L. (2007). *Marketing to the social web: how digital customer communities build your business*. Hoboken, NJ: Wiley & Sons.

Wei, C. (2004). Formation of norms in a blog community. In *Into the blogosphere. Rhetoric, community, and culture of weblogs*. Academic Press.

Weibel, D., Wissmath, B., Habegger, S., Steiner, Y., & Groner, R. (2008). Playing online games against computer- vs. human-controlled opponents: Effects on presence, flow and enjoyment. *Computers in Human Behavior*, *24*(5), 2274–2291. doi:10.1016/j.chb.2007.11.002

Wellman, B. (1997). *An electronic group is virtually a social network. In Culture of the Internet* (pp. 179–205). Hillsdale, NJ: Lawrence Erlbaum.

Wellman, B., & Wortley, S. (1990). Different Strokes from Different Folks: Community Ties and Social Support. *American Journal of Sociology*, *96*(3), 558–588. doi:10.1086/229572

Wen, W. C. (2014). Facebook political communication in Taiwan: 1.0/2.0 messages and election/post-election messages. *Chinese Journal of Communication*, *7*(1), 19–39. doi:10.1080/17544750.2013.816754

West, M. (2011, February 20). How nonprofits can use social media to spark change. *The Chronicle of Philanthropy*.

White, D., & Winn, P. (2009). *State of the blogosphere 2008*. Academic Press.

Whitty, M., & Gavin, J. (2001). Age/Sex/Location: Uncovering the Social Cues in the Development of Online Relationships. *Cyberpsychology & Behavior, 4*(5), 623–630. doi:10.1089/109493101753235223 PMID:11725656

Williams, C. B., & Gulati, G. J. (2013). Social networks in political campaigns: Facebook and the congressional elections of 2006 and 2008. *New Media & Society, 15*(1), 52–71. doi:10.1177/1461444812457332

Williams, J. L. (2016). Privacy in the age of the internet of things. *Human Rights (Chicago, Ill.), 41*(4), 14–22.

Williamson, O. E. (1991). Comparative Economic Organization: The Analysis of Discrete Structural Alternatives. *Administrative Science Quarterly, 36*(2), 219–244. doi:10.2307/2393356

Withey, M., Daft, R. L., & Cooper, W. H. (1983). Measures of Perrows Work Unit Technology: An Empirical Assessment and a New Scale. *Academy of Management Journal, 26*(1), 45–63. doi:10.2307/256134

Wolfsfeld, G., Yarchi, M., & Samuel-Azran, T. (2013, July). *Media repertoires and political participation: evidence from the Israeli electorate.* Paper presented at the ISPP annual meeting, Herzliya, Israel.

Wood, R., & Bandura, A. (1989). Social Cognitive Theory of Organizational Management. *Academy of Management Review, 14*(3), 361–384.

Woolcock, M., & Narayan, D. (2000). Social Capital: Implications for Development Theory, Research, and Policy. *The World Bank Research Observer, 15*(2), 225–249. doi:10.1093/wbro/15.2.225

Woolley, J. K., Limperos, A. M., & Oliver, M. B. (2010). The 2008 presidential election, 2.0: A content analysis of user-generated political Facebook groups. *Mass Communication & Society, 13*(5), 631–652. doi:10.1080/15205436.2010.516864

Wright, K. B., & Webb, L. M. (2011). *Computer-mediated communication in personal relationships.* New York: Peter Lang.

Wuchty, S., Jones, B. F., & Uzzi, B. (2007). The increasing dominance of teams in production of knowledge. *Science, 316*(5827), 1036–1039. doi:10.1126/science.1136099 PMID:17431139

Wymer, W., & Grau, S. (2011). *Connected Causes: Online Marketing Strategies for Nonprofit Organizations.* Chicago, IL: Lyceum Books.

Xenos, M., Vromen, A., & Loader, B. D. (2014). The great equalizer? Patterns of social media use and youth political engagement in three advanced democracies. *Information Communication and Society*, *17*(2), 151–167. doi:10.1080/136911 8X.2013.871318

Xie, L. (2009). *Climate change in the changing climate of news media: A comparative analysis of mainstream media and blog coverage of climate change in the United States and the People's Republic of China, 2005-2008* (Unpublished doctoral dissertation). Southern Illinois University.

Yang, Y. (2013). Guizhentang suspends IPO application. *China Daily*.

Ye, S., & Wu, F. (2013). Measuring message propagation and social influence on Twitter.com. *International Journal of Communication Networks and Distributed Systems*, *11*(1), 59–76. doi:10.1504/IJCNDS.2013.054835

Yu, H. (2007). Talking, linking, clicking: The politics of SARS and AIDS. *Positions: Positions: East Asia Cultures Critique*, *15*(1), 35–63. doi:10.1215/10679847-2006-023

Yu, H. (2011). Beyond gatekeeping J-blogging in China. *Journalism*, *12*(4), 379–393. doi:10.1177/1464884910388229

Zaman, T. R., Herbrich, R., Van Gael, J., & Stern, D. (2010, December). Predicting information spreading in twitter. In *Workshop on computational social science and the wisdom of crowds, nips* (*Vol. 104*, No. 45, pp. 17599-601). Citeseer.

Zaman, T., Fox, E. B., & Bradlow, E. T. (2014). A Bayesian approach for predicting the popularity of tweets. *The Annals of Applied Statistics*, *8*(3), 1583–1611. doi:10.1214/14-AOAS741

Zammar, N. (2012). *Réseaux sociaux numériques: essai de catégorisation et de cartographie des controverses*. Université Rennes 2.

Zerfass, A., Fink, S., & Linke, A. (2011, March). Social Media Governance: Regulatory frameworks as drivers of success in online communications. In *Pushing the envelope in public relations theory and research and advancing practice,14th International Public Relations Research Conference* (pp. 1026-1047). Gainesville, FL: Institute for Public Relations.

Zerfass, A., Tench, R., Verhoeven, P., Verčič, D., & Moreno, A. (2010). *European communication monitor 2010. Status quo and challenges for public relations in Europe. Results of an empirical survey in 46 countries*. Helios Media.

Zhang, W., Johnson, T. J., Seltzer, T., & Bichard, S. L. (2010). The revolution will be networked: The influence of social networking sites on political attitudes and behavior. *Social Science Computer Review*, 28(1), 75–92. doi:10.1177/0894439309335162

Zhou, Y., Guan, X., Zhang, Z., & Zhang, B. (2008, June). Predicting the tendency of topic discussion on the online social networks using a dynamic probability model. In *Proceedings of the hypertext 2008 workshop on Collaboration and collective intelligence* (pp. 7-11). ACM. doi:10.1145/1379157.1379160

Zignal Labs. (n.d.). *Make intelligence central to your business* [website]. Retrieved from http://zignallabs.com

Zittel, T. (2009). Lost in technology? Political parties and the online campaigns of constituency candidates in Germanys mixed member electoral system. *Journal of Information Technology & Politics*, 6(3/4), 298–311. doi:10.1080/19331680903048832

About the Contributors

Michael A. Brown earned his PhD in Public Administration and Urban Policy, International Business, from Old Dominion University (ODU) in 2011. He is teaching social media and communication online for Florida International University (FIU). He previously taught at ODU and the University of Maryland University College (UMUC). He created three courses for FIU, and all have been recognized by Quality Matters (QM). QM is a nationally recognized faculty peer review organization for online and hybrid course design, signaling the best offerings in education. He is currently the deputy director of Public Affairs for a joint military organization at Fort Eustis in Newport News, Va. This PR professional has more than 40 years of military and civilian experience combined, and is an Air Force retiree who served 24 years in uniform.

* * *

Giulio Angiani received an M.Eng. in Computer Engineering and in Information Technologies from the University La Sapienza of Rome. Currently he is a PhD student at the Department of Information Engineering, University of Parma. He has taught Informatics and Networking for 15 years at High School. His current research activity is focused on social network analysis and sentiment analysis. He is also focusing on recognizing patterns on big data extracted from high school marks.

Liston W. Bailey is a writer, educator and consultant living in Virginia. He earned graduate degrees in the fields of education, organizational development, and public administration. His PhD was earned in the field of education and he has routinely taught college courses in a diverse range of topics related to education, management and leadership over the past decade. He currently serves as a program analyst and strategist for the Department of Defense Army Training and Doctrine Command.

Holly Calvasina currently serves as the community partnerships assistant at CHOICES: Memphis Center for Reproductive Health. She holds an MPA, MA in

African American literature, and a graduate certificate in Philanthropy and Nonprofit Leadership from the University of Memphis.

Nozha Erragcha is a PhD, in marketing, Faculty of Law, Economics and Management of Jendouba-Tunisia. Her areas of interest are e-Learning, Marketing, and online Marketing.

Paolo Fornacciari obtained a laurea in Computer Engineering at the University of Parma in 2015. During his career, he did different tutoring activities on Python and C++. He is currently a PhD student at the Department of Information Engineering, University of Parma. His research activity is focused on Machine Learning Algorithms for Sentiment Analysis Problems.

Leigh Nanney Hersey is an Assistant Professor and MPA Coordinator at the University of Louisiana at Monroe. Prior to joining the university ranks, she worked at numerous nonprofit organizations in fundraising.

Eleonora Iotti is a PhD student at the Department of Information Engineering, University of Parma.

Mitchell E. Marovitz is a collegiate professor and chair of the Public Relations program at the Graduate School of the University of Maryland University College. He is a member of the Universal Accreditation Board and was elected to the Public Relations Society of America's College of Fellows and the National Capital Public Relations Hall of Fame in 2016. Dr. Marovitz led strategic communications teams in support of Intelligence Community and Department of Defense clients while at Booz Allen Hamilton, Inc. from 2004-2012. In 2004, as an independent consultant, he was the primary author of the public affairs plan supporting the release of the Army Inspector General's Report on Detainee Operations in Afghanistan and Iraq, which was conducted as a result of the Abu Ghraib prison scandal. During 2002-2003, Dr. Marovitz was the Director of Entertainment for the USO, Inc., where he oversaw celebrity recruitment and the production of celebrity tours for our troops. He revitalized celebrity visits to U.S. posts and bases and brought the first celebrity tour to Iraq after the second Gulf War in 2003. Dr. Marovitz retired from the Army in 2002 as a colonel after serving 30 years in a variety of public affairs positions including Public Affairs Officer, 5th Signal Command; Chief, Army Public Affairs-Los Angeles Branch; and Director, Media Operations, American Forces Information Service. He also served as the commander of American Forces Radio and Television Service networks in Central America and Europe as well as the Commander/Publisher of European Stars and Stripes.

Monica Mordonini is an associate researcher in the Department of Computer Engineering of the University of Parma. She received a Laurea degree in Electronics Engineering in 1994 and a Ph.D. in Information Technology in 1998, both from the University of Parma. Her research interests are in the field of artificial intelligence, mainly in the study of visual sensors unconventional vision algorithms for autonomous systems and application of video surveillance. More recently, her research also covered the issues of information extraction from distributed multimedia databases and applications for the semantic web.

Tal Samuel-Azran (PhD, University of Melbourne; MA, New York University) is the Head of the international program at the Sammy Ofer School of Communications. His main fields of research are political communication, new media, and media globalization. His book Intercultural Communication as a Clash of Civilizations was published in 2016 by Peter Lang Press.

Gayla Schaefer, MPA, is a freelance writer and leadership consultant currently working in communications for county government. Her work has been published by Gannett News, SCB Media Group, and IGI Global.

Elad Segev is Associate Professor in Digital Media and Communications at the Department of Communication, Tel Aviv University. He publishes studies on culture and national identity, Americanization and globalization, international news, search engines and search strategies, digital divide, network analysis, data mining, and new applications and methodologies in social science and communication.

Aminata (Amina) Sillah teaches at Towson University within the Department of Political Science. She was previously a teaching Fellow at the University of North Texas, Denton. Dr. S also served as a Visiting Lecturer at the University of the Gambia, West Africa. She earned her B.A. from Temple University, her MPA from Northern Illinois University and her Ph.D. from University of North Texas. Her current research projects focus on interdisciplinary applications of metropolitan/urban studies and nonprofit studies exploring the intersections of the three. She focuses on capacity building, leadership, entrepreneurship, public policy, and organizational development. Dr. Sillah is on the board of several nonprofits including Friends of Plano Libraries, and Global Youth Innovation Network (www.gyin.org).

Michele Tomaiuolo received a M.Eng. in Computer Engineering and a PhD in Information Technologies from the University of Parma. Currently he is an assistant professor at the Department of Information Engineering, University of Parma. He has given lessons on Foundations of Informatics, Object-Oriented Programming,

Software Engineering, Computer Networks, Mobile Code, and Security. He participated in various national and international research projects, including the EU funded @lis TechNet, Agentcities, Collaborator, Comma, and the national project Anemone. His current research activity is focused on peer-to-peer social networking, with attention to security and trust management, multi-agent systems, semantic web, rule-based systems, and peer-to-peer networks.

Yuanxin Wang is a PhD candidate in the School of Media and Communication of Temple University, USA. She holds a Master of Philosophy degree in Communication from Hong Kong Baptist University, Hong Kong, and a Master of Arts in International Journalism from University of Central Lancashire, UK. Her research interests include new media studies, environmental communication, intercultural communication, and media effects. Currently she is interested in investigating cyberbullying in various cultural contexts.

Gadi Wolfsfeld (PhD, MIT) is a Full Professor in the Sammy Ofer School of Communication, Interdisciplinary Center (IDC) Herzliya, Israel. His major research interests are in the field of political communication with a special focus on the role of the media in political conflicts. His most recent book is entitled, Making Sense of Media and Politics: Five Principles in Political Communication.

Moran Yarchi (Ph.D., Hebrew University) is a Senior Lecturer at the Sammy Ofer School of Communications, Interdisciplinary Center (IDC) Herzliya, Israel. Her main fields of research are political communication, public diplomacy, media coverage of conflicts and terrorism, and new media.

Index

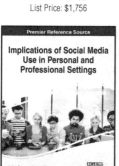

Stay Current on the Latest Emerging Research Developments

Become an IGI Global Reviewer for Authored Book Projects

The overall success of an authored book project is dependent on quality and timely reviews.

In this competitive age of scholarly publishing, constructive and timely feedback significantly decreases the turnaround time of manuscripts from submission to acceptance, allowing the publication and discovery of progressive research at a much more expeditious rate. Several IGI Global authored book projects are currently seeking highly qualified experts in the field to fill vacancies on their respective editorial review boards:

Applications may be sent to:
development@igi-global.com

Applicants must have a doctorate (or an equivalent degree) as well as publishing and reviewing experience. Reviewers are asked to write reviews in a timely, collegial, and constructive manner. All reviewers will begin their role on an ad-hoc basis for a period of one year, and upon successful completion of this term can be considered for full editorial review board status, with the potential for a subsequent promotion to Associate Editor.

If you have a colleague that may be interested in this opportunity,
we encourage you to share this information with them.

Information Resources Management Association

Become an IRMA Member

Members of the **Information Resources Management Association (IRMA)** understand the importance of community within their field of study. The Information Resources Management Association is an ideal venue through which professionals, students, and academicians can convene and share the latest industry innovations and scholarly research that is changing the field of information science and technology. Become a member today and enjoy the benefits of membership as well as the opportunity to collaborate and network with fellow experts in the field.

IRMA Membership Benefits:

- **One FREE Journal Subscription**
- **30% Off Additional Journal Subscriptions**
- **20% Off Book Purchases**
- Updates on the latest events and research on Information Resources Management through the IRMA-L listserv.
- Updates on new open access and downloadable content added to Research IRM.
- A copy of the Information Technology Management Newsletter twice a year.
- A certificate of membership.

IRMA Membership $195

Scan code or visit **irma-international.org** and begin by selecting your free journal subscription.

Membership is good for one full year.

Printed in the United States
By Bookmasters